Painted Mountains

Painted Mountains

First ascents in the Indian Himalaya

STEPHEN VENABLES

Vertebrate Publishing, Sheffield
www.v-publishing.co.uk

Painted Mountains

Stephen Venables

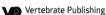 **Vertebrate Publishing**
Crescent House, 228 Psalter Lane, Sheffield S11 8UT, United Kingdom
www.v-publishing.co.uk

First published in Great Britain in 1986 by Hodder and Stoughton (London).
This edition first published in 2018 by Vertebrate Publishing.

Vertebrate Publishing
Crescent House, 228 Psalter Lane, Sheffield S11 8UT UK.

This book is a work of non-fiction based on the life, experiences and
recollections of Stephen Venables. In some limited cases the names of people,
places, dates and sequences or the detail of events have been changed solely
to protect the privacy of others. The author has stated to the publishers that,
except in such minor respects not affecting the substantial accuracy of the
work, the contents of the book are true.

A CIP catalogue record for this book is available from the British Library.

ISBN 978-1-911342-93-9 (Paperback)
ISBN 978-1-911342-94-6 (Ebook)

Produced by Vertebrate Publishing.

Printed and bound by Lightning Source Ltd.

Contents

Part 1

Kishtwar Shivling

1   A Dream

Snow began to fall at dusk. Inside the tent we struggled to cook supper. The stove was an old punctured tin can filled with smouldering lumps of dried yak dung. Our smart pressure stove had been abandoned many miles back, when we failed to obtain petrol for it. In the forest we had managed well, cooking on wood fires, but for three days now we had been above the tree line, forced to improvise, and I had felt slightly ridiculous climbing up to the Himalayan watershed with a large bag of yak turds tied to the top of my rucksack.

Now, on the evening of 11 September 1979, we were camping at 5,300 metres on the crest of the Himalaya, in Kashmir. That afternoon we had for the first time looked north to the brown desert landscape of Zanskar. We had planned to cross the Himalaya and continue through Zanskar to Ladakh; but one look down steep ice slopes, curving down out of sight on the far side, had been enough to deter us. Philip, my brother, had virtually no climbing experience and no crampons to cope with the hard, glassy, ice, so we had abandoned our plan and decided to return the way we had come. As evening was already drawing in and cold damp clouds were swirling around, we had stopped to camp where we were, on the ridge, pitching the tent on a small moderately level patch of snow. Now the wind outside, the horrible black fumes of yak dung augmented by diesel on our makeshift stove, and the cold, seeping insidiously through the tent floor, all intensified our feelings of failure and despondency.

The following day we set off back south. We walked down through grey drizzle and stopped in the evening to camp in a cave, eking out a pitiful meal of dried onions and mashed potato.

Morning transformed everything. The sky was blue; a meandering stream glittered silver in the sunlight; and, as we sauntered down through meadows of edelweiss and cotton grass, the air was filled with the vibrant twittering of a thousand songbirds. Suddenly, failure was forgotten and I could abandon myself to the exuberance of a radiant autumn morning.

We were following the curve of the stream down towards a lower valley, which would eventually lead us back to the Chenab river and the hill town of Kishtwar, where our journey had begun. Gradually, as we rounded a bend, a great mountain came into view, at first only the gleaming white summit, several miles to the south; then ice cliffs, rock buttresses and pinnacles revealed themselves until, finally, the whole mountain was framed in the V of our valley. It was an inspiring sight. The summit was a curved hump of pristine white snow; on either side, ridges fell away in a series of plunging towers; between the ridges, the North Face dropped in a single swoop of 2,500 metres to the valley. Only the elegant snow flutings of the summit ice field were in sunlight. Below that, the face was in shadow; steep slabs of granite, smeared with ice slivers and dusted with powder snow; below them a great barrier of ice cliffs, poised menacingly above more rock walls; further down still, a chaotic glacier tumbled darkly into the valley below us.

I looked back up to the summit, wondering why I had not taken more notice of it on our way up the valley a few days earlier. I knew from our map that it was c.6,000 metres above sea level (about 20,000 feet), quite low by Himalayan standards but, in the context of this Kishtwar region of Kashmir, where few summits exceed 6,000 metres, it was a magnificent mountain. A friend of mine had seen it the previous summer and had discovered that the local villagers called it Shivling, the phallus of Shiva, god of creation and destruction. There is another Shivling in Kashmir, a pillar of ice in a cave, revered by countless Hindu pilgrims. There is also another mountain called Shivling, 200 miles further south-east along the Himalayan chain; it was climbed by the India-Tibet Border Force in 1974, but this 'Kishtwar-Shivling' had never been attempted. On that September morning in 1979 I was in no fit state to climb mountains. After several weeks in the subcontinent, I felt weak and undernourished; and in any case this was a trekking holiday, we were not equipped for serious climbing. For the moment Kishtwar-Shivling was just something beautiful and inspiring to look at, a final reminder of the high peaks before descending to the forests of the Chenab gorge. Nevertheless, as a mountaineer I could not help being intrigued by the idea of trying to climb it. It looked very hard, harder than anything I had done in the Alps or during my first Himalayan expedition to the Afghan Hindu Kush. It would be a fascinating problem and I wondered whether I might return one day to find a way up to that remote gleaming summit.

We returned to England. Kishtwar-Shivling remained at the back of my mind as a vague possibility, a hypothetical scheme. The following summer some friends in Oxford asked to see my pictures of the Kishtwar region. They were planning their first Himalayan expedition and were looking for possible objectives. I showed them a photo of Shivling and they considered making an attempt but eventually opted for a technically easier peak, making the first ascent of Agyasol, a few miles to the south. Although I still had no serious plans for Shivling, I was secretly relieved that it remained unclimbed. I was also relieved to hear from the Oxford expedition that Shivling's south side, which they had seen from Agyasol, looked steep and difficult – relieved, because if there had been an easy way up the back, much of the peak's challenge would have been lost.

There is something very exciting about a beautiful unclimbed Himalayan peak with no obviously easy route to the top. The south side might be slightly gentler, but there was not much in it, and I always returned to my pictures of the North Face, a great mixed climb on snow, ice and rock, a mass of intricate details forming a coherent architectural whole, like some huge and fantastic Gothic cathedral.

In the meantime, other events were occupying my time. In the summer of 1980 I joined an expedition to attempt a new route on one of the highest mountains in the world: the 7,850-metre Kunyang Kish. The mountain had previously only been climbed once, after three attempts, which claimed four lives. Our attempt on the North Ridge failed, but it was a moving and memorable experience. Phil Bartlett, Dave Wilkinson and I spent several weeks isolated amongst the vast glaciers of the Karakoram range, coming quite close to success on a route involving nearly 4,000 metres vertical distance between Base Camp and the summit. In comparison with Kishtwar, the Karakoram is a savage landscape and even the approach march had its dangers, as we discovered when we were caught in a terrifying rockfall in the Hispar gorge. On the mountain, too, there were frightening moments – two falls into crevasses, a near miss when an overhanging cornice of snow broke with a loud bang, and always the nagging fear of avalanches; but it was exhilarating to find a new route on the mountain. Twice we climbed to 6,800 metres; both times bad weather stopped us continuing to the top and we were held down by storms, marooned for several days in a snow cave, before retreating nervously down avalanche-wracked slopes.

Time ran out and we had to admit defeat. I returned to England weary and skeletal, ten days late for a new teaching job in York. Kunyang Kish had been such a compelling objective, in such magnificent surroundings, that we went back for a second attempt in 1981, hoping for better luck. In the event the weather was abysmal and we didn't even reach the highpoint of the first attempt. Dave was so enthusiastic about the mountain that he had persuaded two more climbers to join us. One was an American, Carlos Buhler, who later took a leading role in the first ascent of the East Face of Everest. The other was one of Britain's most experienced mountaineers – Dick Renshaw.

I first heard of Dick in 1973. I had just returned from my first summer alpine season, slightly disappointed with unambitious climbs. In *Mountain* magazine I read about two Yorkshiremen, called Dick Renshaw and Joe Tasker, who had spent the summer systematically climbing some of the most formidable north faces in the Alps. The following summer their names cropped up again and then, in 1975, they made the first British winter ascent of the North Face of the Eiger. Later that year, while a massive British expedition laid siege to the South West Face of Everest, with the assistance of sixty high-altitude porters, Dick and Joe drove out on their own in an old van to the Garhwal Himalaya, in

India, to climb the South Ridge of 7,066-metre-high Dunagiri. This audacious climb of an extremely difficult route, by a two-man team with no back-up at all, received immediate acclaim in the climbing world and set the tone for a revival of lightweight expeditions. Dick published a superb article about the climb in *Mountain*, and reading between the lines of British understatement, one gained some idea of how hard he had been forced to struggle, in an epic retreat from the mountain, descending without food or water, delirious with exposure and suffering from appalling frostbite.

The following year, when his frostbitten fingers had recovered, he teamed up with Dave Wilkinson to make the first ascent, in winter, of the North-West Face Direct on the Mönch, one of the most serious routes in the Swiss Alps, which has still not been repeated. Dave asked him to come on the first Kunyang Kish attempt in 1980, but he had already been booked by Joe Tasker and Peter Boardman for another Karakoram peak – K2. Like us, they were twice driven down from their highpoint by atrocious weather; but theirs was a more pro-longed struggle on a higher mountain, where the storms were fiercer and the avalanches more devastating.

They returned safely and Dick accepted Dave's invitation to come to Kunyang Kish in 1981. It was interesting to meet for the first time someone about whom I had heard so much. I think that I had composed an imaginary picture of some formidably dour spartan and was pleasantly surprised to dis-cover his sheepish grin and friendly manner. During long spells of bad weather, watching and waiting at Base Camp, I came to realise what an ideal person he was to have on an expedition, quiet, patient and self-contained, but also friendly and considerate, with an underlying sense of humour. He clearly loved the mountains but had no intention of dying among them. Some of the risks we had taken the previous year came in for a good deal of criticism and in 1981, when conditions were worse, Dick's caution was a healthy influence. He expressed it succinctly:

'The most important thing about an expedition is to come back alive.'

'What about Dunagiri?' we retorted, reminding him about the time when he had so nearly *not* come back alive. He dismissed it as an irresponsible adventure, carried out in blithe youthful ignorance: but it had obviously been a tremendous experience to have survived and perhaps it was those exces-sively bold adventures of his early climbing career that had instilled the caution, the knowledge of his abilities and the constant awareness of potential dangers that made him such a good Himalayan mountaineer.

Like most people, I found Dick easy to get on with and hoped that we might go on an expedition together again. In the autumn of 1982 I was living with my parents near Bath. I had now stopped teaching, had left York and was hoping to spend more time on expeditions. I had just returned from the Andes, where Dave Wilkinson and I had climbed a number of 6,000-metre peaks – a refreshing change from the slow abortive struggle on Kunyang Kish. One evening the telephone rang and a familiar grunting noise announced that Dick was at the other end. Our hesitant, circling conversation resembled that of two shy lovers trying for the first time to declare their feelings for each other; we were dealing with a less emotive topic, but it took some time to arrive at the conclusion that we were both free the following autumn and that we both wanted to visit the Indian Himalaya after the monsoon to attempt a climb. Dick had just returned from Chris Bonington's ill-fated Everest expedition. Joe Tasker and Peter Boardman had disappeared high on the North-East Ridge, never to be seen alive again; Dick himself had been forced to return earlier, after suffering a stroke at 8,000 metres. Luckily there was no serious permanent injury, but he was advised not to go too high again. It must have been a bitter disappointment, later overshadowed by the loss of two close friends; but he had lost none of his enthusiasm for the mountains. The doctors had suggested a limit of 6,000 metres and now he was looking for an interesting, challenging climb of about that height. I suggested Kishtwar-Shivling.

At the weekend I drove over to Cardiff, where Dick lived with Jan and their son Daniel. On the Saturday evening we projected a slide of Shivling on to the wall and for the first time Dick saw the North Face that I had seen three years earlier. On the Sunday we drove over to Chepstow and spent a dank grey day climbing on the cliffs above the river Wye. Before I returned home, Dick had agreed to attempt Kishtwar-Shivling during the following autumn of 1983.

Himalayan expeditions still hold a certain mystique and many people imagine the difficulties of the terrain, the altitude and the barriers of Asiatic bureaucracy to be almost insurmountable obstacles. In comparison with a trip to the Alps or even the Andes, an attempt on a Himalayan peak does usually involve a lot of hard work, but the difficulties are often exaggerated; after one or two expeditions the organisation becomes quite easy. Our job was to arrive at a suitable Base Camp with enough food and cooking fuel to live there for several weeks. The mountain might require more than one attempt by different routes and we might be delayed by prolonged bad weather; so it was essential to be self-sufficient for long enough to try all possibilities. Our proposed route on the North Face would probably involve several days of hard technical climbing, requiring quite a quantity of rock and ice equipment. If the route proved too difficult or too dangerous, we would have to abseil back down again, abandoning equipment on the abseil anchors; so there would have to be spares to attempt alternative routes. We would have to transport all these supplies and ourselves to Delhi, continue by train and bus up to Kashmir and finally hire mules for the seventy-mile walk-in from the roadhead. Before any of this could happen we had to apply to the Indian Mountaineering Foundation (IMF) for government permission to attempt the peak. For a royalty fee of £330 this was granted and we were assigned the obligatory liaison officer (LO), who would accompany us to Base Camp and who would have to be clothed and fed throughout the expedition.

All this required money. The final cost of the expedition was £2,200, a paltry sum compared with the money spent by many expeditions but, paltry as it may have been, it was more than we could afford from our own pockets, so we were very relieved when the Mount Everest Foundation and the British Mountaineering Council (supported by the Sports Council) agreed to give generous grants towards the cost of the expedition. The Western Daily Press later promised more money in return for an article and photos, manufacturers provided equipment at cost price, and the camping store in Bath generously donated some of our requirements, as did various food companies.

Preparations progressed through the winter of 1982–1983. Every few weeks we met to discuss plans, usually during a day's climbing. So far the only climbs we had succeeded on together were small rock climbs on British crags; so it seemed a good idea to attempt a big alpine climb together before going to the Himalaya. At the end of February we travelled to Switzerland, to the Bernese Oberland.

We had to wait through days of bad weather, until it was safe to set off for one of the most remote, rarely climbed faces in the Alps, the North-East Face of the Finsteraarhorn. Getting to the foot of the face in midwinter involved a two-day approach on skis from the Jungfraujoch railway station. On the second day I fell into a concealed crevasse. The speed of Dick's reaction, pulling the rope tight before I fell any deeper, was a comforting reminder of his skill and experience. We spent three long, tiring days on the face itself, climbing slowly up forty rope-lengths of steep intricate terrain, reaching the summit just as night fell on the third day. On our sixth day we descended the mountain, collected our skis and finally, on the seventh day, skied down the long Fiescher Glacier to the first hint of spring in the Rhone valley, to complete a wonderful adventure. At last we had succeeded together on a serious mountain route. The 4,274-metre Finsteraarhorn in winter was comparable to 6,000-metre Shivling in summer. Of course, on Shivling, the route would be longer and there would be the additional strain of doing technical climbing nearly 2,000 metres higher; but the overall feel of the climb would probably be similar to what we had experienced on the Finsteraarhorn.

Summer came. In England it was the finest summer for eight years. Like Dick, I was earning my living from joinery and decorating and during the long hot days of June and July I drove by moped along twisting lanes, through the abundant fields and woods of Somerset, to a small village where I had been contracted to paint two houses. Occasionally I escaped from the toil of brushes, scrapers and ladders, to join Dick for a weekend on the limestone sea cliffs of Pembrokeshire. Sometimes Jan and Daniel came too and it was fun getting to know the family. Jan was not looking forward to Dick's departure but seemed resigned to the yearly separation. She recalled with retrospective amusement the time when Dick arrived back from K2, only just in time for the birth of his son. Apparently he had been so dazed and exhausted by the long struggle at high altitude that it took some time for him to register what was happening and show his natural joy and excitement at Daniel's birth.

By July everything was ready for Shivling. Another expedition from Cardiff was kindly freighting out some of our luggage to Delhi and we were due to fly with the rest on 5 August. I managed to fit in a week with three friends in the Lake District, where it was so hot that we only climbed in the shade of north-facing crags and we swam in the crystal waters of Lingcorn Beck and Stickle Tarn; even Wastwater had lost some of its customary chill. Then there was just time to return to London and paint one more house during a tiring week of fourteen-hour days, with the paint glaring fiercely in the harsh sunlight.

Setting off for Heathrow on the underground, I felt the usual last-minute pangs of doubt about leaving home for all the discomforts and possible dangers of a Himalayan expedition.

Dick was waiting at the airport, sweltering in double climbing boots and laden with grotesquely bulging rucksacks. We talked over the final details, checking that all the last-minute shopping had been done. Dick seemed as enthusiastic as ever about the trip and in the excitement of departure I quickly forgot my earlier doubts. It was exhilarating to be setting out for a single, precise, compelling objective, which I had dreamed about intermittently for four years; and I felt again a sense of commitment and excited anticipation as we pushed our overladen luggage trolleys towards Terminal Three for the flight to India.

2   Causeway of Distress

A large black vulture sat perched atop the headquarters of the IMF. Dick and I burst into laughter, puzzling the taxi driver, who saw nothing funny in the spectacle of this ominous creature, settled with such proprietorial assurance on the very pinnacle of the fortress-like building which is the starting point for nearly every expedition to the Indian Himalaya. But for us it was a marvellous moment of black comedy – one of the many absurdities which enlivened a week of mundane drudgery.

We had just returned from a morning's shopping in the bazaar and the taxi was crammed with boxes of food. We humped the boxes into the IMF building, relieved to return to the showers and electric fans which provided a cool haven from the relentless humid heat of Delhi. The chokidar brought tea and we ordered our lunch.

In the afternoon we rested in the dormitory, sprawled under the fans. I had almost fallen asleep when the IMF secretary came in to introduce our liason officer. Reluctantly I got to my feet, yawning dopily, but just conscious enough to be aware of the fact that Dick and I were dressed in nothing but underpants. Our LO was seconded to us from his duties in Garhwal with the India-Tibet Border Force, the paramilitary group responsible for patrolling India's long Himalayan border with China. He was a big man in his early thirties, his hair immaculately groomed and he wore a freshly laundered shirt, tailored trousers and shiny black shoes. I shook hands, smiled through the yawns and let Dick do the talking. Everything was very polite and formal, underpants notwithstanding, and it was rather daunting to think that this pukkah man was to be our constant companion for the next few weeks. A sense of awkwardness was accentuated by communication problems: he had a very thick Indian accent and had to repeat everything he said several times, so that it took some time to establish that his name was Patial. He found us equally incomprehensible and when in doubt said yes to anything we said. He could be excused, though, for incomprehension, because Dick is notorious for his *sotto voce* mumbling and my articulation often isn't much better.

After a few minutes of confused small talk, Patial started to work round to the moment we had dreaded:

'May I see the equipments?'

'We've packed all the equipment in those bags.'

'Yes – I am packing the equipments?'
'No – that is already done. It is ready.'
'Yes – I am ready.'
We decided on a different tack:
'Perhaps we should go to the bazaar now – there is more shopping to do.'
'Yes … '
There was another pause, Patial looked perplexed; he tried again:
'I shall be seeing personal LO equipments?'
'Sorry?'
'Sorry … ?'
'Can you repeat what you said, please?'
'I am wanting to see personal LO equipment articles.'

The message had finally got through and Dick and I exchanged shifty glances. We knew that every LO joins a foreign expedition with high expectations of LO perks. We had brought a motley selection of clothing and camping equipment, which just complied with the IMF regulations and which would be more than adequate for Patial's requirements at Base Camp; but he had friends who had worked for heavily sponsored Japanese expeditions, lavishly equipped with all the latest in mountaineering fashion and technology. He made no attempt to disguise his disappointment when we produced a well-used rucksack containing an old tent of my parents, my brother's walking boots and a down jacket of Dick's which was extremely warm but had a slightly déjà vu appearance. Patial fingered our offerings disdainfully. However, our sponsors had kindly provided a few compensatory items – a brand new karrimat, pristine thermal underwear, some luxurious loopstitch socks and a gleaming red Swiss penknife – which seemed to cheer him up a little. We also assured him that we had packed the regulation ice axe, crampons and climbing harness – items which we knew he was unlikely to use, but which we were glad to have with us as spares.

We repacked the rucksack and handed it over to Patial, promising to buy him some denim jeans and a transistor radio. Dick and I put on trousers and shirts, then the three of us went into the glaring heat outside. In the course of another laboured conversation we explained that Dick and Patial would continue with the shopping, while I took an auto-rickshaw to the tourist office near India Gate to reserve berths on the following day's night train to Jammu.

I met Dick again in the evening. Patial had returned to army quarters. Dick looked disconsolate and I asked how the shopping had gone. He had procured the extra rice, flour and dried fruit, but apparently Patial had been little help.

'He was useless!' Dick exclaimed in his bluntest Yorkshire accent. 'I had to carry all the heavy stuff on my own, while he just watched. He didn't seem to have a clue what was going on – did nothing but ask about his bloody jeans. It's going to be awful stuck with him, prancing round Base Camp in his new Levis ...'

It was depressing and we were both worried that Patial was going to be a terrible liability. However, as so often happens, our first impressions were wildly inaccurate: within a few days Patial had accepted the fact that he had been consigned to two slightly eccentric Englishmen with very little spare cash and he was trying to make the best of a disappointing situation, obviously doing everything he could to be helpful. As the expedition progressed, we often heard his favourite aphorism – 'Communications Is Must' – and by dint of meticulous articulation and growing familiarity we built up a good rapport. By the end of the trip we were agreed that Patial had coped most cheerfully and efficiently with what must have been an exceedingly boring job, acting as negotiator, interpreter and Base Camp guard for two foreigners who were neither willing nor able to take him on the mountain.

We had arrived in Delhi on a Saturday morning, hoping to leave for the mountains the following Monday. However, Patial's late appearance delayed us slightly and we didn't leave until the evening of Tuesday 9 August. We had now bought all the basic foodstuffs to supplement the rations donated in England, and it only remained to find paraffin and cooking utensils in Jammu and fresh vegetables in Kishtwar. Three taxis came to the IMF to take us and our eighteen pieces of luggage to the railway station and we left, driving through the spacious avenues of New Delhi, past all the embassies and India Gate and Lutyens' grandiose presidential palace and on into the borderland of New and Old Delhi, seething with a noisy mass of people, cars and cows. The station porters in their uniform red shirts welcomed us with an outrageous price for carrying our luggage to the platform and they seemed in no mood for negotiation. So Dick and I astounded them all by picking up two twenty-five-kilo loads and setting off ourselves. It was a long journey, across the lethal taxi stand, through the teeming entrance hall, up over a footbridge and down to our platform. Patial guarded the diminishing pile of luggage outside while Dick and I alternately humped loads and guarded the growing pile on the platform. After half an hour of hard labour we had stubbornly relayed all the loads and could rest, sweaty and exhausted.

The Frontier Mail was two hours late. Unlike British Rail, the Delhi station authorities do not announce publicly the late arrival of their trains. The expected time of arrival remains a subject for rumour and conjecture, while the public address system is used for more educational purposes: every few minutes its impeccable tones would cut through the hubbub, exhorting people to be sensible, asking them to refrain from carrying too much luggage or riding on the footplates or entering an air-conditioned carriage without an AC ticket. The best announcement went something like this:

'Please do not sit on the platforms, which is uncomfortable, and a nuisance to other people; instead, please use the seats provided.' It seemed an unreasonable request, when our platform boasted perhaps four small bench seats for a waiting crowd of hundreds of passengers, not to mention the scores of people who just happened to live there, sprawled on the platform in dense mounds of sleeping bodies.

The train arrived. We had treated ourselves to the luxury of an air-conditioned carriage, where a small bribe to a porter enabled us to stow all the luggage, illegally, in the compartment. It was wonderful to retreat into the delicious coolness of the carriage, settle into comfortable bunks and wait for the gentle swaying motion of the train to rock us to sleep, as it trundled through the night across the immense plains of Northern India.

Jammu lies right at the foot of the Himalaya, at the southern extremity of the state of Jammu and Kashmir. We arrived in the late morning and once again had to shift all the luggage, a tedious process which seems to be repeated endlessly during the early days of every expedition. It was a day of heat and drudgery and that evening I summed it up in my diary:

> Sitting in 'retiring room' No 9 at the bus station, trying to write by the dingy light of a single yellow bulb. The constant din of scooters, auto-rickshaws, taxis, lorries and buses, and the frenetic shouting of thousands of people, the smell of cow shit and stale urine and curry and rotting mangoes. The smell of sewage in our shower room and the sweet little brown rats scurrying in the rubbish cupboard ... all this is starting to make us just a little weary. In the morning a skinny mangy horse pulled a cart with our 300+kg of luggage to the bus station. Staring at its festering fly-infested sores and watching its pathetic attempts to shake its head, I felt depressed by the hopeless cruelty of it all – the horse, the people in the squalid huts by the station, the grotesque head of a man perched on a tiny legless torso on the floor of the bus station, the coolies carrying 100kg loads to our room, the soft-eyed scrawny cow ambling nonchalantly round the bus station, oblivious of all the noise – it all seemed utterly hopeless and futile.

The romance of India seemed to be eluding us.

Of course, it hadn't all been as bleak as my diary suggests. We had completed the first part of our journey and we were booked on to the next day's bus to Kishtwar. We had managed a successful shopping trip to the bazaar, buying paraffin, pots and pans, a large polythene sheet for our Base Camp kitchen and a transistor radio for Patial. There had even been moments of beauty like waking up at dawn to stare out of the train window at the gold and green fields of the Punjab and, in the evening, escaping from the bazaar to the twilit peace of a Hindu temple, where children played in the courtyard, while their parents prayed. Now we were back in our room, about to go to bed. There was a loud knock on the door and Dick went to open it, to find an enormous beturbanned man prowling around the corridor with an axe in his hand. Dick said hello and hastily shut the door, but Patial told him not to worry, assuring us that the man was just a resident security guard doing a check of the rooms.

Every long-haul bus in Jammu and Kashmir is adorned with one of two mottos, either 'Trust in God' or 'Best of Luck'. I cannot remember which ours was, but it negotiated without incident the first stretch of the journey into Kashmir, along a road decorated liberally with road safety slogans: 'Better late than never'; 'Dazzle him and he may dash you – Puzzle him and he may crash you'; 'Keep your nerves on sharp curves'.

We climbed up through pine forests and over a mountain pass, crossing the Pir Panjal range to Batote, where the main road continues north over another pass to Srinagar, and a rougher road winds its way tortuously eastward, following the twists and turns of the Chenab river to Kishtwar. We were to take the latter road, but first we had to stop overnight at Batote. I am always glad of a chance to sleep, but at Batote I was disappointed. Just after we had settled into our beds in a five-rupee hotel, giant fleas began to advance at high speeds from every chink and crevice in the beds and the surrounding walls of the room. The three of us fled downstairs, to balance precariously through the night on narrow benches, islands in a sea of voracious bugs; but they had already done their worst in the bedroom and we were all suffering from furiously itching red weals.

In the morning we continued on the long road to Kishtwar, bouncing for most of the day along the rough track high above the Chenab. We had almost reached Kishtwar when the bus stopped abruptly at a bend. Several other buses and trucks were also waiting. Round the bend, a section of the road had disappeared, swept down in a great slice of rain-loosened earth and rock into the turbid waters of the Chenab, 200 metres below. Landslides are a constant expected hazard during the monsoon and already a bulldozer was at work, trying to re-excavate the track. It was obviously going to take some time, so I settled in the shade beside the bus to continue reading V.S. Naipaul's tale of darkest Africa, *Bend in the River*. After two hours little progress had been made and people were starting to carry their luggage across the breach. Reluctantly we took down from the bus roof our packing cases, kit bags, rucksacks and scratchy hessian sacks, to start on yet another luggage relay. It was frightening work, stumbling across a fifteen-metre stretch of boulders, glancing nervously up at more boulders poised precariously above, imagining what it might be like to be crushed and swept down the steep gully into the river.

Once all the luggage was across we were safe; but by now a queue of trucks had built up on the far side for several hundred metres, and as evening drew in we had to trudge back and forth, humping load after load past a long line of old Bedfords. Although we were now about a thousand metres above sea level and the air was less humid, it was still very hot and I was developing a raging thirst. As I put down the last load, I thought how nice it would be if we could all go off to the pub to drink several well-earned pints of cool dark beer, and I remembered sitting in Wasdale, only three weeks earlier, doing just that. However, this was the Chenab valley and all we had was suspect water, which Dick was boiling on the primus, and I had to content myself with scalding tea.

We slept by the road and in the morning a relief bus took us to Kishtwar. The first Westerner to visit Kishtwar was an Englishman called Godfrey Vigne (pronounced Vine), who came here in 1839, in the course of extensive explorations which took him along the length and breadth of Kashmir. His *Travels in Kashmir, Ladak and Iskardoo* describes how he found a town of about one hundred houses, containing a mixed population of 'Mussalmen' and 'Hindoos'. The Rajah of Kishtwar had once controlled all the land to the north and east to Ladakh. By Vigne's time it had all been swallowed up in the expanding empire of Gulab Singh, the Rajah of Jammu. The Kashmiris of Srinagar held the region of Kishtwar in ridicule, and their contempt was illustrated by Vigne in a translation of one of their songs: 'Kishtwar is the causeway of distress, where people are hungry by day and cold by night; whoever comes there, when he goes away is as meagre as the flagstaff of a fakir.'

Kishtwar perhaps lacks the lush abundance of the country round Srinagar, but it is a pleasant enough town, situated on a broad shelf of land above the Chenab, surrounded by fields and wooded hills. We saw no signs of gross malnutrition, and people seemed to be as prosperous and thriving as they had been in 1979. The town, which has grown slightly since Vigne's day, is the trading and administrative centre for a large area of isolated villages. Villagers may travel over a hundred kilometres on foot, to visit the bazaar's thriving tailors, ironmongers and chemists. There is a police station, post office, District Commissioner's office, offices for forestry and agricultural officials, and both mosques and temples to cater for a mixed population of Muslims and Hindus, who in the 1980s were still living peacefully side by side.

Three hotels surround the main square in Kishtwar. When Dick, Patial and I arrived in the morning we heard that there would be no bus to the roadhead until the next day, so we asked to stay at one of the hotels and crammed all our luggage into a tiny room upstairs.

An irritating roughness at the back of my throat was developing into a cold, and now the familiar ache of flu was seeping through my body, intensifying as the day wore on. I lay on my wooden bed, feeling sorry for myself, while Patial took Dick to the police station to report the expedition's arrival. In the evening they persuaded me down to a smoky cafe, where I struggled unsuccessfully with chapattis and a leguminous mush stewed in searing chilli juice. I returned to bed and dosed myself to sleep with Paracetamol and Piriton; but in the middle of the night I woke again, aching, shivering and filled with a loathing for the canine population of Kishtwar. Himalayan dogs bark like no other dogs, and on this night every hound, bitch and puppy for miles around was competing in a frenzied howling that echoed relentlessly around the mountains.

I lay awake, hating dogs, hating India, hating the Himalaya, and wondering why I had come on this horrible expedition. Of course I knew that flu makes people miserable, that travelling through India in August is always hot and difficult, that drudgery and discomfort are unavoidable elements of any expedition; I knew that we had in fact come to climb a wonderful mountain and that these little irritations would pass; but at the time it was hard to believe that there was enjoyment ahead.

Near Kishtwar-Shivling there is a village called Machail. In the village there is a temple. We were told that the temple is dedicated to a goddess called Chendi. The name is unfamiliar and I have not been able to trace it, but it may perhaps be a local name for one of the celebrated Hindu goddesses like Parvati or Lakshmi. Whoever she is, a large group of women and girls were setting out on Sunday 14 August, to pay homage at her temple. Like us they were taking the bus from Kishtwar to Galhar, where the road ends and we would have to start walking. The pilgrims were accompanied by a gentle, courteous, grey-haired man, who appeared to be their group leader and chaperon. It was he who persuaded the bus driver to leave for Galhar. The road was undergoing repairs, so was officially closed and in an even worse state than usual. The driver refused to leave until the chaperone had done a whip-round among all the prospective passengers, collecting enough money to bribe him on his way.

As we rumbled out of Kishtwar the pilgrims started to sing Hindu songs. The youngest girl, who looked about ten, sang with boisterous enthusiasm, never flagging during the five hours it took to cover the twenty kilometres to Galhar. She had a shrill powerful voice and seemed to be trying to sing an octave above the others, but she usually only managed something like a seventh, adding a wonderfully discordant descant to the songs. The women's exuberant singing made a delightful antidote to my brooding hypochondria. It was also heartening to see people going contentedly about their business as we drove out of town, past the spacious maidan (the Indian equivalent of the municipal park or village green) bordered with majestic plane trees. Bumping along at ten miles an hour in billows of dust, we passed men with saws, boys leading donkeys laden with firewood, a woman bowed under bundles of maize leaf fodder and a tethered ram being dragged reluctantly past a group of bewildered ewes. All along the track there were road-menders at work with pickaxes, crowbars and shovels. Many of them were children, glad of the chance for a brief rest while the bus passed through. Frequently we all had to get out and walk, while the driver inched the straining vehicle over a particularly rutted stretch of earth and boulders; then we would all climb back on board and the singing would start again.

Galhar was as I had remembered it: dusty, smelly and buzzing with flies. We drank sweet sticky tea outside one of the huts, while Patial entertained the locals. He was entering thoroughly into the spirit of things, acting as our self-appointed PR man, proudly telling everyone about the Shivling Expedition and brandishing our one photo of the mountain. Neither Dick nor I spoke more than a few words of Hindi, so we were glad to have an interpreter, and as Patial talked with two old men he translated for our benefit. Apparently they came from the Darlang Nullah, a remote valley to the south of Shivling. One of them claimed to have climbed part of the way up the mountain: metal in his boots had stuck to the magnetic rocks … the mountain had glowed iridescent with many changing colours … he had heard the sound of melodious voices and the music of conch shells … He also knew of a sadhu, a holy man, who had left his cave one day, to walk towards Shivling. At nightfall he had lain down to sleep at the foot of the mountain, but the following morning he had woken to find himself back in his cave. Later, reading Vigne's account of his visit to Kishtwar in 1839, I found an almost identical story. Vigne writes about 'the Brimah … a very lofty range, covered with eternal snow' – another holy mountain, now usually spelled Brammah. He was told about a fakir who made numerous attempts to climb Brammah. The fakir would always make his first bivouac beside a little lake, part of the way up the mountain; but he invariably woke to find himself right back at the bottom. Dick and I were slightly concerned that there might be objections to our aspiration to set foot on the summit of the holy Shivling, but both the two old men from the Darlang Nullah and other local people we met later seemed to have no objections; they were, on the contrary, amused and curious at our plans. There was also business to be done. We had to transport 410 kilos of supplies to Base Camp, seventy miles away. Patial opened negotiations with a muleteer called Mohammed Ikbar, who reckoned that he could handle the job by using his five mules and subcontracting a genial older man, Ruph Singh, to provide two 'little mules', which appeared to be ordinary donkeys. After a heated discussion, during which we realised what a hard-hitting negotiator Patial was, we arrived at a price of 2,600 rupees (about £170) for the five-day journey. (Mohammed was a mean obstreperous man and we were infuriated to hear later that he had only paid Ruph Singh a niggardly 300 rupees for his share of the work.) Patial concluded negotiations, securing at our insistence a written contract, and then announced proudly that 'Tomorrow, after packing all the articles, we shall proceed to our destination.'

By evening the repacking of all the articles was complete. Mohammed had sewn all the loads into special double hessian sacks to be slung across the mules' backs, and had agreed to appear with Ruph Singh and the animals at dawn the next day.

Kishtwar-Shivling lies just south of the Himalayan crest. To the north of the Himalaya lies Ladakh, the arid region once known as Central Tibet, ethnically and culturally very close to Tibet proper, but politically part of India. Through Ladakh flows the Indus river, dividing the Himalaya from the Karakoram range further north. The Indus actually rises some way east, in Tibet, to flow north-west through Ladakh, along the southern flank of the Karakoram, which feeds the river every day with millions of tons of glacial meltwater, swelling it to a mighty swirling torrent before it carves its way south, round the western bastion of the Himalaya, Nanga Parbat, and on inexorably down to feed the great fertile plain of the Punjab, the land of five rivers, where the Indus is swelled by its five main tributaries – the Beas, Chenab, Jhelum, Ravi and Sutlej.

Since we left the fleas at Batote, Dick, Patial and I had been travelling up the Chenab. From Galhar we had to continue east up the same valley for another thirty miles to the village of Atholi, where we would turn north along a tributary river called the Bhut.

The journey to Atholi takes two days – two days of walking high above the river, constantly climbing up and down the beautifully engineered hairpins of the mule track, which consists in places of steps and gangways built out from sheer cliffs. Occasionally one hears the muffled roar of the river, enclosed thousands of metres below by the steep walls of the valley, but for most of the journey one is alone with the sounds of the forest – crested tits twittering among the pine cones, the occasional screeching of a flock of emerald parakeets, monkeys scampering through the undergrowth and branches above, the strange tongue-clicking, whistling and grunting of muleteers driving their laden beasts along the path, and the polite 'Good-morning-what-is-the-time-by-your-watch-please?' of a government official, stopping to say hello, before continuing on his way, briefcase and furled umbrella in hand. The river gorge is densely coated with an abundant forest of chestnut, holly oak and deodar – the Himalayan cedar, with its inimitable heady scent – and the forest floor is carpeted with pungent wild cannabis.

Walking peacefully through the filtered green light of the forest, it seemed no less wonderful than it had done four years earlier, and I was able for a while to forget the wearying ache and chesty cough of the flu. On the second day we descended to river level and walked through terraced fields of rice, maize, beans and potatoes. Children played in the shade of ancient walnut trees. Three girls, smiling coyly, worked a revolving mustard seed press. At this point, the confluence of the Chenab and Bhut rivers, the valley opens out, and Atholi lies on a gently sloping plain, in the midst of fields and orchards, encircled by wooded hills. We camped just outside the village and in the evening children came to stare wide-eyed through the door of our tent.

We continued up the Bhut Nullah ('nullah' is Hindi for river valley), enclosed again by steep walls of forest, which hid the high snow peaks from view. We passed a forestry camp, where labourers were felling cedars and adzing the timber into square-cut beams. It was heartening to learn that this tree felling is carefully controlled and that the Indian forestry department, in this area at any rate, seems to be avoiding the kind of devastation that has wreaked such havoc in many parts of the Nepal Himalaya. (Like the road authorities, they exhibit a penchant for educative slogans and I remember one charming plaque nailed to a wayside tree, proclaiming 'Wood is good but tree is better.') They are helped by the fact that there is as yet no road, so all the timber has to be felled by hand and floated down the river to Kishtwar – a slow process which has hardly affected the luxuriant abundance of this silvan paradise.

The villages, too, make little impact on the forest, isolated as they are in small clearings of terraced fields. Children stared at us from the flat earthen roofs of timber houses with exquisitely carved doorposts and lintels. Later, on the way home, we stayed at one of the houses, sitting on the large verandah, facing out over the valley, while our host plied us with food, maize spirit and hashish. After supper he took us into the inside room, where a fire was burning in the hearth. We coughed and spluttered in the acrid fumes, understanding painfully why so many of the people suffer from eye and lung infections. Our host explained that during the winter the whole family lived round the fire in this one room. Huge wooden-lidded bins lined two walls and were being stocked with food for the long winter, when the house would be half-buried in snow. Animal fodder was already being stacked on the roof and later more would be piled up on the verandah, helping to insulate the house. The animals themselves would live in the house, penned behind wooden rails on two sides of the room, adding another layer of insulation.

After returning to England I sometimes thought of that family, incarcerated through four or five long winter months in their dark smoky house, totally self-sufficient and isolated, with nothing much but cooking, sleeping and weaving to keep them occupied. The fourth day of our walk-in was interminable. A cold grey drizzle turned the path into a quagmire. Mohammed was surly and irritable, threatening to turn back when we were confronted by an avalanche chute left from the winter, and we had to cross a great mound of old grey snow, embedded with the splintered remains of pine trees. The mules baulked at one greasy slippery tree trunk that blocked the way, and the five of us had to heave it down into the river. As the day wore on I lagged far behind the others, sneezing and coughing, reluctantly dragging my wobbly legs and pausing frequently for ever-longer rests. However, at least the rain stopped in the afternoon I tottered into Machail, to find Dick and Patial waiting with tea. The beautiful pilgrim women were also there, garlanded with flowers, dancing and singing their way through some joyful religious ceremony. Not restricted to the pace of a mule train, they had travelled quickly to Machail, arriving there before us. They looked healthy and happy and the sixty-mile walk through the forest had not blemished their immaculate saris. In comparison, I felt a very feeble specimen of humanity –ill, haggard and splattered with mud.

On the morning of Friday 19 August, two weeks after leaving England, we left Machail on the last leg of the journey to Base Camp. We walked east for three miles to the entrance of the Darlang Nullah, but then turned north up another nullah which would take us round to the north side of Shivling. Towards midday we stopped at a tiny hamlet, whose name I didn't know but which I called Potato Village, because four years earlier Philip and I had been treated here to a meal of new potatoes, flavoured with lumps of rock salt. The people in this and the last village, Sumcham, are Tibetan Buddhists, who must originally have crossed the Himalaya from the north, to settle in this high valley on the south side. We halted outside the house I remembered which now had an extension in progress – new walls made from layers of rock and mud, sandwiched between lateral timbers. Members of the family appeared, their round slit-eyed faces smiling warmly. I recognised one of the girls, who was now about fourteen, and then her mother appeared. The mother had aged very slightly, but there was still the same welcoming twinkle in her eyes and the same elaborately jewelled pendant hanging from her nose. She didn't recognise me until I spurred her memory by producing an envelope of photos. Suddenly the family were all crowding round, laughing and giggling and pointing excitedly at their pictures. Possibly it was the first time they had ever seen photographs and they were clearly delighted with the present. For my part it was good for once to be giving instead of taking: giving something in return for the hospitality that I had so often received in the Himalaya. However, the lady of the house would not accept our present without giving us one of their precious goat cheeses to take to Base Camp.

At Sumcham the bridge over a side river had been washed away and replaced by a single plank. A few days earlier a mule had drowned trying to cross this plank, and Mohammed was certainly not going to subject his mules, his livelihood, to the same risk. The alternative course was to cross the main river below the village, where a mound of old hardened winter snow had formed a bridge; but Mohammed didn't like that either.

'We halted for an hour, while Patial tried to cajole Mohammed into action, and Dick and I walked back and forth across the snow bridge, pointing out how safe it was. Eventually Mohammed agreed to proceed to our destination and brought the mules across.

However, he was now in a surly intractable mood and the minor obstacle of a small wood of silver birches was cited as another reason for stopping. I remembered the phrase coined by the Oxford Agyasol Expedition, 'stubborn as a muleteer'. Mohammed was clearly hoping to set off home at the first opportunity, without completing his contract, and it was left to Dick and me, bemoaning the bad industrial relations which seem to taint every expedition, to rush back and forth through the trees, alternately reconnoitring the route and rushing back to help Patial cajole our caravan forward. After a weary afternoon of ill-humoured argument, we reached a suitable campsite, unloaded the mules and paid Mohammed his 2,600 rupees. Ruph Singh, the older muleteer, was his usual charming self-effacing self, almost apologising for Mohammed's behaviour, for which he was in no way responsible, and giving us his address so that we could meet him in more congenial circumstances in Kishtwar, at the end of the expedition. It was only then that we learned how shamefully he had been treated by Mohammed.

We could not have asked for a better Base Camp. A stream burbled down from a copse of silver birches on to a level meadow, where we pitched our three tents. A large granite boulder formed the back wall of our kitchen, supporting one end of the roof, the large polythene sheet we had bought in Jammu. The other end of the sheet was supported on birch posts, held tight by guylines.

After the constant travelling of the last ten days, it was a relief to settle into a permanent home, and the three of us spent a contented evening pitching tents, unpacking loads, building the kitchen, lining the floor with hessian sacks and moving in to prepare rice, lentils, onions, spices and potatoes for an enormous supper. We were granted a rain-free evening, but the monsoon was still very much in evidence and low cloud was hanging over the valley when we retired to bed. Shivling remained hidden, lurking, unseen, somewhere above us.

3 Monsoon

I was woken very early by the patter of drizzle on the tent, and spent the next hour trying vainly to sink back into the blissful oblivion of sleep; but it was no good, so as soon as the rain stopped I got up to escape the claustrophobic tent. Outside, my feet were quickly soaked in the wet undergrowth, the birch trees were dripping and granite cliffs glistened darkly in the bleak grey light. Beyond the trees I could see the gravelly grey surface of a glacier and now clouds were drifting upward to reveal bigger, blacker cliffs, the shattered profiles of ice séracs and snow gullies gouged by avalanche furrows. As the clouds continued to rise, higher bands of rock appeared, where snow, not rain, had fallen during the night, leaving a dusting of cold grey powder. Whatever this mountain was, it looked very unpleasant and I hoped that Shivling, just round the corner, was less hostile.

Dick emerged from his tent, looked up disapprovingly at the cliffs above and asked, 'Is that it?'

'I don't think so,' I replied hopefully. 'Well, I don't think we've come that far up the valley. Don't you think it's just round that shoulder?'

'I'm not sure. This looks like a big mountain. It looks a right bugger, doesn't it? Can you remember if there was anything like this to the right of Shivling?'

My memory was vague, I had forgotten the details surrounding the mountain and I began to wonder if this monster above us actually *was* Shivling.

'We'd better have a look at that photo and find out which mountain we're meant to be climbing,' Dick said, so I crawled back into my tent to rummage among books and maps, eventually finding the photo that I had taken four years earlier from a higher, more distant viewpoint. Dick studied it: 'Yes, you see those big ice cliffs above the glacier? Well, aren't they these ones here, half-way up the face? And look, that's the snow gully on the right and that's the right-hand buttress. That snow arête going up to a sort of tower is the one in sunlight on the photo ... '

It all began to make sense. We were indeed camped right at the foot of our North Face, seen now from a different angle, foreshortened so that it seemed a squat ugly travesty of the vision in the photograph.

Dick was muttering things about how horrible it looked, reinforcing my own feelings of pessimism and fear. It all looked very steep and difficult, and the ice cliffs, about which we had pondered so much at home, now seen from close quarters, looked much more extensive and threatening than the photo had suggested. We stared up at the buttress on the right-hand side of the face, which we had considered as a possible route. It would give some very steep, possibly overhanging, rock climbing and the approach up the glacier looked hideous – a chaotic jumble of leaning ice towers and dark jagged crevasses, all liberally splattered with rocks that had fallen from above. Later we were to see the rocks bouncing off the cliffs high above and winging out through space to plummet hundreds of metres on to the glacier, and at all times of day and night it was threatened by the band of ice cliffs which jutted out from a hanging glacier higher on the face. More ice cliffs further round to the right threatened other approaches to the West Ridge of the mountain.

I was depressed by this formidable battery of defences, but Dick was now being more positive and rational, continuing to search the mountain for weaknesses, and it was he who pointed out the snow arête leading up on to the left side of the face. Speaking solemnly, analysing a job of work to be done, he described the route. Above the far side of the glacier a gentle-angled snowfield, now highlighted by morning sunshine, appeared to lead without hindrance to a sharp snow arête, which in turn led up to the crest of some complex snow towers. Beyond the towers hung the ice cliffs, guarding the hanging glacier; but at this left-hand end they seemed slightly more amenable. Beyond the shelf of the hanging glacier was the headwall of steep granite, seamed with the spidery lines of snow and ice runnels, which offered a number of possibilities, all of them no doubt involving difficult technical climbing. The most prominent runnel led straight up to the summit ice field, a final topping of elaborate snow flutings, capped by an enormous cornice. The cornice seemed to be a permanent solid structure, in which case the headwall, although very difficult, would probably be free from avalanche threat. It was the lower part of the mountain, particularly the basin of the glacier, which was dangerous; and Dick's route, sneaking in from the left, was a safe prow above the avalanche funnels. There were all sorts of problems, but they were technical climbing problems which could be investigated in relative safety, free from the threat of avalanche. As for reaching the start of the prow, we could see on the far side of the glacier a long moraine of overgrown boulders curving up towards an area of moderately angled cliffs, gullies and scree slopes, through which there would almost certainly be a route up to the start of the snowfields, completely avoiding the dangerous glacier.

In half an hour we had moved from a position of fear and pessimism to one of rational hope, and it was reassuring to discover that there was perhaps a route up the North Face which we could make our first objective. For the time being, however, we would not be climbing very high. Our camp on the valley floor was only about 3,500 metres above sea level; the summit was 2,500 metres higher and most of the hard climbing would be in the last thousand metres, between 5,000 and 6,000 metres. Before tackling strenuous climbing at that altitude we would have to acclimatise, and before I could contemplate anything remotely strenuous I had to recover from the flu. The worst symptoms seemed to have passed but I was still very weak, particularly as I had eaten virtually nothing during the walk-in. The cuisine at the wayside chai houses had been rudimentary to say the least and I hadn't managed to raise much enthusiasm for the interminable bowls of overcooked rice and dahl, flavoured with nothing but the ubiquitous chili, and washed down with endless cups of 'tea', a saturated solution of tea powder, dried milk and sugar, boiled long and hard. My first priority now was to rest and eat, and I intended to start on the job right away, with a large breakfast and my long-awaited pot of strong black coffee.

We were camped in a particularly delightful spot. Wild raspberries and strawberries grew among boulders at the edge of the wood. We had fresh running water and on the first morning, when the sun had reached us, after introducing Patial to the delights of porridge for breakfast, we were able to have a good wash in the tingling water. Afterwards, I went for a walk round the meadow, photographing the luxuriant carpet of flowers.

When the sun became hotter I settled in the shade of the trees with a fat book. Acclimatising on an expedition, away from distractions, provided just the right conditions for absorbing Proust's long convoluted sentences, albeit in English, and during the next twelve days I spent many happy hours immersed in the first thousand pages of *Remembrance of Things Past*. Occasionally, however, the high seriousness of this monumental work began to pall, and I would escape for light relief to a chapter of P. G. Wodehouse. Dick, meanwhile, was glued to *The Forsyte Saga*, an unusually light book for someone with his austere tastes. Although he trained as a scientist, reading Geology at Manchester University, Dick's sympathies seem to lie more towards the arts and he must be one of the best-read climbers around.

If Proust at Base Camp suggests an atmosphere of rarefied intellectualism, we also took great pains to nurture our bodies. Days at Base Camp always started with a leisurely breakfast. I insisted on making a pot of real coffee, so thick and dark that Dick always insisted on diluting it. We also had a big bowl of porridge, followed by bread rolls; the dough was made from coarse flour and dried yeast and was deep fried in ghee over the primus, so that the end product was a sort of wholemeal doughnut, which we spread lavishly with tinned Danish butter and, until it ran out, fragrant honey made by Dick's bee-keeping father from the heather of the North Yorkshire Moors. Dick had been a vegetarian for several years and although I like to eat meat when it is on offer I was quite happy to go without it during the expedition. In the evening we usually made a large stew of beans or lentils, with carrots and potatoes, cooked in the pressure cooker and flavoured with onions, garlic, an elaborate selection of spices and various other flavourings which Dick had procured in one of Cardiff's more recherché wholefood shops. We had one bottle of whisky that was sometimes brought out for a pre-prandial drink, to be savoured with a cigarette. There was also a can of Tom Caxton's home-brew beer concentrate, and one of the first jobs on arrival at Base Camp was to dilute the concentrate, yeast and sugar in forty pints of warm water. The brew was mixed, in the absence of the bucket which had been crushed by one of Mohammed Ikbar's mules, in one of the heavy- duty polythene sacks donated by Carsons camping store. We kept it propped up with sticks and at night covered it lovingly with hessian sacks to insulate the precious fermentation against the frost.

On Sunday, our second morning at Base Camp, the weather was fine, so Dick set off to investigate the lower part of the mountain, carrying ice axe and crampons in a small rucksack. I was taking my resting very seriously and was quite happy to let Dick, who is always infuriatingly fit, do the reconnaissance. He returned in the afternoon looking pleased.

'How was it?'

'It's okay.'

'Did you reach the col?'

'Yeah. There's a good spot for a tent and the first part of the route looks all right … well, there are a few dips you can't see into, but it should be all right. There's a big boulder slope at the back of that rock peak, so you can walk round to the start of the snow slopes.'

'What about the ice cliff?'

'I'm not sure, you can't really tell from the col, but it should be all right.'

He had skirted round the foot of the glacier, just behind our camp, then climbed up the long moraine on its right bank, up into a large gully which was filled higher up with snow. From Base Camp it appeared that the top of the gully was blocked by a cliff, but he had found a way out to the left up loose rock and earth ledges, awkward but not unduly difficult. Above that, steep scree slopes had led to the col, a saddle on the crest of a rocky peak at the foot of our snow slopes. The col would be an ideal starting point for the climb proper, about 1,000 metres above Base Camp and 1,500 below the summit.

While Dick had been exploring, I had been making the acquaintance of some of the valley's other temporary inhabitants. Just above our camp, three men had diverted the stream into the hollow bole of a tree, where they were washing their blankets. They were semi-nomadic shepherds who own houses near Jammu, 300 kilometres distant, but every spring set off north with their enormous flocks of sheep and goats and with ponies carrying tents, bedding, brass cooking pots and basic foodstuffs, to spend two months travelling slowly up to the high valleys, where they remain until September, when they begin the long return journey to Jammu. Patial gave a rather disparaging analysis of their existence: 'They are a very rich people – one of these men owns 300 goats! But they do not know anything – they are just going hither and thither.'

The shepherds, known as the Jammu wallahs – or *gujars* –, are Muslims. They have the long Semitic-looking faces typical of most Kashmiris, in marked contrast to the Tibetan faces of the Buddhists in Sumcham and Potato Village, just down the valley. This particular sect or tribe do not adhere to the more oppressive dictates of Islam and the women neither wore veils nor showed any shyness about visiting our camp. We were particularly taken by one girl with unusually dark skin. Her hair was plaited into tight locks, like a Rastafarian's, and she wore elaborate jewellery.

Unfortunately, she had a young baby, which meant that there was presumably a husband lurking nearby, but she did sometimes drop in to see us, with her baby, a cousin and her younger brother, a boy of about fourteen who already had his head shaved and encased in an enormous turban, like all the men. He had a vibrant engaging personality and would spend many an hour talking and joking in Hindi with Patial, questioning him about our absurd plan to climb Shivling.

Other shepherds came to see us, often complaining of headaches. This seems to be a common problem among these people, possibly caused by some dietary deficiency; but all we could do was to give them some pain killers, warning them to go easy with them because supplies were limited and we had to keep some for ourselves, in case of high-altitude headaches or an accident.

There were other visitors to the valley. One evening, as the shepherds were rounding up their flocks, we noticed an encampment of enormous tents on the far side of the river. Patial told us that they belonged to the army. I turned to Dick and said: 'Who else would have such enormous tents?'

'Chris Bonington!' he replied, with a deprecating grin, but then went on, 'Actually … I wouldn't mind … ' and there was a faraway look in his eyes as he remembered the luxurious Base Camp of the previous year's Everest expedition, a necessary place to recover from the exhaustion of extreme altitude, with the big frame tent, the stereo cassette player, the cases of wine and champagne, the Americans dropping in for cocktails. According to Patial the army was investigating the possibility of building a road all the way up from Galhar to this valley, which would almost link up with the Zanskar road on the other side of the watershed. Apparently they were hoping to make a start on the road in ten years' time, and I thought sadly of how irrevocably the area would be changed.

If the road is built, it will provide an easy approach to the Umasi La, a high glacier pass which crosses the Himalaya just to the north-east of Kishtwar-Shivling. The pass is used frequently by Ladakhi and Zanskari traders. One evening we met two such men, who had crossed the Himalaya to trade salt for wool. They had bought the wool from the shepherds, and now it was all bundled on to the back of a shaggy yak which was being allowed its fill of grass before starting the strenuous journey back over to Zanskar. Our business was exclusively on this side of the Himalaya but we decided after three days at Base Camp to walk up to the Umasi La, not to cross it, but just to see some new country and get some exercise. It would also be a good opportunity to acclimatise, because the pass is over 5,000 metres above sea level.

Four years earlier, Philip and I had tried to cross the Hagshu La – another pass, now disused, immediately north of Shivling. I now knew that we had followed the wrong glacier branch at the head of the Hagshu Nullah, reaching the watershed well to the right of the correct pass, hence our disappointment and failure to cross to Zanskar. The Umasi La, however, is much better known and lies at the head of a parallel nullah. To reach it, Dick and I would have to walk further east up our valley, cross the river by another snow-bridge, then strike north up the Umasi Nullah.

I felt much better after three days' rest and was glad to be on the move again. We left after breakfast, carrying tent, sleeping bags, gas stove and food for an overnight stop somewhere near the Umasi La. It was a beautiful morning, with the birch trees shimmering and the pink flowers of Himalayan balsam backlit by the still low sun, which had just broken out from behind the cirque of peaks at the head of the valley. As far as I knew, the only people to have explored the glacier at the head of the valley were Fritz Kolb and his companion. They were Austrian mountaineers who had taken part in a highly successful Austro-British expedition to Lahul in 1939. Having made the first ascent of Mulkila, they descended to the valley to be confronted with the news that Britain and Germany had just declared war. The British climbers rushed off to join the war effort; the Austrians, however, were now aliens in British India and were immediately arrested, to be interned for the duration.

At the end of the war Kolb had to wait another two years before he could get a sea passage back to Europe. During that time he worked as a schoolteacher and, during his last summer leave in 1947, managed to fit in a quick expedition to the largely unexplored Kishtwar region. It was the ultimate shoestring expedition: two men with only the slenderest finances, meagre food supplies and the worn remains of equipment they had brought out to India eight years earlier. Yet they succeeded in locating the highest mountain in the area and gave it the name by which it still goes – Sickle Moon. They climbed two small peaks but inadequate equipment precluded an attempt on Sickle Moon itself, so they returned to Machail, taking note of another fine peak across the valley, Agyasol, which my Oxford friends were to climb thirty-four years later. Then, with only a few days' leave remaining, Kolb and partner set off up the valley below Shivling, to the glacier at the head of the valley. They climbed up to a high pass called the Muni La. The 1945 Survey of India map marked this pass in the midst of some very conjecturally depicted mountains, crossed by a dotted line, labelled 'old deserted road'. Kolb hoped that this pass would cross the watershed to Zanskar, but what he found was a difficult gap, which had probably never been a road to anywhere and certainly didn't cross the watershed. Instead it led them back south to the Darlang Nullah. Kolb was still very keen to reach Zanskar, but the idea of returning simply to the well-known Umasi La seemed too tame, so he suggested to his companion a more ambitious plan. During a gruelling three-day marathon the two men travelled over a hundred miles through little known terrain, with no adequate map, crossing the main Himalayan axis twice. They walked for many long weary miles up the Darlang Nullah, to find the remote Poat La, which did cross the range to the fabled land of Zanskar. At the capital of Zanskar, Padum, they only allowed themselves the briefest halt before continuing up the Doda river to locate the entrance of a valley which would take them, via some secret steps carved in a cliff, back over the Umasi La to their starting point. On the third day they reached the famous pass, descended the glacier on the south side and stumbled down through the darkness, late at night, to the first trees in the valley, where they could finally make a fire to cook their last morsels of food.

Now the crossing of the Umasi La is a popular tourist trek – quite understandably, because to cross from the harsh arid landscape of Ladakh and its southern province, Zanskar, over the monsoon barrier of the Himalaya, to the green abundance of Kishtwar, must be a very rewarding experience. As Dick and I set off from our camp, we noticed one such party, a large caravan coming down from the Umasi Nullah on the far side of the valley. We had some letters which they might be able to post, so Dick dashed ahead to cross the snow bridge and rush down the other side of the valley to catch them. He caught up with a French girl who claimed to be the group leader but who apparently had no clue where her party was heading, had never heard of Machail and didn't even know the direction they were travelling in. All initiative was left to an army of competent Ladakhi porters and guides, who assured Dick that they were heading for Kishtwar, where our letters could be posted.

Later, Dick caught up with me at the top of a steep path which zigzags up into the Umasi Nullah. In the afternoon we reached the Umasi Glacier and walked easily up its smooth surface of gravel-encrusted ice. Above us several glacier branches descended from out of the clouds, but we were not absolutely sure which of these branches led to the pass. No doubt one can buy guidebooks which explain these things, but we had no such sophistication. However, we did suspect that the pass was at the head of the easternmost branch, and in the evening the discovery of copious yak dung at the foot of a scree slope heading that way confirmed our suspicion.

Here we camped, glad of the tent as hail started to fall. The following morning, however, was fine and we continued up the scree slope and on to the upper glacier, with a small rucksack for spare clothes and some food. As we set off from the tent, Dick noticed my slow speed.

'Shall I take the sack?'

I answered irritably: 'I'll be slow whether I carry the sack or not.' But in his flat unruffled tones he insisted: 'I'll take it anyway.'

He was only trying to be helpful, but I was still feeling weak from the flu, sensitive about my slowness and perhaps slightly resentful that Dick always seemed to be taking the initiative. These feelings were quickly forgotten as we reached the crisp snow of the upper glacier and climbed steadily towards the pass, an improbable notch in the serrated ridge at the head of the glacier cwm. Just before we reached it, I noticed the prayer flags fluttering in the sunlight. A few minutes later we climbed out beside them and stopped on the crest of the Himalayan range at 5,342 metres.

We stayed for a while to enjoy the wonderful early morning view north-east over unknown, unclimbed, blue mountains, then descended to the tent and packed up for the return to the valley. On our way down we passed some Ladakhi men who were on their way up to the Umasi La. One of them was struggling to carry three enormous wooden beams right over the Himalaya to Ladakh, where timber is in such short supply.

The weather was still fine that evening and the Jammu wallah's ponies were silhouetted in the sunlight as they cantered around Base Camp. Our beer was frothing beautifully but not yet ready for drinking, so we started on the whisky while Dick cooked supper. Life seemed much better than it had done a few days earlier. I had climbed, albeit slowly, to over 5,000 metres without any ill effect and our walk to the Umasi La had given us the chance to examine Shivling from a new angle. Looking across from the north-east, we were able to see the upper part of the North Face in profile. The headwall certainly looked steep, with an average angle of about seventy degrees. We could just make out the hanging glacier below it, with the ice cliff jutting out from the face. The cliff would obviously give us some hard, vertical, ice climbing, but it did not look impossibly high. On the left, the East Face was glowing in the morning sunshine, a smooth bastion of brown-grey granite. More interesting to us was the South-East Ridge, further left, on the skyline; if the North Face proved impractical, this ridge might be a magnificent alternative, a steep buttress which, once reached, would provide a difficult but safe rock climb. However, this route did have two disadvantages: firstly, there was the long tedious approach, culminating in a snow gully which was almost certainly threatened by rockfall; secondly, if we did climb the buttress above the gully, it would not take us directly to the summit, for from its top we would have to continue over a long, almost horizontal ridge, spiked with complex towers, which would be very time-consuming. For the moment it seemed best to stick to our plan for the more direct North Face, and that evening we told Patial that we hoped to go up the next day to inspect our route.

We did not go up the next day. In the morning we sorted out food and equipment to take to Advance Base on the col, but by midday clouds were massing and just as I finished packing my rucksack the sky darkened and a fierce wind came rushing up the valley, tearing at the tents and thrashing through the trees. Then came the rain, heavy and persistent and accompanied by thunder, rumbling around Shivling. We retired to our tents and the following day the weather remained bad. On the third day the monsoon weather still hung over the valley, as I recorded in my diary:

> *Saturday 27 August – Our eighth day in the valley and still I haven't set foot on the mountain. It rained during the night and today we rose to a grey humid sky, Patial dressed up in his smart new jeans to go and visit another encampment on the far side of the river where resides a beautiful woman, who treated him to pirhata, ghee and tea and gave him two precious hen's eggs to bring back. Desperate for exercise, I went for a walk up the valley, reached the snout of the main glacier and stared up at vague dark shapes of mountains, disappearing into thick clouds. I walked back in the driving rain, getting increasingly wet and cold and glad to be returning 'home' to dry clothes, bread and butter and Earl Grey tea. Dick cooked an excellent supper of rice, dahl and potato curry, with roast flakes of coconut. Afterwards all I could do was retire to bed, light a candle and, propped up on a large pillow of clothes, read a few pages of Wodehouse, before rolling over and falling asleep.*

Sunday was again cloudy but on Monday morning, getting up at 5.30 to stagger out of the tent for a pee, I was surprised by a myopic vision of Shivling, rose-tinted against a pale blue sky. Sleepy as I was, I had to make the effort to fetch my glasses and bring the wonderful vision into focus, before returning again to the tent, to the luxury of lying in bed with an empty bladder, savouring an hour of sleepy relaxation before breakfast, secure in the happy knowledge that the day was going to have a purpose.

Later, having in the words of Bertie Wooster 'got outside' a large breakfast, we repacked the rucksacks and set off slowly under the weight of twenty-five-kilo loads. Dick quickly drew ahead, his short legs pounding inexorably up the hill, while I gangled along behind, stopping for frequent rests to photograph flowers, which included the translucent azure petals of a Himalayan Poppy and a pale cream Aquilegia. After two hours of steep struggle, aided by a pair of ski sticks, I found Dick waiting at the bottom of the snow gully. We unpacked ice axes and donned helmets as protection against any rocks that might fall from the wet walls overhanging the gully. Luckily the snow was soft enough to kick steps in, so it was easy work to reach the top of the gully; but the way out to the left looked awkward; steep loose rocks, broken by earthy ledges. It was the sort of terrain where delicacy is paramount; delicacy is hard to achieve with a heavy sack on one's back, so to guard against a possible fall we roped up, and afterwards left the rope fixed in place to safeguard any future journeys up and down that stretch.

While rooting around a dank corner of rock for a belay, I came across a cluster of *Primula macrophylla*, a plant which I had first seen in the Hagshu Nullah four years earlier. It only grows well above 4,000 metres, has thick fleshy leaves, insulated against the cold, and is crowned with a head of rich purple flowers. This was just one of many primulas and other species, like the exquisite *Paraquilegia microphylla*, with its pink cupped flower and delicate fern-like leaves, which grew near Advance Base. Finding all these flowers growing in such profusion in their natural rock gardens amongst the cliffs and boulders was a delightful distraction from the hard chore of climbing to the col, a climb which on this first occasion took me a full five hours.

Dick had been to the col before, but I had the excitement of seeing the face above at close quarters for the first time. It was very foreshortened and it was difficult to gauge the angle of the runnel on the headwall, but the lower part of the route – the ramp leading up to the ice cliff – looked reasonable. We were now at least a thousand metres above Base Camp and the birch trees in the valley looked a very long way down. At the head of our valley in the east the unclimbed peaks round the Muni La were luminous orange-pink against a dark lurid sky, and in the west the setting sun pierced shafts of light through towering cumulus clouds piled high over the turreted summit of Arjuna.

We had with us a tiny bivouac tent, a relic of Dick's early alpine days, which we might be using on the wall. For the moment it did service as our Advance Base, pitched on a small platform which we excavated from the snow and earth on the col. It was horribly cramped and we spent a restless night squeezed inside, uncomfortably aware of the ominously warm air temperature. When we set out just before dawn to investigate the lower part of the route, swirling clouds made us uneasy. The snow had not frozen during the night and at dawn, after we had climbed up a soggy gully, the clouds were firmly descending.

We stopped at the top of the gully to sit in the wet snow and discuss what to do. Dick suggested going back down but I remonstrated:

'This is easy ground; we're not going to come to any harm.'

'I just don't like climbing in these conditions,' he insisted.

'Yes, well it's not very pleasant, but I don't think it's actually dangerous.'

'Would you set out on an alpine route in these conditions?'

'No, not a big route – not to go to the top – but why can't we just go a bit further to see what it's like? This isn't the sort of slope that's likely to avalanche and if the weather gets really nasty there's nothing to stop us going back down straight away.' As usual I was impetuously anxious to get to grips with the mountain and impatient with the notion that climbing in bad weather should never be considered, as a matter of principle. But Dick was adamant that we were wasting our time.

'Look, it was nowhere near freezing last night. It's all wrong. We've got to wait till this monsoon weather's over. The mountain's not ready for climbing.'

I remembered the incident on the Finsteraarhorn, when we had argued about what to do during a break in the winter weather. We had continued, but that had been different, because we had already been committed, halfway up a big face where retreat would have been difficult; and the clouds then had proved, as forecast, to be a short break in a long fine spell. Now, on Shivling, it was a case of the whole weather pattern being wrong. Dick was right: we had ample time on our hands and the climb could wait; so we returned to Advance Base, leaving a cache of all the food and equipment, and descended to Base Camp for a late breakfast.

Once we were down in the valley, the clouds lifted tantalisingly, prompting Patial to chide us for our supposed cowardice and procrastination. He seemed to be impatient with our slow progress and this was perhaps a reflection of his own boredom, isolated as he was, away from his army colleagues and his wife and children. He couldn't even have the dubious excitement of going to Advance Base, because we dared not leave a man with no climbing experience to descend alone back down the snow gully, where a slip could result in a very long slide, with painful, or possibly fatal, consequences. Sympathising with his unenviable job, we had said all along that we would have no objection to his going to Kishtwar for a break and coming back to fetch us at the end of the expedition; but he insisted on staying to guard our camp, bored and lonely and mourning the transistor radio, which had died a quick death shortly after arrival there.

Two days later Patial did walk down to Machail to chat with the equally bored police officers doing their stint in the wilds. He returned in the evening in high spirits, slightly drunk after helping the villagers celebrate Krishna's birthday. We also had been drinking, starting on the home-brew beer, which still had a certain yeasty rawness but was just palatable and quite potent. Patial had procured some cigarettes, which we pounced on greedily, eager for every stimulant we could lay our hands on.

I was still reading Proust and was enjoying his yearning remembrance of sitting on the seafront at Balbec, in Normandy, one golden evening, watching with delighted curiosity the happy, boisterous, beautiful girls wheel their bicycles past along the front. There were no girls walking past our camp and the beautiful shepherdess was nowhere to be seen, but alcohol and nicotine induced a warm serenity, heightening genuine feelings of happiness, as I gazed out over our valley with the shredded bark of the birch trees gleaming white in the evening sunlight. In twelve days I had become very fond of this spot, and this growing intimacy with a particular corner of landscape recalled childhood camping holidays on the coast of Wester Ross, under the cliffs of a Norwegian fjord or among the forests of Ticino. Our comfortable well-stocked kitchen, nestled in the corner of the meadow, was so redolent of domesticity and security that it would almost be a wrench to leave it for the mountain waiting above. However, there had been no rain during the last two days and it seemed that we might be witnessing a change in the weather pattern. We had spent the day sorting out additional food rations, climbing equipment and gas cylinders. I had cut marker wands from the branches of a birch tree, while two floppy-eared goats watched curiously, occasionally plucking up courage to sniff my trousers. Now we had everything prepared so that if the weather remained fine in the morning we would be ready to climb back to Advance Base. We would now be equipped to stay on the mountain for at least two weeks and we hoped that, with a little luck, when we next came down to the valley we would be returning from the summit.

4 Getting to Know the Mountain

In the morning we were disappointed: the weather looked unpromising, but it was not actually raining, so we climbed back up to the col. The clouds built up during the day, and we were glad this time to have brought up a comfortable Salewa dome tent to replace the tiny bivouac shelter at Advance Base. Well aware that we might be spending some time there, we pitched the tent carefully on the col, securing the base and guylines with boulders. Before going to sleep that evening, we set the alarm for 2.30 a.m., just in case the morning should be fine enough for climbing.

At midnight we were woken by violent thunder and lightning. Rain started to beat on the nylon flysheet, announcing that we would not be going climbing that day. No matter how enthusiastic I may be about a climb, when it comes to the awful reality of getting up in the middle of the night, bad weather always comes as a blessed excuse to remain thankfully in bed with a clear conscience.

Boredom and frustration might come later, but for the moment I was content to lie in bed and enjoy listening to the fury of the elements from the warm security of a sleeping bag in a dry tent.

The patter of rain on nylon dragged on for hour after hour, only interrupted by occasional grunts of conversation, as I had a turn with *The Forsyte Saga* and Dick immersed himself in the appropriately titled *Bleak House*. Higher on the mountain we heard the clatter of stonefall and roaring snow avalanches. Because the face was so steep, new snow did not stick for long. The steam of Earl Grey tea filled the tent with memories of home, and I only wished that one could add a drop of milk from the fridge, instead of dried Anikspray.

On Saturday evening the rain finally stopped and we escaped with relief from the tent. As we ate supper outside, the clouds had gradually drifted apart to reveal Shivling, stark against a deep blue sky. The upper part of the face was plastered with new snow, but lower down only rain had fallen, compacting further the old snow leading up to the arête. If it froze hard during the night, it would be in good condition for climbing. By dusk the last clouds had evaporated and we hoped for some action in the morning. If the sky remained clear we would set off before dawn to investigate the lower part of the route, hoping in one day to reach the top of the snow arête and ascertain whether or not the towers and ice cliffs above looked a reasonable proposition. If they did, we would leave a cache of all the climbing equipment at our highpoint, return to Advance Base and then set off again on Monday with food and bivouac equipment for a summit push.

Our plan for a reconnaissance, followed by a full-scale attempt, was not in the purest modern tradition of Himalayan mountaineering. Over the last few years there has been a growing practice, helped by vastly improved lightweight equipment, of tackling difficult Himalayan peaks in 'alpine-style' – in other words setting off from the foot of the mountain with a rucksack full of everything required for the climb and moving up in one continuous unprepared push to the summit, as one would normally do in the Alps. It is a refreshing reaction to the older Himalayan tradition of enormous cumbersome expeditions, laying siege to a mountain with a line of camps and fixed ropes – a tactic used with great efficiency, for instance, on the first ascent of Everest in 1953, on the South Face of Annapurna, the West Pillar of Makalu, and the South-West Face of Everest in 1975. But 1975 had also seen the ascent of a new route on 8,068-metre Gasherbrum I by Reinhold Messner and Peter Habeler, who climbed and descended the world's eleventh highest mountain in a mere three days, carrying the minimum of equipment, rejecting even the weight of a rope, each man relying instead on his superlative skill and experience for security. And that same year there had been Dick himself, with Joe Tasker, on Dunagiri, 1,000 metres lower than Gasherbrum I, but technically harder and uncompromisingly alpine style.

Since 1975 even more audacious climbs have been achieved in the Greater Himalaya, some of them demanding an extraordinary level of confidence and commitment. Alpine style has become something of an obsession. For some pundits, only a true alpine style ascent is worth considering, and alpine style strictly precludes reconnaissance of the route: the ascent must be made in one push, with no recce, no safety line of fixed ropes, no hiccups in the single continuous upward progress. (The logical inference is that if you discover, shortly after leaving Base Camp, that you have forgotten your ice axe, going back to fetch it disqualifies you – sorry mate, if you want to do a real alpine-style ascent now, you'll have to come back again next year.) In reality, however, most people employ the tactics that seem best for them at the time. Some of the biggest, hardest recent climbs, like the daunting South Face of Lhotse, have been achieved by full-scale sieges. Other climbs have been done with the help of limited sections of fixed rope, nibbling slowly at the lower part of the rope, before leaving the top of the ropes for a quick dash to the summit.

One change that the alpine style ethic has wrought is to stimulate a revival of small expeditions. Most mountaineers nowadays prefer the ambience of a small team of two to four climbers, where decisions are made more easily and members all have a significant share of the leading, the satisfaction of being responsible for their own actions and a degree of intimacy with the mountain which is hard to find on a massive expedition. Tactics depend largely on how far people are prepared to stick their necks out; most of us are content to settle for some sort of compromise between the desire to survive and the desire to retain an element of uncertainty and adventure, adapting our tactics to a particular mountaineering problem, rather than trying to adhere to some precise dogmatic statement.

This was the case on Kishtwar-Shivling – a modest climb compared to some of the hardest routes being done on much higher peaks, but still a difficult route which was going to involve us in some slow technical climbing. Both the climb and the descent were going to require a considerable weight of climbing equipment. The weather was still uncertain, the ice cliff might involve us in long delays and it might be best to establish an intermediate camp in its vicinity. We might decide to use our limited supply of fixing rope.

As well as the climbing equipment, we would have to carry bivouac tent, sleeping bags, spare clothing, stove, fuel and several days' food supply. This all added up to an enormous weight of gear, and for the moment it seemed best to do two carries up the lower part of the route. It would give us the chance to explore the area round the ice cliff with comparatively light sacks, while we waited to see what the weather was really going to do. It would help us to acclimatise better to altitude and it would enable us to have adequate food and fuel supplies high on the mountain, so that we could, if necessary, sit out another storm and still be in a position to continue to the summit. We were also very conscious of our isolation – two people utterly alone on a steep face, with no possibility of a rescue. Patial might be able to summon a helicopter to Base Camp, but we would have to get down there ourselves. Even a simple injury, like a broken arm, would result in a slow desperate retreat, where adequate supplies of food and gas for melting snow could make all the difference between surviving and not surviving.

Possibly our approach was a little cautious, but it seemed the best way of ensuring a reasonable degree of safety and a high level of enjoyment on the mountain. As if to re-affirm that this was the best approach, Dick spoke on that Saturday evening at Advance Base of his experience on Dunagiri. It was the first time I had heard him talk in any detail about his descent from the mountain. By the time he and Joe had started down from the summit they had run out of food and fuel for the stove – the only effective means of melting snow for water. Several days later, during the long, gruelling, thirst-racked retreat, Dick had found some old scraps of paper in his rucksack and had desperately lit a tiny fire: 'I had already dropped the pan, but I was so far gone I tried melting snow in a plastic mug!'

He went on to describe his appalling frostbite, his wild hallucinations resulting from serious exposure, and the enormous effort of will required, each time he collapsed for a rest, to force himself to get up again, knowing that if he didn't he would die. Then he chuckled over the postlude: walking back on his own from Base Camp to the road to seek medical help, still desperately dehydrated, he discovered that all the streams had dried up. One morning, waking up with a raging thirst, he had been reduced to scraping off the frost on his sleeping bag and spooning it into his parched mouth.

It was a wonderful story of courage and endurance, but understandably not a story he wished to repeat, and he seemed reconciled to a more cautious approach to our attempt on Shivling.

We set off on our recce at 3.30 a. m., climbing up the boulder field behind the camp, picking out rocks in the beams of our head torches. At the snow we stopped to fit crampons to our boots, put on climbing harnesses and tie on to a fifty-metre rope. This time the snow was beautifully frozen, crisp and firm under our crampons. We quickly reached the highpoint of our abortive recce five days earlier, then continued up the humped back of the ridge, zigzagging our way up the hard snow crust. Across the valley to the east there was a faint purple glimmer of light behind the spiky silhouettes on the horizon, but we were still in darkness, using the light of our head-torches to fix a rock belay below an awkward section of the ridge. I continued while Dick paid out the rope; by the time he came up, dawn had broken and the snow ridge had form and colour, poised above a background of drifting valley clouds. Far away in the north-west, above the clouds, the high summits of Sickle Moon glowed orange. It was the first time we had seen this famous peak and I was excited to pick out the crescent-shaped snow saddle which gives the mountain its name.

Soon after dawn we discovered our first serious obstacle: the ridge was blocked by a forty-metre cliff, a great bulge of glacier ice, split into semi-translucent fins, which jutted out over space on the right side of the ridge. Dick traversed leftwards to see if there were any easy options, but the cliff continued uniformly steep and we dared not continue left into an easier snow gully, because it was one of the mountain's main avalanche chutes. We preferred to stick to the safety of the ridge and that meant climbing directly up this ice cliff which had been invisible from below. We were being forced into technical climbing sooner than we had expected.

We hammered an ice screw into the base of the cliff and I tied on, paying out the ropes through a friction brake while Dick led without his rucksack, carrying just ice axe and ice hammer and clipping one of the ropes into ice screws for protection. This section of our route, projecting like a prow from Shivling's North Face and pointing slightly east of north, caught the first sunlight of the day so that the ice cliff was now glowing a rich lambent cream colour, suffused with green and blue. It was a wonderful spectacle, with Dick's red Gore-Tex suit brilliant against the ice and, far above, the dark headwall leaning against an even darker deep blue sky.

Dick disappeared over the top of the cliff and I heard the distant sound of an ice screw being driven home. Then I just heard him shouting down:

'I'm safe, I'll pull up the sack.' It bounced and slid its way up the cliff; then he pulled my rope tight. 'Okay, you can come up.' I climbed up over the sharp fins of ice, stopping to unclip and remove a screw. The angle steepened and by the time I arrived at the second screw I was only just standing in balance. Above, the cliff bulged out and my rucksack pulled me backwards as I reached up to whack ice axes into the brittle ice.

'Tight!' I shouted, as the ice pushed me outwards and I leaned out to look down and see where I was kicking in my crampon points, before swinging ice axes in a metre higher, arms aching with the strain of my weight. 'Tight, I said!' At nearly 5,000 metres above sea level, it was strenuous work, in spite of the tight rope, and as I pulled out over the top of the cliff I was panting heavily.

We continued up a more relaxed forty-five-degree ramp, crossing at one point a dubious snow bridge over a crevasse and planting one of the birch wands to mark the crossing point.

After three more rope-lengths we reached a great snow terrace, almost flat and about the size of a football pitch. We had arrived at the foot of the snow arête, a sharply sculpted line between light and shade, curving elegantly, logically, up to the snow towers – elaborate encrustations on a rocky crest which abutted against the main ice cliff of the hanging glacier. It was now 8.30 in the morning and already the snow was becoming soft in the heat of the sun; but the west side of the arête was in shade, its snow crisply frozen and ideal for kicking steps in. So we continued, hoping to reach the snow towers. We made steady progress, moving one at a time up six rope-lengths, stopping every fifty metres to belay to a Deadman – a snow anchor plate.

At the top of the sixth pitch we traversed right to the foot of a little rock cliff below the towers, belaying to a rock peg hammered into a crack. At last we were making progress on the mountain: we had gained about 700 metres height and only the first ice cliff had given us any real difficulties. So far the route had unfolded naturally, but Dick was anxious to ascertain whether the snow towers and ice cliff really would 'go', before we dumped all the climbing gear and set off back down; so I led one final pitch. The angle was now steeper and there was interesting work to do, pulling up on flakes of granite, with my cramponed feet biting on patches of snow and ice. I moved right into a snow gully which steepened to nearly seventy degrees. Near the top I hammered in an ice screw, clipping in the rope to protect the final steep insecure moves on to a crest of sugary snow. There was just enough rope left to step round the corner on to a ledge. I was now immediately below the snow towers, strange bulbous encrustations like fantastic giant white fungi. On their left side, the melting action of the sun had exposed a narrow rock ledge and at its far end, about a hundred metres distant, I could see the ice cliff. Part of the ledge was hidden, but it seemed that we would probably be able to follow it all the way to the ice cliff. I now saw that this cliff was in fact in two sections: we would have to climb up one vertical wall of green ice to gain the ridge crest at the far end of the towers; above it easier-angled ground led up to another wall, the lip of the hanging glacier, striated by the horizontal layers of glacial ice, but also split vertically by the dark slot of a crevasse. It was hard to judge the width of the slot, but it might just be possible to climb up inside it; otherwise we would have to go straight up the bulging striated face. All this might take time but it would certainly not be impossible, and it was encouraging to discover that we would be able to bivouac near here, on the rock ledge. First, however, we had to return to Advance Base to collect all the food.

I slotted two wedge-shaped nuts into a crack, clipped one end of the rope to their wire loops and abseiled back down to Dick.

We left our climbing gear hanging from a rock peg, taking down just what we needed to safeguard our descent. It took four hours to climb back down to Advance Base. We reversed the arête and the ramp to the top of the first ice cliff, where we had left one of our 7 mm fixing ropes hanging from an ice screw. We abseiled down, leaving the rope in place for our return the next day, then continued down the ridge, moving carefully on the wet mushy snow. At the boulder field we dumped crampons, axes and harnesses, before descending the last stretch to Advance Base.

We had been gone twelve hours, twelve hours of almost continuous climbing which had left us feeling very tired. Suddenly the prospect of another predawn start in another ten hours' time did not seem very appealing. We would only have a few hours of daylight to try and dry sodden clothes and boots, soaked in the wet afternoon snow, and sort out all the food rations for the climb, before fitting in four or five hours' sleep if we were lucky. I think it was Dick who suggested: 'Shall we wait a day?' and I agreed readily, glad of the chance to get thoroughly dried out and organised before setting off on the route. We designated Monday a rest day, deciding to leave at 2 a.m. on Tuesday.

Later that afternoon Dick went over to collect our food box from a boulder cave nearby. There was suddenly an anguished cry from the cave:

'Oh no, something's been at our food!'

'Something' had ripped open the large cardboard box and scattered the remains of food and packing over a wide area, strewing the ground with burst tea bags, Crunchy Bar wrappers and piles of coffee and milk powder. It seemed to have taken a special liking to milk powder and tea bags. Luckily we were well stocked and the losses were not serious, but we were intrigued by the possible identity of the thief. The usual ubiquitous choughs, notorious scavengers, had been flying around, but they did not seem powerful enough to rip open a securely tied box, so we wondered if it might be an eagle.

The mystery was solved later that evening. At nightfall I went outside the tent. The first stars were just appearing in the sky and, far below, the blackness of the valley was broken by the orange flicker of Patial's fire. Suddenly I noticed two luminous green eyes scurrying across the snow towards the cave. I went over to investigate, shining my torch into the cave. Two green eyes stared back with a look that was both inquisitive and petulant – curious, but indignant at the interruption and annoyed that all the food had been safely bundled into a sack, weighted down with stones. The eyes belonged to a furry animal, like a large stoat, dark brown with a long bushy tail and a pale cream chest. It looked like a pine marten, which for some reason best known to itself (or had word got around about the rich pickings to be had on the col?) had decided to spend the summer right up here, far above the tree line. It darted in and out of the cave, peering inquisitively, then retreating, then plucking up courage again to thrust its face out from behind another rock. After checking that all the food was really secure, I returned to bed.

Dick was in one of his hyperactive moods the next morning and announced that he was nipping down to Base Camp to post a letter. He had been writing prolifically ever since we left England and he wanted to send off one more letter to Jan before we started the climb. We now had an arrangement with the police station in Machail to send on our mail to the post offices in Atholi and Kishtwar; the Kishtwar office had also been asked to forward any incoming mail to Machail, but unfortunately they delayed sending it up until the day we returned to Kishtwar at the end of the expedition, and somewhere in the forest we must have passed our precious long-awaited letters heading in the opposite direction on the back of a mule, never to be heard of again.

While Dick was away I enjoyed a day of peaceful domesticity. Even at 4,500 metres it was too hot for clothes and I soaked up the luxurious heat sunbathing, reading, writing my diary, fetching water from a trickle just above the camp, and sorting out food rations for the climb, juggling with different quantities of butter, cheese, oatcakes, tea, coffee, sugar, milk powder, soup, potato powder, noodles, glucose, Crunchy bars and chocolate.

Dick returned in the afternoon.

'How's Patial?'

'I think he was glad to see me, he seems very lonely. Mind you, he has been to visit his girlfriend over the river again.'

'Did you stay long?'

'Just a couple of hours. We had a meal – Patial cooked some really good dahl.' He reached into his rucksack. 'Here's your supper.'

And he pulled out a large hot tin, smelling richly of garlic and garam masala. I asked him how the beer was and he gave one of his most guilty sheepish smiles: 'Er ... yes, I did try a bit ... it's very good. It's cleared and the flavour's much better.'

I told Dick to come and inspect the food rations, proudly displayed in neat rows of bags and packets, along with several blue gas cylinders, the most important supply of all. We planned to set off with ten days' food and fuel. We reckoned that the climb would take four or five days, with another two days for the descent. That left three or four days spare, so that we could if necessary sit out a prolonged spell of bad weather in the bivouac tent, high on the face, and still have the option of continuing to the summit.

The summit still seemed very remote and hypothetical. So much depended on having some luck with the weather and, even if we were lucky, there was still the doubtful runnel on the headwall. The previous night I had lain awake, tormented by visions of jibbering hopelessly up ever thinner, hollower ice, vainly searching blank rock underneath for belays. I had imagined ice blocks smashing down from the summit cornice and had visualised with horrible realism a failed belay – the long bouncing plunge into the dark abyss of the glacier far below – or perhaps a short fall, held by the rope, but leaving one of us in agony with a shattered leg … Would we really manage to get down safely?

On this night, however, I managed to suppress morbid fantasies and it was only excitement that kept me awake, an impatient longing to get to grips with the mountain and unlock some of the secrets of the route. I turned over and over in my sleeping bag, switched on my head-torch to read more of *The Forsyte Saga*, tried sleeping again, lit a cigarette, read a few more pages. Eventually I realised that I wasn't going to sleep and, while Dick snored beside me, I watched the minute hand of the clock move slowly round to one o'clock.

At last it was time. I crawled out of the tent's sleeve entrance, lit the stove for a brew and sat down to put on double boots and gaiters. The air felt suspiciously moist and our ready-packed rucksacks were coated thickly with frost, but the sky was perfectly clear, luminous with thousands of stars. I woke Dick and he joined me outside for a quick breakfast. We packed the remaining odds and ends for the mountain in our rucksacks and shut up the supplies we were leaving in the tent, zipping up the door to deter the pine marten, and at two o'clock on the morning of Tuesday 6 September, we shouldered our sacks and set off into the darkness.

5 On the Wall

I moved alone, isolated in a pool of torchlight, enclosed by the heavy sound of my own breathing and the crunch of crampons biting on the frozen crust underfoot. Once again the rope jerked me forward and I shouted angrily to Dick, fifty metres ahead; 'Slow down – I can't go that fast!'

He slowed down and asked: 'Is that better?'

'Yes, thank you – that's perfect – just keep it like that and I'll do fine.' We continued at a slow measured pace, settling into a steady rhythm which allowed my lungs to keep pace with my legs, stepping endlessly, repetitively up the humpback ridge. Now that I was not gasping for breath, I could start to enjoy the unique thrill of moving smoothly upwards, alone in the darkness, happy to be setting out at last on a great adventure.

We halted at the first ice cliff, peering with our torches to find the end of the fixed rope. 'I'll go first,' I announced, 'and send the jumars down afterwards.' I had never before used jumars to climb up a rope though, like most people, I had seen television shots of famous mountaineers sliding the handles with apparent effortless ease, as they made their way smoothly up fixed ropes on some vast mountain face. But I quickly discovered, fumbling in the dark, that it is actually an exhausting process, and the final struggle over the ice overhang left me gasping for breath and sweating profusely.

On the ramp above, I clipped into the ice screw, took off my rucksack and clipped that in too, then attached the jumars to the rope with a karabiner and slid them down to Dick, waiting below. I quickly became cold and took out my duvet jacket. Having put it on, I sat down again, leaning against the slope and staring out over the valley. Dick was invisible, hidden below the cliff, and only the tension on the rope and the distant muffled clink of ironmongery hinted at his progress up the rope. The only clouds were a few benign silver wisps hanging innocently in the valley. The immense sky above was still brilliant with stars; on the far side of the valley there was again the faintest purple glow, near the Umasi La. It was one of the few occasions in my life when I have been prompted to remember lines of poetry. I have an appalling memory for words and it is usually only music that sticks, but that wonderful glow over the Himalaya did stir memories of some lines from Shakespeare – something like, 'Look where the morn ... all russet ... no – in russet ... in russet mantle clad ... steals o'er something or other ... ' It was poignant to recall, albeit imperfectly, those lines first heard long ago at school, and to wonder whether I had then imagined that fourteen years later I might be standing alone in the darkness, tied to an ice screw on an unclimbed peak, watching the first glimmer of dawn appear over the crest of the Himalaya.

The growing noise of clinking equipment and crampons scraping on ice and the dim glow of torchlight reflected below the lip of the cliff announced that Dick was about to arrive and my sense of poetry gave way to a more prosaic concern for my cold body and a longing to be on the move again.

We stopped for a second breakfast at the terrace. While we ate our Crunchy Bars and drank orange juice laced with Glucodin, the surrounding mountains came to life and the sun burst on us, full of effulgent promise. Once again we climbed the snow arête, so reminiscent of the famous arête on the Frendo Spur on the Aiguille du Midi high above Chamonix; but there was a difference – that arête comes as the climax of the route, whereas ours on Shivling was just one more incident before the real difficulties started. We had a long way to go, but already on this first morning there was an exhilarating sense of height and space, and the birch trees of the valley, nearly two thousand metres below, looked tiny, remote, abstract, almost lost in the swirling patterns of grey river channels.

At the top of the arête we jumared up the rope which I had left two days earlier to the snow towers, and continued round the corner, edging along the narrow rock ledge. After one rope-length we belayed to a large granite block and inspected a lower ledge, poised like a balcony above overhanging rock walls. This ledge was not absolutely flat, but it was spacious and would make a reasonable bivouac site. It was only midday and rather early to stop, but already the ice cliff was starting to trickle with water, so we decided to wait here and leave the cliff for the frozen cool of the morning. We dumped our rucksacks, returned to the fixed rope, descended it to collect all the cached climbing gear, jumared back up, pulled up the rope and returned to the Balcony, to settle down for an afternoon of sunny relaxation.

There is a lot to be said for an early stop. It gives you ample time to fix a secure belay, hang up all the equipment, tie in everything (including yourself) safely, and get organised and comfortable for a good rest, eating, drinking and sleeping well before starting the next day's work.

Later that afternoon, while drinking one of many brews of tea and eating biscuits and cheese, we discussed what to do next. I was worried that the lip of the hanging glacier might conceal a complex maze of crevasses above. I still thought that the ice wall of the lip, hanging above us, might cause long delays, and I wondered whether we ought to do two ferries to a base on the hanging glacier, before tackling the headwall. Dick was keen to be more mobile, setting off from here in one push, instead of wasting time and effort to-ing and fro-ing. As he pointed out, if we ran into desperate difficulties we could always return to the Balcony for more supplies. I began to agree that we should discard the fixing ropes and set off with just the two 9 mm climbing ropes and enough gear to get us up and down the headwall. As the sun dropped round towards the west, leaving us in shade, we worked through all the food and gear, packing a small sack with the things we could afford to leave.

'What about the butter?'

'Just take half the tin.'

'Milk powder – I don't mind going without it. We can drink black tea.'

'No, let's take it. It's very light and full of protein.'

'Twenty karabiners enough?'

'Twenty-four.'

'Okay, twenty-two. Do you think we can leave these three pegs?'

'Yes, but we'd better take all the ice screws – we're probably going to need them to abseil down the icefields.'

'Cheese – this Edam has really improved … tastes more like Gruyere now …'

'We'll have to leave some of it. Why don't we leave the Edam for the way down and take up the smoked stuff? You know, this is still going to be quite a weight of food.'

'Yes, but we can always dump another reserve at the next bivouac. I'm all for having meals waiting for us on the way down.'

And so it went on – a careful, methodical paring down of supplies, to bring our rucksacks down to something like an acceptable weight. Everything was organised by the evening. I climbed up to the higher ledge, taking care to remain clipped into the belay, to scoop up more water from a trickle of melting ice, then clambered back down to cook supper. It was still light when we turned in, building up the ledge with ropes to make it more level, before settling into down sleeping bags for a contented night's sleep.

We failed to hear Dick's alarm watch in the morning, so we were a little late and the sun had already risen when we moved off along the ledge. I led to the end of it and belayed to a screw right at the foot of the ice cliff, the second ice cliff on the route. I have always found steep ice unnerving and was glad when Dick volunteered to lead the pitch. He stepped straight off the ledge on to vertical ice, glassy, brittle and unyielding. After a couple of metres he gasped, 'This is hopeless. I'll have to take my sack off,' and he came down to leave the rucksack tied to one of the ropes.

He returned to the fray, moving more easily now, battering the ice to remove loose brittle flakes and find secure placements for ice axe picks and crampons, stopping about five metres above me to hammer in an ice screw and clip in one of the ropes, leaving the other free for hauling up the sack. Later, after he had disappeared from sight, belayed and pulled up the sack, I followed on the second rope, leaning back heavily on it when I had to stop and twist out the ice screw. I continued up the unrelenting ice and as I hammered one of the axes above my head the slewing movement swung me out of balance, pulling my weight on to the rope again. Dick's ice climbing technique, as well as his equipment, seemed to be better than mine and I was glad to be on the blunt end of the rope.

He was waiting in the middle of a fifty-degree slope of glittering snow. I stopped, took off my sack, grabbed some screws, karabiners, slings and a Deadman, and set off for the third ice cliff, wondering if I was going to cope.

It proved to be a pitch of delightful surprises. At the base of the striated cliff I found hard ice, where I could place a protecting screw before balancing leftwards to the vertical slot, a chimney wide enough to climb inside. I shouted down to Dick, 'It's fantastic!' as I made my way up inside the chimney, with my back pressed against the left wall, crampons gripping on the right wall and ice picks providing handholds. The ice here was beautifully soft after the brittleness of the second cliff, and my picks stabbed easily into the smooth opaque surface like proverbial knives into butter. Higher up, the crevasse narrowed and I crawled out on to the face on the right. Now I was above the overhanging bulge, the face was only about seventy degrees and I could kick steps up the steep snow. The angle relented and I emerged over the top, on to the hanging glacier, to discover another wonderful surprise: there was no maze of séracs and crevasses, just a smooth shelf, sloping gently up and then steepening into the first ice field of the headwall. We had successfully climbed one of the main obstacles of the route and resolved one of the big question marks.

I couldn't wait to share my euphoria with Dick, so I was disappointed when he appeared, looking cross.

'I sometimes wonder at you,' he said in tones of weary resignation. I smiled innocently and asked what he meant. 'What do I mean? You know you had the rope way to the right of the chimney? It was desperate: I had to climb straight up the overhanging part and then wade up that snow, when there was a bloody great line of bucket steps four feet to the left!'

'I'm sorry,' I replied, suitably chastened. Luckily he quickly forgot about the mistake, dismissing it with one of his grunting laughs, and enthused about the encouraging prospects ahead. We could start work on the headwall right away and it looked as though we might find somewhere to bivouac at the top of the ice field, before moving right under rock walls to the runnel.

We walked across the glacier shelf then zigzagged up steepening snow and finally reverted to a facing-in position below the bergschrund, the big crevasse separating the hanging glacier from the steep ice field above. It was my turn to lead and the bergschrund gave some good sport, hacking and excavating my way over the upper lip and swinging up on to firm ice above. We climbed three pitches up the ice field, first following a rib of snow, then, when it became unstable, moving left into a glazed avalanche furrow, which steepened to at least sixty-five degrees. At one point, when Dick was leading, one of his crampons – smart new contraptions called Footfangs which clip on to the boots with ski-type bindings – came loose and he had a worrying few moments, balanced on one foot while he refitted the errant Footfang.

On the second afternoon we again stopped early, taking advantage of what might be the last reasonable bivouac site for a long way to come. We worked hard to create a ledge underneath a little rock overhang. Patches of snow on the granite wall above, melting in the afternoon sun, had produced a steady trickle, which seeped down into the back of the overhang, dripping on to the ledge; so we called this second bivouac Drip Ledge; but the drips could be avoided and by evening they were frozen static, so we were quite comfortable, perched on a snow ledge about three metres long by sixty centimetres wide.

We had a wonderful evening, again eating and drinking well and puffing contentedly at a cigarette, while we watched the landscape change in the shifting evening light. Immediately below us the ice field funnelled down dramatically to the hanging glacier and below that the red blob of our spare provisions bag was just visible on the balcony, perched improbably above steep cliffs. Two choughs were flying and hopping around it curiously. Across the valley, slightly to the right, I could see the meandering stream of the Hagshu Nullah, where Philip and I had been four years earlier. Dick was very taken with the monolithic flat-topped pyramid at the head of the nullah, commenting: 'You know, that's one of the most impressive mountains in the area.'

'What about this mountain?'

'You mean Shivling? Oh yes, this isn't a bad mountain.'

Further left, we could see the Barnaj peaks, where friends of ours had been climbing a few years earlier. We could also just make out some of the rock needles above the Chiring Nullah, climbed by Lindsay Griffin, whom I had been with in Afghanistan in 1977. Sickle Moon, climbed by the Indian High Altitude Warfare School in 1975, still dominated the landscape in the north-west, massive above the complexity of deep hidden valleys. South of it, the summit of Brammah, the mountain which Vigne's fakir attempted but which was eventually climbed by an Indo-British expedition in 1973, was now piercing through diaphanous orange clouds, glowing in the setting sun.

As the sun sank from view, the clouds evaporated, giving us hope for another day of fine weather. Dick had become infectiously optimistic, persuading me that we should aim the next day, Thursday, to climb right to the top of the runnel, to a bivouac on the shoulder of the East Ridge. On Friday, if all went well, we would travel light, climb quickly to the summit and back, and perhaps start down the same day from the top bivouac. We decided to take food and fuel for two nights, which could at a pinch be stretched to three. The bivouac tent we would leave at the ledge; if we were caught in a storm we would have either to try to dig a snow hole on the ridge or hurry back down the North

Face to the shelter of Drip Ledge. Climbing gear was also slightly reduced, because we knew some of it would have to be kept in reserve to make abseil anchors back down from Drip Ledge to the Balcony. We were now going to continue with seven ice screws, two Friends (adjustable camming wedges), three small nuts, three large nuts, eight rock pegs, twenty-two karabiners, a selection of tape slings and two climbing ropes.

Now that we were approaching 6,000 metres, the air was colder and the time had come to don another layer of clothing. I had in reserve a pair of thermal long johns which I decided to put on that evening before it became impossible higher up; already changing was awkward. It was a delicate process: taking off boots and carefully clipping them into the belay; then fixing a loop round my chest to clip in so that I remained attached to the mountain while removing my waist harness; then perching, stork-like on the ledge, to remove overtrousers and the one-piece fibre pile suit, stow them carefully at the back of the ledge, put on long-johns and pull back on the outer layers; then rebuckling my waist harness, tying it back into the belay, removing the temporary chest loop and putting on my down jacket. Dick was already settled in bed, facing me from the far end of the ledge, with the umbilical cord of his belay loop protruding from his sleeping bag and clipped into a peg on the wall above. I arranged my foam karrimat on the remaining space at my end of the ledge, sat down, adjusted my belay loop for length, wriggled into my tube of goose down, and then lay down, to sink luxuriously into the warm blur of sleep.

On Day Three we were determined to leave at first light. Dick started the first breakfast brew at 1.30 a.m., waking me half an hour later with a mug of tea. Before starting a day's work in the thin dry high-altitude air it was essential to drink plenty of liquid; so we made three large brews before leaving the warmth of our sleeping bags to get packed and ready. As always on these pre-dawn starts there was a strange juxtaposition of the sublime and the mundane: on the one hand, a Wordsworthian awareness of solitude under the immense silent starlit sky; on the other, the chore of lacing up stiff frozen boots with cold fingers, of sorting out the confused tangle of ropes and slings and the sleeping bag which refuses to fit into its stuff sack; the rumbling of a belly which has been forced into an unnaturally premature breakfast – and the need to relieve yourself, however cold and awkward it is, fumbling with buttons and zips and leaning out backwards over the dark drop, reminding yourself that it is better to get it over and done with now, rather than run the risk, later in the day halfway up some steep precarious pitch, of a sudden fear-induced loosening of the sphincter.

Dick started the first pitch at five o'clock. Dawn had not quite broken, so he moved off by the light of his head torch, traversing right across the top of the icefield.

We followed a meandering route that day, deviating from the original plan to climb straight up the runnel. The ice field was fine – three full rope-lengths of steady sideways progress, across a band of sixty-degree snow and ice, suspended between steeper rock walls, with the security of good belays on dependable tubular ice screws. On the fourth pitch I traversed round a tongue of rock and moved up into the runnel. Then we struck difficulties.

Dick continued higher, muttering things about hollow ice. There was an abortive scratching, as he searched unsuccessfully for a running belay. He led out the full fifty metres of rope, then spent an age fixing up a main belay, before I could follow.

The ice was indeed hollow, with a pocket of air between its thin skin and the smooth, ice-worn granite underneath; higher up there was unconsolidated snow and when I joined Dick he pointed out that the belay was very sketchy. He also pointed out how hard the continuation of the runnel looked: it reared up above us, a faint shallow gully, smeared with thin slivers of ice, too thin for ice screws. Where the rock showed through, it looked blank and smooth, offering little hope for pegs and nuts. The final steep bulge, plastered with the thinnest streak of ice, looked particularly repellent and the thought of attempting that kind of precarious climbing with only marginal protection was not appealing. We were also concerned, now that we were so close underneath it, about the summit cornice: just supposing it was unstable – we would be exposed in the line of fire for many hours.

It took Dick a few minutes to bring me round to his way of thinking, persuading me that the runnel was unacceptably risky, enticing me away from the direct logical line with the lure of solidity and security on the rock walls to the left, where cracks and chimneys offered the promise of safe nut and peg placements.

So we changed course, moving back left away from the runnel. I made straight away for a large rock spike, draping it with a sling and clipping in one of the ropes, to make a secure running belay. It was reassuring to have this good runner, so that if I did fall off we would not be reliant solely on Dick's flimsy belay. I continued up a pitch of my favourite type of climbing, typical of north faces all over the Alps and the Himalaya – a mixture of rock, snow and ice, where there is sufficient snow and ice to need crampons on one's feet, but where the rock adds a complexity and variety missing on pure snow-ice slopes. Ice axes, instead of just being whacked into ice, are used to excavate handholds on a snow smothered block, or to scrape clear a little nick on which one can stand in crampon points, or to reach up and hook a flake of rock which hands cannot reach.

I moved up into a chimney. Now the ice axes were dangling on their slings and I was climbing with gloved hands on the rock, jamming fingers in a crack and bridging up with cramponed feet on each side. The chimney narrowed and I squeezed more awkwardly upwards, my bulging rucksack catching in the constriction. It was difficult, but the ropes below were running through several karabiners, clipped reassuringly to pegs and nuts in the rock. I had almost reached a suitable belay ledge, but first I had to gain another metre of height. I strained up with my left hand, reaching for a block, while my right elbow pushed against the wall behind, right foot wedged in the snow at the back of the chimney and left foot scrabbled at the left wall, struggling to hook a crampon point on to a nick of rock. The crampon stuck and with an ungainly panting heave I pulled up on to the ledge.

After leaving the runnel we climbed four pitches, zigzagging leftward up the rock wall, following in the line of least resistance, but never quite sure where the line was leading us. First there was my chimney pitch, then Dick disappeared round a corner to the left, then I, too, continued left, evading the steepest rock and following a sloping snow-covered shelf, balancing round underneath over- hangs. By the time Dick had joined me at the end of this pitch the sun had crept round on to the wall and for a while we enjoyed its brightness and warmth.

It was already mid-afternoon and we were nowhere near the shoulder of the East Ridge. Now that we had wandered so far left we were not sure where to go next. Perhaps we should have headed straight up one of the steep cracks we passed? Perhaps we should go further left and climb up an icy chimney to one of the great towers on the East Ridge? But that would leave us with a long traverse back right along its intricately turreted crest. Immediately above us, steep granite slabs curved up out of sight. They looked very hard but it seemed that we would have to climb them and try to break back right higher up towards the summit. There did seem to be a line, starting with steep cracks leading to a chimney. Unfortunately, the chimney was capped by an overhang, which might require slow artificial climbing; but above that there was a vague suggestion of a break, which looked as though it might be a ramp leading back right. It all looked very hard and it threatened some slow technical rock climbing. We were obviously going to be another day on the wall and it was too late now to start on the overhang pitch, so for the moment all we could do was climb a steep snow ramp to the foot of the pitch and hope to find somewhere to bivouac there.

At three o'clock we started to excavate our bivouac ledge. Half an hour's hacking at a lump of hard ice produced little in the way of a ledge, so I climbed higher, pulling strenuously up on to a rock pedestal, crowned with a blob of snow. It wasn't much but I could dig a small ledge in the snow, thirty centimetres wide by a metre long, like a small bench seat. Dick was not impressed but agreed that it would suffice in the absence of anything better; so we spent the night there, sitting upright, with our backs leaning against the vertical rock wall behind, and our feet hanging over the sloping snow bank, resting in rope loops for support.

By the time we were organised it was nearly dark. We sat side by side, in our sleeping bags, tied to two rock pegs, surrounded by festoons of climbing gear and our rucksacks, also suspended from the pegs. Dick commented that it was like sitting on a window ledge on the ninetieth storey of a skyscraper. When it became dark we flashed our torches to show Patial where we were. Far, far below we could see the tiny flash of his torch beside the yellow flicker of the fire. Further down the valley there was a light in Sumcham and we wondered what the villagers thought about our improbable lights on Shivling. Most of the Jammu wallahs had now left for home, but a few remained and we could also see their fires. Later Patial told us that one of them, a hadji who had twice made the pilgrimage to Mecca, had prayed for our safety.

We placed the stove on the ledge between us, melting snow to make a meagre supper of soup and noodles. After supper I had work to do: my overtrousers needed mending. They were a fine pair of trousers, made of Helanka, a warm, wind-and-snow-resistant fabric. They had started life in 1956, in Austria, made for my father by a Kitzbühl tailor. Then they had been the height of skiing fashion, with a tailored waist and tapered legs stretched down to heel loops. My father had used them for about twenty years before a sudden attack of fashion-consciousness forced him to discard them, whereupon I took them over, setting to work on the sewing machine, extending the waist with a sort of cummerbund and adding darts, gussets, braces and zips, to make an excellent pair of mountaineering overtrousers. With their thigh-length leg zips, they could be taken on and off over crampons, and they were bulky enough to wear over long johns and fibre pile trousers. They had done good service on many expeditions, but today one of the zips had finally broken, leaving the right leg gaping open. The zip was beyond repair, so I now had to lace up the split with a length of string. It was far too cold to get out of the sleeping bag, so the repair had to be done inside the bag – an awkward process which entailed leaning over, reaching down with my arms into the restricted tube of the sleeping bag and, working by feel alone, boring holes in the trouser fabric with my penknife and then threading through the string. The final result looked like some medieval peasant's leggings, but it worked, keeping out most of the snow during the days ahead.

Between supper and breakfast we had about five hours' rest on the Window Ledge. We slept a little, but never for more than a few minutes at a time, always longing to be able to lie down flat instead of leaning uncomfortably against the unyielding wall.

It was my turn to lead in the morning. I left my rucksack tied on the ledge and set off, armed just with ice axe, ice hammer, all the climbing hardware and my camera. First I had to stretch out from the pedestal to reach the start of the cracks; then I began to gain height, pulling up on finger jams in the crack. Higher up, as I moved right to another steep wall split by a crack, I started to enjoy myself. I had been very apprehensive about this pitch, but the sudden rush of action had brought warmth to stiff limbs and filled me again with enthusiasm for the climb. The rock became steeper and almost devoid of snow, so I stopped to remove crampons, hanging them on the back of my harness. Then I started up the next steep section, bare fingers wrapping round features in the cold rock, the huge unwieldy Vibram soles of my double boots gingerly testing tiny ledges. After hammering in a peg for protection, I moved left to a corner which offered more protection and a route up into the chimney. The overhang proved to be a huge flake of granite hanging out over the chimney. I hit it with the palm of my hand and it made a deep booming noise. In underneath it was a wide flared crack where I could place our largest Friend; it cammed perfectly in the slot, providing protection for the moves ahead.

We had feared that the overhang might require artificial climbing, but once again the mountain surprised us with a delightful passage of free climbing. The rock was solid and rough, covered in knobbly rugosities, wonderful to climb and suddenly reminding me of Scafell, where I had been climbing a few weeks earlier. It was possible to tiptoe sideways, with my hands underclinging the lip of the flake, until I could reach up higher to handholds and pull up on to the top of the flake. I stopped to blow on numb fingers, then climbed up leftwards over a wrinkled slab to a small footstep, where I could just stand in balance and fix up a belay. I hauled up the rucksack on the blue rope (a laborious job) and then Dick came up, carrying his sack and collecting all the runners clipped into the purple rope.

As he pulled up on numb fingers to the belay, I said: 'Sorry I was rather long leading it.'

'I thought you were quick.'

'Really?'

'Yes. I thought it was hard; you're climbing well … do you mind leading the next pitch? My fingers seem to be really cold.' Perhaps his old Dunagiri frostbite injuries were impairing circulation. My fingers were warm and raring to get to grips with more interesting climbing, so I was glad to lead another pitch. There would no doubt be occasions later during the climb when I would be glad to rely on Dick to take over my lead.

We climbed eight pitches that day, our fourth day on the route. Once again the sky was blue and the summit snowfield, growing closer and closer on the right, was brilliant white in the sunshine. It was possibly the best day's climbing I have ever had, giving us a succession of difficult, fascinating, wonderfully varied pitches. We could never see far ahead, so there was the continual excitement of not being sure what we would find round the next corner; but the route always unfolded with a logical continuation, obvious but never easy; each move was a new problem to be solved.

The first pitch up the overhang gave us some fantastic rock climbing. The second was more mixed, climbed in crampons up some steep cracks, then following the rightward ramp, up steep shelving snow, searching the granite wall above for handholds. The third pitch was a diedre – an open, square-cut corner – led by Dick. While I leant back in my harness at the belay, using one hand to take photographs and the other to pay out the ropes through my friction break, Dick stepped across into the corner, formed by a thirty-metre-high pillar leaning against the wall. He climbed the Renshaw Diedre with great panache, cramponed feet biting at ice on the left wall, hands searching for holds and nut placements on the right wall. Higher up the ice on the left wall became thicker and he took out his ice axe to supplement the ice hammer and complete the pitch with some very steep ice climbing. Waiting at the belay, I felt utterly content, paying out the ropes and smoking a cigarette, while I watched Dick perform above. Few things could give more pleasure than spending such a perfect day in this extraordinary vertical landscape, totally absorbed in what we were doing, living entirely for the moment.

Above the Renshaw Diedre there was more fascinating variety for me to explore: a delicate traverse right on steep snow-smothered slabs, a pause to take off crampons, then a steep wall split by a single crack, recalling the famous *Grandmère Crack* on the Aiguille du Plan near Chamonix; then another move right, size twelve boots tiptoeing on minute nubbins, and then a final chimney, strenuous and brutal, leading to a sort of resting place and a belay.

It was midday and the sun had swung round on to the North-West Face. Away to the south-west the usual afternoon clouds had begun to mass in the valleys, but the familiar shapes around us of Brammah, Barnaj, Sickle Moon, Arjuna, Chiring and Hagshu were all clear, and the sky above was deep blue. Far away in the north-west, beyond Sickle Moon, we could now see the two bulky summits of Nun and Kun, the highest and most famous peaks in the Kashmir Himalaya, visited every year by numerous expeditions. On Shivling we were now hanging above tremendous depths, with the headwall funnelling down to the great jutting shelf of the hanging glacier, apparently suspended in space above the dark crevasses of the main glacier much further below. Further right, the snow ridge which we had climbed on the first day now looked completely flat, distorted by a new dramatic perspective. We had come up a long way and had now almost reached the shoulder on the East Ridge, where we hoped to emerge from the North Face and find a spot, among towering snow mushrooms, to dig a comfortable bivouac ledge.

Before continuing we stopped for a short rest, sucking orange and Glucodin juice from the ice-encrusted neck of the water bottle. Then we plastered our faces with sun cream before Dick started up the fifth pitch.

We had almost worked back round to the line of the runnel which emerged on to the summit snowfield a short way below us to the right. We intended to avoid the fragile flutings of the summit snowfield, heading instead for the East Ridge directly above us. Dick led across a precarious snow ledge into a concave wall composed of granite blocks and snow. It looked short and straightforward and I imagined that we would reach the ridge above in no time at all. I started impetuously up the sixth pitch, not even bothering to collect all the gear from Dick. I quickly discovered that I was in fact moving into very steep terrain, putting in more protection than I had intended, and rapidly running out of gear. A short wall, which had looked innocuous from below, held me up for nearly half an hour, as I tried in vain to reach up and place a peg. Eventually I managed to lodge the pick of my axe, stretched high above my head, into a thin crack and pull up on it, while I flailed with my left arm and leg at a vertical snowdrift on the left, gradually heaving up past the wall and swimming up horribly steep unconsolidated powder to a little cave, where I collapsed to regain my breath. I used my last karabiner to clip into a Friend belay and brought up Dick.

He led the seventh pitch, using nuts and pegs for direct aid to climb over a steep wall and a vicious corner. While he engineered this pitch, the sun swung round the west tower of the mountain, sinking towards a gathering mass of clouds. They now looked more serious than the usual afternoon cloud – vast turbulent cumulus, with ugly missile-shaped streaks of cirrus above. Suddenly, just as we were getting really high and committed on the mountain, so close to the summit, the weather was threatening to wreck everything.

I followed Dick, struggling in the corner, where you had to step in a sling suspended from a nut, reach up high, thrust ice-axe shafts into a pile of loose snow, and pull up strenuously on to an apology for a ledge. I hurried on, racing the approaching darkness. The huge snow mushrooms of the ridge bulged out just above us, forcing me to shuffle sideways along a sloping rock ledge, driving picks into the ice above for balancing handholds, until it was possible to climb straight up through a slight break in the bulges. I managed to place one ice screw – the only protection on the pitch – before thrashing up a seventy-degree wall of snow, precarious and loose, forcing me to thrust deep with axe shafts and to lift legs high above knee level to kick steps which would not collapse. It was a strenuous athletic finish to a long day and, now that we were approaching 6,000 metres, it was hard on the lungs. The sun was sinking rapidly, deep red, into a seething mass of clouds as I kicked and shoved up the last stretch, to emerge from the North Face on to the crest of the ridge.

It had been a hard day. After the uncomfortable night on the Window Ledge, we were longing to lie down. While Dick came up, I peered through the fading light, looking around for a suitable spot to bivouac. The narrow crest of the ridge was overgrown with huge snow mushrooms, bulging out over the steep drop on both sides. A few feet away, towards the summit, the crest of one mushroom seemed quite solid and not quite so undercut as some of the more fantastic formations. When Dick arrived we put on our head torches and started to investigate. We fixed up a safety line, tying a length of rope from the rock belay to a Deadman, dug into the snow of the mushroom; then we started excavating.

The missile clouds were still spreading from the south-west in sinister dark bands reaching across the sky, and a vicious cold wind was blasting across the ridge from the north-west, so we dug down on the south-east side, making a large ledge, protected by a snow wall. When the ledge was large enough, we started to get ready for the night, spreading out karrimats and laboriously brushing snow from our clothes and boots.

Later, after poking our heads over the ridge to flash Patial, we got into our sleeping bags and I began to prepare tea, slowly melting snow to produce a full pan of water. When it began to heat, I added tea bags and sugar, then lay back to wait for it to boil. Eventually came the long-awaited bubbling noises and I turned round to pick up the pan. There was a sudden orange flash and a hiss of steam; then darkness and the tinkling sound of metal bouncing down over snow crystals; then a distant clatter, followed by silence. The stove was clutched firmly in my hand, but the precious pan full of tea had gone, knocked over the edge by a clumsy swipe of my elbow.

'Sorry – the saucepan's gone.'

'You bloody idiot!' Dick stared incredulously at me from behind the merciless beam of his head torch. What were we going to melt water in now? Without water we could not go on. I apologised abjectly, humiliated and angry with myself for ruining what had been a perfect day. Up till now everything had gone so smoothly and we were close to completing the hardest and most enjoyable climb that I had ever attempted.

Luckily there was a solution to the problem. We still had one full spare gas cylinder and the cylinder on the stove was almost empty: it would have to suffice as a saucepan. I removed it from the stove and set to with my penknife, hacking open the domed top of the empty cylinder. It was not ideal, but balanced on the stove, it did slowly melt small quantities of snow, and laboriously I produced half cups of tea, soup and orange juice.

Dick made one of his grunting laughs and said: 'At least you didn't drop the stove.' Eventually he got bored with waiting for brews and fell asleep. I sat up late, working sleepily to fill the water bottle with liquid for our summit climb. I was still hoping desperately that we would be going to the summit the next day; but I had to admit that that was now in doubt. The wind was still blowing over the ridge, just above our heads; the sky was murky with clouds and there were more in the valley, lapping menacingly at the foot of the mountain. Looking out across the towers of the South-East Ridge I could see lightning flickering in the sky away to the south, illuminating more dark bands of cloud. It was sinister and depressing.

6 The Summit

Saturday 10 September – a joyless predawn. After only three hours sleep, I was woken at two o'clock to start brewing. Reluctantly, I pulled myself into a sitting position, switched on my torch, found my glasses and started again to dig with the spoon, scooping lumps of snow into the torn gas cylinder. We had little left to eat but we did make a point of drinking as much liquid as our new improvised pan would allow, before leaving for the summit. I don't think that either of us ever mentioned that morning the possibility of *not* going to the summit. Presumably, if it had actually been snowing we would either have dug into a better shelter or set off down; but it was not snowing – at least not yet. The sky at dawn was heavy with the threat of stormy weather: in the south, range after range of peaks were disappearing under the clouds; in the north, the familiar panorama was still just visible, surreally clear against a narrow strip of intense pale blue, isolated between bands of dark cloud above and seething grey waves billowing up from the valley. Evil lenticulars hovered high in the north-east. When the sun appeared it was wan and brief.

It was a menacing start to the day and by all normal criteria we probably should have abandoned the climb. However, we carried on, determined apparently to complete the job. The existence of reserves of food and fuel and a bivouac tent below slightly reduced the seriousness of what we were doing: descending in a storm would be miserable and difficult, but at least we would be heading for creature comforts. So we carried on, hoping that the storm would hold back awhile or be short-lived, not really expecting to enjoy ourselves as we had done on the previous four days, just determined to take what might be our last chance of going to the summit. It was going to be hard work and we hoped to get the job done as quickly as possible.

Looking up from the bivouac towards the summit, we changed our minds about following the top part of the East Ridge. It was composed of elaborate towers of very steep brittle ice, riddled with holes, and it looked repellent in the bleak grey light of dawn. So once again we made a slight change of plan: we would traverse back on to the North Face and follow the fluted snowfield to the top, hoping that it might be slightly more amenable than the ridge. There would be a good deal of traversing, but we only had to gain about two hundred metres of height and with any luck we should be up and down in time for afternoon tea. We left almost everything on the Mushroom, taking just one rucksack containing the sun cream, water bottle, spare mittens and Dick's duvet jacket; I wore my duvet all day, underneath my Gore-Tex anorak. Before leaving I wondered about putting in a head-torch, then squashed the idea, carried along by Dick's optimistic notion of the 'quick dash' to the summit and back.

Our first job was to reach the snowfield. To get there we thought we would have to travel down and along the ridge to a little col below the final summit tower; but the ridge was hopelessly blocked with overhanging snow mushrooms, so we abseiled down on to the East Face, pulled the ropes down and traversed round a rocky ledge to a peg belay, level with the col. Then the climbing started in earnest.

I led the first pitch, crossing rock and ice to the col, where I sat astride the crest and gawped nervously down the North Face. After a pause to pluck up courage, I rammed axe shafts deep into the snow crest and lowered myself down on to the North Face, kicking through sugary snow to force my front crampon points into the brittle ice underneath. Then I set off sideways, moving slowly, step by step across the face, rightwards towards the summit. After a few metres I stopped to hammer in an ice screw, clipped in one of the ropes and then continued sideways, repeating the same laborious sequence over and over again: reach out wide with right arm, swing ice hammer hard, bashing the pick into the ice; step across with right foot, kick hard until crampon points grip in the ice; move left foot across and kick; pull out ice axe with left hand and drive pick further right; then pull out the ice hammer and start the routine all over again.

I stopped to hack out a tiny foot-ledge and hammered in two screws for a belay. After I had pulled in the slack rope Dick came across.

When Dick joined me at the end of the first pitch he commented grimly: 'It's going to be like this all the way.' 'This' was a relentlessly steep slope, never less than sixty-five degrees, frequently steeper, with powder snow plastered on top of crusty sugar, plastered on top of hard black ice – the sort of conditions where every move is hard work and it often takes repeated blows of the ice axe to make the pick stick; and all the time we were traversing, leader and second equally exposed to the risk of falling off in a big pendulum. After the previous days of mixed climbing, it felt unnerving to be isolated suddenly in a world of snow and ice, without a single comforting rock in sight, relying all day on the tenuous attachment of ice axe picks and crampon points, and only occasional widely spaced ice screws.

The day had an element of unreality. We moved across a strange landscape of weird and fantastic snow flutings, with the towers of the ridge above us appearing dimly through swirling clouds. Sometimes the clouds below would part briefly to reveal the valley, a remote abstract pattern, impossibly far below; then the clouds would move in again, isolating us in whiteness. Lack of oxygen and the effects of two days with very little food or sleep produced in me a strange heightened awareness, where everything seemed slightly surreal. I also experienced strange moments of dreamlike paranoia: once during the day I suddenly saw a dark shape swinging over my head and I ducked, frightened that I was being attacked, only to realise that it was just my own ice axe, which I was swinging into the wall. On another occasion I suddenly began to worry about our belongings on the snow mushroom: it was as if we were climbing on Scafell, had left our rucksacks at Mickledore and were worried about picnickers stealing them. I was about to ask Dick if our bivouac things would be safe, when I returned to reality and realised that we were the first, and probably the last, human beings ever to visit this spot, and that if I did ask the ridiculous question he would probably think that I had gone completely mad. To add to the confusion, I was troubled all day by a theme from Mahler's Fifth Symphony, hammering strident and persistent in my head.

On the second pitch we started to cross the flutings, elaborate formations that reminded us of climbs we had done in the Andes. The snow had built up into great pillars, protruding from the face at ridiculous angles, so that we had to burrow across each one, scooping with our arms and stamping down a ledge, shuffling across, with the remains of the pillar above pushing out against our chests, wondering, as we stamped on the bottomless powder underneath, what, if anything, was holding it all up.

On the third pitch I had to break trail across more flutings; then I started to gain height, suddenly finding good conditions, soft white ice where picks sank in perfectly every time, and I could move smoothly, quickly up a seventy-degree wall, with legs and arms outstretched in a cross shape for stability.

Dick continued to the foot of an ice overhang, then traversed right across an eighty-degree wall and disappeared over the crest of another fluting. When my turn came to follow, I began to feel frightened. The ice was again iron hard and after crossing the fluting I had to climb diagonally down another steep wall. My crampon points were badly blunted from all the rock climbing lower down and were shattering the ice instead of cutting it. Dick was several metres further across, with the rope between us hanging in a wide horizontal arc. Below the potential swing, the ice face dropped steeply into the clouds.

'Come on,' Dick shouted, 'It's not that bad. Use your feet.'

'They won't stick in the ice.'

'Yes, they will.'

'I hate this,' I shouted back, weary with the constant strain on wrists and calf muscles, tired of the unrelenting steepness of it all. Dick, however, was bursting with optimistic urgency when I finally teetered across to the belay:

'Look, that's the summit up here!' He pointed up to the huge cornice, appearing dimly through the clouds just above us. We could just make out the gap to its left and a vague gully leading up to it; but first we had to traverse a little further and climb up a steep band of glassy grey-blue ice, which stretched right across the face. I climbed a few metres right, then placed an ice screw. I was loath to leave the security of the screw, but we had to hurry on to the summit and Dick was telling me to get a move on, so I pulled up on to the almost vertical wall. Twice my feet came off, leaving me hanging by my arms from ice picks. I hated those few metres and was relieved to reach a shallow runnel, where the angle was a little gentler and the ice softer.

Snow was falling and the summit had disappeared. Dick was a blurred dark shape in the swirling whiteness. I called down to ask, 'How much rope?' Dick shouted back, 'Ten feet.' So I stepped left on to a snow rib, where I could kick a tiny ledge. I fumbled clumsily with mittened hands to unclip an ice screw from my harness and hammer it in. It was tempting to leave it at that, but a really good belay was essential, so I forced my weary arm to hammer in a second screw. Then I pulled off mittens, exposing thin inner gloves for the fiddly work of clipping in karabiners, tying myself into them, pulling the ropes tight and feeding them into the friction brake. Spindrift had poured into my mittens and I had to tip it all out before putting them back on over numb hands. Once everything was ready, I slumped back against the slope, sitting heavily in my harness, resting my weight on the two ice screws, and started to bring up Dick.

He came up quickly and continued straight past me, Footfangs hammering away at the ice. He headed straight up towards the murky cornice, then disappeared from sight, eventually shouting down for me to follow. It was a relief to be climbing straight up at last, with the rope taut above me. There was no need now to check every axe placement: instead I could rely on the rope for security and hurry upwards, ice axes just scratching the surface. It was exhilarating to be racing up so close to the summit, kicking and scraping up through the driving snow, following Dick's marks past the enormous cornice and into a gap, where glassy ice lay underneath deep powder and my blunt crampons skidded as I rushed at it, shouting to Dick to pull the rope tighter, impatient to see over the top.

The slope eased off. Dick was belayed below a final snow slope.

'There you are,' he said. 'Off you go.'

I started to kick steps, longing to go faster, but having to stop and pant heavily every few steps. 'Why do I get so tired?' I grumbled and Dick provided a reassuring excuse:

'You've hardly eaten for three days.'

I kicked a few more weary steps, then suddenly I stepped out on to the top. I expected the summit to be on the right, above the cornice; but it was set back, slightly to the left, a white mound rising above a broad plateau, barely visible against the enveloping cloud and falling snow. Dragging the rope behind me, I plodded across the plateau, peering through the clouds to make sure that this really was the highest point. It felt strange to be on the flat after five days of walking verticality.

I stopped at the highest point, sat down in the snow, pulled the rope tight and gave it three jerks to inform Dick that he could come up. A few minutes later he appeared on the plateau, walking towards me with the faintest hint of a smile on his face.

We didn't stay long on the summit, just time for a drink of orange juice and a couple of photos. It had taken most of the day to reach the top and in four hours it would be dark. Our 'quick dash' had turned into a prolonged epic, and suddenly our situation began to seem very serious. I suggested digging a snow hole and waiting for the morning to descend, but Dick didn't like the idea.

'What – stay up here without sleeping bags!'

'It'll be cold, but we'll survive.'

'Maybe; but what if the storm gets bad? It'd be desperate getting back and we'd be a day later starting down from the mushrooms. We've got to get back to the bivouac tonight.'

I didn't think that we could make it before dark, but Dick was adamant that we should descend immediately: 'We'll just have to be quick: you'll have to pull all the stops out!' So we set off back down.

We walked back across the plateau and I belayed Dick as he descended back on to the North Face. I hurried down his steps to find him waiting beneath the cornice, with a tape sling tied round a pillar of icicles – our anchor for the first abseil. We untied from the ropes, threading an end of blue through the anchor sling and tying it to an end of purple with a fisherman's knot, also tying an enormous knot in the other end of the ropes, so that there was no danger of sliding off the end, at the bottom of the abseil; then we threw down the double rope.

As I left, Dick reminded me: 'Don't forget to check the ropes at the bottom, will you? It's Pull Purple.' I clipped the ropes into my friction brake and set off, sliding down the ropes and walking my crampons across the ice wall, working diagonally left, frightened by the tension that threatened to swing me back across the face. Fifty metres lower, I reached the knot in the end and leaned back in my harness, while I hammered in an ice screw for the next abseil anchor. Once I was clipped safely into the anchor, I took the ropes out of the friction brake and tested them, pulling purple, to make sure that the blue would pull through the sling fifty metres above. I heard Dick's voice, distant and remote in the clouds:

'Okay, I'm coming down.'

It was snowing heavily and spindrift was pouring down the face in a continuous torrent, driving down our necks, clogging up glasses and pouring into mittens when we took them off to struggle, numb-fingered, with knots and karabiners, and pull down the ropes, threading them through the anchor sling for the next abseil. When the circulation had returned, painfully, I started down the next abseil, sliding diagonally through a steep torrent of spindrift, flailing with knees and elbows to burrow across flutings and keep working left, eyes screwed up to peer through misty glasses at ghostly half-remembered shapes, trying to pick out the route of our ascent. Halfway down I placed an ice screw and clipped in the ropes, to check the diagonal tension, then continued to the knot at the bottom.

Now we had to move horizontally left. Dick volunteered to lead and climbed sideways on to a great pillar of snow. He belayed on the crest and brought me across, shouting urgently: 'Quick, come on, hurry up. Come and have a look at this.' I wondered if he had suddenly seen some wonderful poetic vision which he wanted to share with me. He pulled me up on to the crest and said: 'Right, look over there.' It was no poetic vision, but there was a slight clearing in the clouds and he wanted me to check the landmarks.

'Is that the ridge?' he asked, pointing to ghostly ice towers.

'Yes, I think so,' I replied. 'Yes, it must be … yes – and the col is down there. We're still too high. If we head down from here we should hit the traverse line on that second pitch you led.' So we abseiled again, suspended on the ropes from a single ice screw. I went first again, sliding through space over an overhanging ice cliff, then continuing in contact with less steep ice, pulling diagonally left towards the col. One more abseil took us down to the lowest line of steps remaining from the morning.

Dick led a short pitch back across the worst of the flutings and I joined him at the belay, overlooking the final stretch back to the col.

We were very lucky: the clouds were lifting, the snow had stopped and it looked as though the storm was over. However, we were still not home and dry; between us and the haven of sleeping bags and stove lay forty metres of steep ice, which we had to cross before we could climb back over the col and up to the bivouac. The light was fading fast and we would have to hurry. I knew that I wouldn't be able to do it quickly and I was terrified of the possible fall, so I was very relieved when Dick said, 'Shall I lead it?'

During the earlier days of mixed climbing I had sometimes been frustrated by his slowness, knowing that I could cope more quickly with the technical problems; but today, on the ice, he had been the competent one, climbing with unflagging assurance, and now when it really mattered, he had the reserves of strength and the nerve to storm across that final wall of brittle ice, confident that he would not fall off.

'I'll be as quick as I can,' he promised. Then he added: 'How are you going to manage in the dark?'

'I'll leave this screw and karabiner, with the ropes through it. I'm not doing it without a backrope! We'll just have to hope to God that the ropes pull through afterwards!'

Dick set off to do a brilliant lead, racing the encroaching darkness. He had time to place one poor screw runner halfway across; but if he had fallen it would probably not have held, and he would have tumbled in a huge swing across the face before the ropes came tight on my belay. Stars had already appeared between the parting clouds, when he reached the col, pulling over by the last glimmer of daylight and shouting exultantly: 'I'm there!' Then he disappeared over on to the East Face, to search for the rock pegs that we had left in place that morning.

It took him ages groping in the darkness to find the belay. I waited on the ice face, damp, cold and shivering, longing to be back on the comfortable bivouac ledge, tucked up in my sleeping bag.

Down in the valley, two and a half kilometres below, Patial flashed his torch frantically; but we were powerless to reply and I felt frustrated by our foolish decision to leave the torches at the bivouac.

Eventually Dick found the belay and shouted the good news. Stiff and numb, I started to prepare for the traverse, forcing my mind to concentrate on the sequence of operations: first, check that I am tied in with a sling to the karabiner; second, pull in some slack rope, tying off a loop, to ensure that when I untie the ends from my harness I do not lose the ropes and find myself stranded; third, feel in the darkness for the ends of the ropes, to untie the frozen knots attaching them to the harness; fourth, blow hard on fingers, warming them sufficiently to tie the two rope ends together and clip them into the karabiner on the ice screw; fifth, peer through the darkness to make sure that the ropes really are attached to the screw, then untie the temporary loop, leaving the ropes hanging in a clear line across the face, ready to be pulled through later; sixth, wrap my left arm securely round the ropes, then with my right hand unclip my belay sling from the ice screw and transfer its karabiner to the ropes, ready to safeguard my journey across the face.

I was about to set off when I peered through the darkness again and noticed with horror that the karabiner gate was open; frozen and encrusted with ice, it had not sprung shut. I hastily shut it, checked everything again, blew hard to rewarm my fingers, pulled on frozen mittens and clutched the rope handrail.

I had hoped to rely entirely on the ropes, pulling across with my hands and putting my weight on the sliding karabiner attached to my harness; but it didn't work – there was too much stretch in the ropes and the face was concave, threatening me with a big swing into space; so I actually had to climb across, using the rope just as a safeguard and searching in the darkness for the footsteps and ice axe slots, forcing weary arms and legs to hammer and kick and retain contact with the ice. Halfway across I had a long blind struggle to remove Dick's ice screw runner, then I continued, scraping in the darkness, while Dick shouted words of encouragement.

After much jibbering I eventually re-joined Dick on the far side of the col. Mercifully the ropes pulled through. Then, standing amongst heaps of equipment, we cursed and swore, tired and irritable, struggling in the darkness to sort out the tangled frozen knitting and prepare for the final climb back on to the Mushroom.

After Dick's magnificent lead across the ice face, it was my turn to take the initiative. I climbed over rocks to a sloping ledge immediately under the Mushroom and pecked nervously at a steep wall on the right, retreating to try round to the left; but that was worse, with a huge snow bulge hanging out over space, so I went back round to the right wall. It looked steep and difficult, but I knew that the point we had abseiled down in the morning, further right, was steeper, so there did not seem any alternative way of getting to bed.

Later Dick admitted that he had been very worried, waiting at the belay while I climbed up the Mushroom, in the darkness of a moonless night, with no running belay for protection. If I had come off it would have been a big fall; but I think that I was far too absorbed in the climbing even to consider the possibility of falling off.

I reached up in the darkness, to poke ice axe shafts into the hard snow, then pulled up to stand precariously in a little scoop. Then I repeated the process. The wall was steep and I had to put all my weight on the ice axes, relying on them as I pulled up and kicked new footsteps. There was one more pull up, then I could reach over the bulge, plunge axes in once more, pull over and collapse on my knees on the crest of the Mushroom, just beside the bivouac ledge from which we had set out seventeen hours earlier. We were safely home.

Bringing up Dick, I had to blink hard to stay awake. Late that night we finally got to bed. At this stage there was no great sense of joy at our achievement, more a profound relief to be safely back at the bivouac. We were badly dehydrated and were longing for something to drink before going to sleep; so I placed the stove carefully at the back of the ledge and filled the cylinder pan with snow. Unfortunately, after a long search, I could not find the cigarette lighter. Unperturbed, I reached in my rucksack for the lifeboat matches, a sealed container full of windproof waterproof matches, guaranteed to light in a force ten gale, which I had carried up numerous climbs, ready for just such an emergency; but they proved to be useless, because the igniting paper had worn off the lid. I tried desperately to light the matches on a metal zip, but they were safety matches and would not produce a single spark.

Dick didn't know whether to laugh or cry.

7 Return to the Earth

While we slept on our hard beds of compressed snow, at the top bivouac, the last clouds vanished and the temperature dropped to about −20 °C. I woke late to a bleary-eyed sensation of dazzling whiteness. The sun was already on the mountain but it was devoid of warmth, so we remained in bed, huddled in our sleeping bags with down hoods drawn tightly over our heads. My limbs were heavy, my lips were swollen and cracked and my throat was parched.

Later the sun brought warmth and we sat up to begin drying out gloves and mittens, sodden and frozen from the previous afternoon's storm. Facing me from the other end of the ledge, Dick looked haggard. Behind him, the summit tower was dazzling against a deep blue sky. It looked ridiculously steep. I could see some of our tracks from the previous day: an improbable line of neat black holes in the white crust, where we had made that final desperate traverse twelve hours earlier. We had grossly underestimated the difficulties of the summit climb, our decision not to take torches had been absurd and we had been lucky to get back down to the bivouac. We had also been very lucky with the weather; the storm, which had looked so threatening, had proved just to be a temporary aberration in a long spell of fine weather. If it had continued, our position now would be very serious. As it was, even without the difficulties of driving wind and snow, the descent was going to be long and tedious. The summit was only a turning point in the climb and only when we had returned to the safety of the valley could we begin to relax and enjoy the sensation of success.

We delayed the evil moment of descent, reluctant to start on a day of hard work. I sucked a trickle of water, a few drops melted from pieces of ice in my water bottle, which had been sitting in the sleeping bag all night. Eventually we started to pack up. I had stopped to spoon some pieces of ice into my dry mouth when Dick suddenly exclaimed: 'Have a look at this!' Lifting up the Karrimats, he had found, lying on the compressed snow underneath, a small red plastic object – the cigarette lighter. Suddenly life was transformed.

I said: 'I don't know what to say.'

Dick suggested jovially in broadest Yorkshire: 'Why not try feeling thoroughly ashamed.'

We postponed the descent and eagerly unpacked the stove and the cylinder pan, to make tea and coffee, spooning in all the remains of our sugar to try and give ourselves some energy for the day's work.

Once the nagging thirst had abated, I started to enjoy myself again and began to appreciate the fantastic view of mountains in every direction. Now for the first time we had a clear cloudless view out to the south-east and could see the silver ribbon of the Darlang Nullah, winding eastwards, with blue mountains beyond, stretching far away to Kulu. The descent was now less daunting; now that we could use the stove again there was not such a desperate urgency to get off the mountain to running water, and we could stop at Drip Ledge, where it would now be too cold to find any drips but we could melt as much snow as we liked, resting there and eating up all the cached food supplies.

We made twelve abseils that day, our sixth on the route. We worked our way carefully back down the landmarks of the ascent, now transformed by a plastering of new snow from the previous afternoon's storm. First we dropped steeply down the concave wall, then worked diagonally round to the Renshaw Diedre and on down past Booming Flake and Window Ledge.

Just below Window Ledge we took a direct line down new terrain, heading straight for Drip Ledge and eliminating the weaving detours of the third day's climb. The ropes were looped through a tape sling on a peg, which was linked to another back-up peg, hammered into the rock a little higher. I went first, leaning out backwards and walking down snow-plastered slabs. After I had gone about twenty metres, Dick shouted down to warn me that the peg was moving. 'Can you make yourself safe?' he added, 'and I'll transfer the ropes.' So I stopped on a snow patch and drove in my axes to support myself, while he rearranged the slings, transferring the weight of the ropes to the back-up peg. I continued down on to a steep wall, swinging left and right, as I neared the end of the rope, searching for another abseil anchor. I was disappointed to find only fragile flakes, cemented loosely to the wall by ice. Finally, right at the end of the rope, I tensioned far over to the right, reaching out with one hand to grab the top of an enormous flake, a great plaque of granite, weighing many tons and booming with a hollow sound when I hit it. It seemed a little suspect, but it was so enormous that I had to assume that it was attached firmly to the mountain, firmly enough, at least, to take our weight. I cut off a length of abseil tape, tied it into a loop, draped the loop over the lip of the flake and clipped in.

When Dick arrived, we repeated the methodical routine of preparing for the next abseil – first untying the safety knot in the bottom end of the ropes then feeding the end of the purple through the anchor sling, while we hauled it down and nervously watched the blue end snaking up the cliff, and breathed a sigh of relief when it pulled through the previous sling fifty metres above, to come whipping down about our heads, then gathering up the ends and tying them together again, before flinging the ropes down the wall, ready for the next abseil.

Determined to prove that I was not totally incompetent, I went first on the abseils, taking the responsibility of fixing up the anchors. I set off down again, disappearing after twenty metres over the lip of an enormous overhang – a great roof jutting out fifteen metres from the face – spinning gently down through space, mesmerised by the circling view spread out beneath my feet, coming to rest finally on more granite slabs and continuing down to the end of the ropes, where I found a suitable crack for one of our dwindling supply of pegs.

We continued down and down, towards the midway haven of Drip Ledge. I finally arrived at the top of the icefield, swung across into a rock corner and spent an age searching for an anchor, peering and poking at a thin crack until I found a little pocket to take one of our last pieces of gear, a tiny 'micro' nut on a wire loop. It was a perfect fit and made a safer anchor for the last abseil down to Drip Ledge.

It was wonderful to return to all that food stowed in a bag underneath the overhang. We gobbled up biscuits and cheese, made brew after brew and ate our first decent-sized cooked meal for four days. When darkness fell, we signalled to Patial to indicate that we were safely on our way down. The new snow on the walls above sent down a steady tinkling shower of crystals, so for the second time we used the bivouac tent, rigging it up from the overhang and sheltering underneath, warm and secure. It was good to relax after a day of hard concentration, pleased that we had coped smoothly and efficiently with all the abseils, so fraught with potential dagger.

The weather was fine in the morning and I was tempted to linger on the mountain, savouring our last moments amongst its spectacular rock and ice architecture; but Dick was determined not to hang around and kicked me awake for a 4.30 start. 'I want to get the job finished,' he explained. 'I don't see mountains as friendly things: as far as I'm concerned they're hostile and dangerous, and if you hang around you just lull yourself into a false sense of security. In fact, all the time you're hanging around you're burning up energy to keep warm, weakening yourself and increasing the chances of a mistake … the longer you stay on the mountain, the more chance it has of killing you. I used to shut my eyes to all the dangers, but now I can't stop thinking about them … '

It was a long speech, but behind this apparently joyless assessment of mountaineering there was a deep respect for the mountains, born of many years' experience. I think that Dick has probably found more pleasure and satisfaction in mountaineering than most people but that enjoyment is qualified by a highly developed instinct for survival, and he was quite right, on that seventh day, that we should descend as quickly and efficiently as possible.

From Drip Ledge, we did four abseils down the icefield, leaving behind more of our expensive ice screws, sliding quickly down past a marker wand which we had left near the bergschrund five days earlier, in case we should find ourselves descending blindly in a white-out.

We walked back across the hanging glacier and stopped at the lip of the third ice cliff to place a Deadman in the deep snow. Neither of us had ever abseiled off a Deadman and we were a little nervous about trusting our lives to the small metal plate, so we used the second Deadman as a back-up, while I went down, testing the anchor. It did not budge an inch, and Dick was able to bring down the second Deadman safely for the next abseil over the vertical blue wall of the second ice cliff.

Dick allowed us a brief rest at the Balcony to devour as much food as we could manage and pack up the spare equipment we had left there, before hurrying on to make another abseil down on to the snow arête, arriving just in time before the snow became dangerously soft. It was tempting to solo down the arête, but, determined not to risk an unchecked fall, we moved one at a time, belaying each other down the six rope-lengths to the terrace. On we went, down on to the ice ramp, where we grew bored with downclimbing and hammered in an ice screw to abseil down to the top of the first ice cliff. There we paused to hammer in our last screw. While we sorted out the ropes, Dick observed that, although both my axes were firmly embedded in the ice and attached to my body, I had not also clipped into the ice screw. He said: 'I should clip into the screw. What am I going to say to your mother if you get killed?'

'You'll say,' and I put on my best attempt at a caricature Yorkshire accent,' 'E was a silly bugger and 'e 'ad it coming to 'im. 'E chucked everything off mountain and when there was nowt left to chuck 'e chucked 'isself.' To reassure my mentor, I clipped into the screw, while I prepared for the next abseil.

Lower down we were allowed another short rest and a quick brew, before continuing down the snow ridge, pausing repeatedly to knock our feet with ice axes, removing the heavy clods of sticky snow which were dangerously balling up our crampons. Finally, we slid in a wild glissade down the last soggy slope to the boulder field and clambered over the rocks to Advance Base, where we pulled off overtrousers, boots and socks, tipped open our rucksacks and spread everything in a great sprawling heap to dry in the sun.

It was half past two in the afternoon and there was time for a good rest and several cups of tea before packing everything up again to leave for Base Camp. I had been looking forward to a large bowl of porridge; but we discovered that we had accidentally left one of the tent's inner doors open, allowing the pine marten to walk off with all the food. It had also apparently helped itself to our spare medical supplies, which included a substantial quantity of very strong painkillers.

Later we burned all our rubbish, before packing the tent and all the clothing and equipment into bulging rucksacks and setting off for the valley. At the awkward rockstep we paused for one final abseil, our twenty-sixth since leaving the summit two days earlier. Then we continued down the snow gully and on, wearily, down earth and scree, delighted to be back amongst the brilliant colours of alpine flowers and to see the trees of the valley growing closer, their green leaves now tinged with autumnal yellow. That evening, as we stumbled down the long moraine, our knees straining under thirty-kilo loads, we saw a lone figure coming up to meet us. It was Patial, beaming and bubbling and welcoming us with a superbly hyperbolic speech: 'You have achieved your aim and you have gained the victory for which you have travelled many miles.'

At dusk, walking happily down through the trees and bushes of the valley, it was wonderful to stop and look back up at the intricate spidery lines of the headwall and the white summit, now distant and remote again, far above us, and know that 'we were there'.

Now that his lonely vigil was over, Patial was anxious to be home with his family. Dick, too, was anxious to get back to Jan and Daniel, so we only spent two days at Base Camp resting and getting organised. Patial had hired four contract labourers who had been helping out with the harvest in Sumcham to carry our loads back to Kishtwar. But first there was a food surplus to dispose of, for we had only spent twenty-six days in the valley and had provisioned ourselves for a possible two months. So Patial invited over a man from Sumcham called Hari Lai. We had heard much about this man: his warm hospitality, his scrapbook full of cards and letters from previous expeditions, his beautiful house and his great wealth – 'twenty laks of rupees' (two million) Patial kept reminding us. As a young man he had made his fortune, setting off from the sapphire mine above Sumcham (now closed and under government control) and travelling many hundreds of miles to Bombay, Delhi and Calcutta, to sell the precious jewels. Now he had chosen to return to his old village, high in the Himalaya, where there was no opportunity to spend his enormous wealth. Patial had enjoyed his hospitality on several occasions, so we gave him first option on the surplus food. He arrived in the afternoon, dressed in the traditional local tweed drainpipe trousers and jacket. Helped by his two sons, he went through the sacks of flour, rice and sugar, packets of tea and biscuits and unopened tins of jam and butter, loading into large boxes everything that took his fancy. Several of the villagers also appeared to glean among the leftovers and gather up delightedly all the old empty tin cans.

We left on a brilliant morning. At first light I got up to photograph Shivling, catching the brief pink glow on the summit flutings. Above Sumcham the leaves of wild rhubarb were already touched by autumn, turned to a fiery crimson. Some of the birch trees had lost most of their leaves, the few remainders hanging like pendants, silhouetted against the silver shimmer of the river.

On the far side of the river I walked across the springy turf of a meadow, recognising the spot where we had camped four years earlier. I stopped to take more photos of Shivling, with different foregrounds – emerald ferns, russet leaves of dwarf willow and a magnificent bush of lime-green Euphorbia. Then

I climbed up the hillside to find a better viewpoint for the entire North Face of the mountain. It was four years and two days since the day when I had first conceived the tentative notion of climbing the face. Once again it was a radiant blue morning and the sun was slanting across the East Tower of the mountain, just catching the summit flutings and the snow arête, lower down. The rest of the face was still in blue shadow. Now that the days were getting colder, the snow at that altitude was hardly melting and the headwall was still plastered with the remains of the snowstorm; but I could pick out the permanent white lines of the ledges and corners which we had followed up the wall. To the left, at the head of the valley, were more mountains, sharp blue silhouettes, still waiting to be climbed. Hidden behind them were countless other mountains, waiting for future adventures.

It was time to leave. I ran back down the hillside and continued down the valley, following the path between granite boulders, to emerge amongst barley fields surrounding the small cluster of wooden houses that was Sumcham. The air, heated by the climbing sun, was heavy with the scent of wild herbs and spices. I headed for the largest house in the village, which of course belonged to Hari Lai. He was waiting on the verandah with Dick and Patial. One of the sons brought tea on a gleaming brass tray, then we were taken into a small room to sit on carpets, while a woman brought bowls of curry, redolent with the wild herbs and spices of the fields outside. While we were eating, Hari Lai showed us his scrapbook, filled with messages of thanks and letters of recommendation from past visitors, trekkers on their way to and from the Umasi La, and some of the rare climbing expeditions that had visited this valley.

We added our own words of thanks.

After lunch we stayed for more tea, carrying on a halting conversation with Patial translating. Then we shouldered our rucksacks, said goodbye and left. As we walked out through the fields, men and women were at work with sickles, cutting the harvest. Above the village there was a small Buddhist shrine, a chorten, built on to the top of a boulder. Behind it, steep walls of mountainside slanted up out of the valley, almost obscuring Shivling; but the very top was still visible, hanging high in the blue sky. I stopped to take one last look at the white summit, then turned round and headed for home.

Part 2

Rimo,
The Painted Mountain

8 An Invitation

The Alpine Club
74 South Audley Street
London W1Y5FF
October 1984

POSSIBLE EAST KARAKORAM EXPEDITION

The club has been negotiating with the Indian Mountaineering Foundation about the possibility of an AC party visiting the East Karakoram during 1985. This area of northern Kashmir has been closed to foreigners for many years, and therefore contains a large number of unclimbed peaks. While the club has not, in the past, sponsored expeditions, the committee feel it appropriate to do so on this occasion. No detailed plans have yet been formulated, and formal permission for the expedition has yet to be granted. However, it is expected that the expedition would be a joint venture with Indian participation and would attempt a major objective during the summer of 1985. The expedition would be self-financing, with no call on club funds. The number of participants is likely to be limited. Anyone who would like to be considered for membership of this venture is asked to contact the Honorary Secretary.

When I first read this notice in the Alpine Club newsletter, my knowledge of the East Karakoram was hazy. I had heard of Saser Kangri, the most easterly of the great Karakoram peaks. I had heard of the Shyok river and the legendary Karakoram Pass, the historic trade route linking the plains of India to the old Silk Route in the heart of Central Asia; and I had heard of the Siachen Glacier, one of the largest glaciers in the Greater Himalaya, flowing over seventy kilometres from its head, east of K2, to its snout, the source of the Nubra river. That was the sum of my knowledge.

During the autumn of 1984 I had been climbing with Dick Renshaw again in the West Karakoram, in Pakistan, plagued by bad weather and avalanche conditions. We had climbed three small peaks, but achieved nothing to compare with the previous year's excitement on Kishtwar-Shivling. Soon after we returned to England, Dick announced that Jan was expecting another baby the next summer and that he would, this time, be staying at home with her. I had returned to discover that my love life had disintegrated in my absence. Life seemed a little bleak but I was at least making an effort to immerse myself in work, drawing up plans for a large, complicated set of mahogany bookcases and cabinets for a customer in Harrow. Other contracts were under way and I was priding myself on my ability to settle down to some reasonably well-paid employment; I was even considering a whole year of uninterrupted work, with a summer free of Himalayan commitments. Then came the Alpine Club newsletter.

The temptation was hard to resist. It was not a specific mountain that tempted me: apart from Saser Kangri, which had been climbed by the India-Tibet Border Force in 1973, I hardly even knew the names of any peaks in the East Karakoram; but I was tempted by the area as a whole, because it had the allure of the unknown and the mysterious. Later research revealed that there had in fact been considerable exploration and a number of fine ascents; but, in comparison with the other areas of the Karakoram there was an unusually large number of high unclimbed peaks and there were valleys which were still virtually unknown. I was also keen to approach the range from Ladakh, the Buddhist province in northern Kashmir which we had failed to reach in 1979. This expedition, if it happened, would be a good excuse to visit Ladakh's capital, Leh, before heading north, over the highest road pass in the world, to the remote Nubra valley, which had for so long been – and which still was for most people – forbidden territory.

In November I went up to the Lake District, to a gathering of the Alpine Climbing Group – an offshoot of the AC, representing younger climbers interested specifically in high-standard mountaineering in the world's greater ranges. It was a typical evening, characterised by indifferent food and plentiful beer, with the hyperbole flowing more freely as the evening progressed and the supposed elite of British mountaineering talked over past climbs and future plans. Various people were interested in the East Karakoram proposal and were questioning the AC secretary, Steve Town.

He made no attempt to disguise the potential difficulties. The AC was most anxious that the expedition should happen, but its support would be moral rather than financial. The expedition had to be a joint one with as yet unspecified Indian climbers. We would be climbing in a disputed area where India and Pakistan were unofficially at war; so any plans might well have to be aborted at the last moment in the event of a sudden military crisis. The IMF were demanding a hefty royalty fee of $2,000, in return for which we would officially have to restrict ourselves to a single named peak; but we had no knowledge of the area and little photographic record on which to base a choice of objective, and we had no way of knowing the competence of the Indian climbers who would be assigned to the expedition. The problems in India would clearly be formidable; in Britain what we had so far was a number of people tentatively interested but as yet uncommitted to an expedition which had no objective, no leader, no specified Indian members, and which might never happen.

The next AC newsletter printed a list of about twelve people, myself included, who had 'expressed an interest'; beyond that, little progress had been made. I knew several of the other interested people. One of them was Dave Wilkinson, with whom I had climbed on Kunyang Kish. Another was Victor Saunders, who by virtue of his position on the AC committee had access to knowledge and power, and had appointed himself 'co-ordinating secretary' of the proposed expedition. By the new year of 1985 it was becoming apparent that not much co-ordinating had been going on; but Dave and I were now determined that the expedition should go ahead.

At the beginning of February, while Victor applied for financial support from the Mount Everest Foundation and the British Mountaineering Council, naming Saser Kangri II, an unclimbed peak of 7,513 metres, as a possible objective, I sat down to draft a prospectus to send to potential sponsors. I had been studying the few available photos of Saser Kangri II and agreed that it would make a fantastic challenge. Later that month we learnt that a Bombay climber, Harish Kapadia, well known as editor of the *Himalayan Journal*, had been asked by the IMF to lead the expedition and that we would probably be climbing with a team from his club, the Bombay Mountaineers. Unlike most Indian climbers, they were not soldiers. We had already met one of them, Meena Agrawal, a surgeon who works in London. We had liked her and she had assured us that Harish and the others were an easy-going team, whose style of climbing would fit in with our mildly anarchic approach, and who would not try to impose the rigid, hierarchical structure typical of most army-based Indian expeditions. However, they made no pretence to be brilliant technical climbers and did not want to confine themselves to a single highly technical route on Saser Kangri II. Harish proposed instead a more wide-ranging journey of exploration, with several unclimbed peaks to aim for. We continued to press for Saser Kangri II, because it seemed such a compelling single objective, but it became clear that Harish was not going to swallow it, so, just as the prospectus was about to be printed, I hastily re-wrote a section, substituting for Saser Kangri II some of the unclimbed summits further west, near the Teram Shehr/Siachen Glacier junction, and fund-raising began in earnest.

After the elegant simplicity of the Kishtwar-Shivling expedition, the 'Siachen Indo-British Expedition 85' was in its early stages an unnervingly nebulous, rambling affair. Even when we left England at the end of May, the IMF had still not confirmed the Indian team and had said nothing about our objectives. Meanwhile we had been forced to prepare for a continually changing set of possibilities, while we tried to present an image of single-minded purpose to the world at large. Because we were visiting such an unusual area and because this was an international expedition, we found an enthusiastic response. Grindlays Bank, the first British bank to be founded in India, offered to support us. Victor enlisted the help of British Airways, who generously offered two free return tickets and free carriage of all our baggage. Numerous individuals donated money. Barclays Bank gave a donation and Alan Tritton, who has done so much to help British mountaineering, agreed to our using the Barclays headquarters in Lombard Street for a fund-raising lunch and lecture. Inspired by Barclays' generosity, other companies donated cash. Meanwhile, the MEF and the BMC had been deliberating and decided between them on a grant of £1,450, for which we were extremely grateful. Finally, at the end of April, the British expedition members gathered one cold, blustery, snowy day at Derbyshire's most famous gritstone outcrop, Stanage Edge, for a sponsored climb, the proceeds of which would be shared between the expedition and the charity Intermediate Technology. It was the first occasion when the whole team met.

The expedition team had undergone several changes since January. There had always been a nucleus of Dave, Victor and me. Various other people had come and gone, but we had now been joined definitely by Jim Fotheringham, a dentist from Cumbria, and Henry Osmaston, a senior lecturer in Geography at Bristol University. Henry was the most recent addition and I had only met him the previous weekend. Jim we hardly knew as yet, but the other three of us had known each other for some time.

I first met Dave Wilkinson in the spring of 1976. Later we climbed together two consecutive summers on Kunyang Kish, and in 1982 made several new routes in the Bolivian and Peruvian Andes. For over fifteen years now, Dave has devoted most of his spare time from his job as a mathematics lecturer at Birmingham Polytechnic to climbing, spending most term-time weekends on the British crags and going away during vacations to the Alps, the Andes and the Karakoram. Like many others, he had been plagued by bad weather in the Karakoram; but he had a formidable repertory of Andean and Alpine climbs, including spectacular new routes in the Bernese Oberland. He makes no pretence to be a brilliant rock climber but is extremely deft on ice and mixed ground and enjoys cultivating his image as the steady, cautious mountaineer, at thirty-nine the older wiser man who exerts a calming influence on younger impulsive elements of an expedition; the image of solid reliability is enhanced by his physical build, which keeps him warm when other skinnier climbers are shivering on some miserable high-altitude bivouac. There is a touch of northern directness about him, exhibited in his curt contempt for pomposity and hyperbole; but when the occasion demands, he is quite adept at handling the most tiresome Asian bureaucrats, is meticulous about filling in all the correct forms and only occasionally allows exasperation to get the better of him, exploding in a melodramatic display of temper.

Victor Saunders had, at thirty-five, been indulging in serious climbing for only a few years. Like me, he had first visited the Alps as a privileged child on ski holidays, but he did not begin climbing until much later. The interest was there, but he did not dare to take up such an addictive occupation until he had safely qualified as an architect. Since then he has made up for lost time, making the most of his natural ability: small, light, agile and strong, he is ideally suited to difficult rock climbing; but he also has the stamina, nerve and zest for the less immediately rewarding world of big mountains. I first met him one summer's afternoon in 1979, halfway up a cliff in the Avon Gorge. It soon became apparent that he was a talkative sort of chap, as he told me at some length and with bubbling enthusiasm about his recent winter ascent of the Eigerwand. I next bumped into him in the Mall, in Rawalpindi, when he was en route for a bold alpine-style first ascent of Conway's Ogre in the Karakoram. Eighteen months later we skied together at Mürren and I was infuriated to discover that he was more competent than me in the powder snow. Since then we had met often, but had never actually climbed together. Victor had been climbing at ever-higher standards and had recently, with other members of the highly competitive North London Mountaineering Club, been developing a perverse new branch of the sport: climbing with ice axes and crampons on the chalk, sand and mud cliffs of England's south coast. In 1984 he had returned to the Pakistani sector of the Karakoram, to attempt 7,330-metre Bojohaghur Duanasir. The attempt failed, but Victor's final bid, with Phil Butler, involving thirteen days of almost continuous climbing and descent, in indifferent weather with very little food, was a fine display of determination and perseverance. Between all these climbs he had maintained his job as architect with the Lambeth Council and had become the proud father of a son, Ben.

Jim Fotheringham, thirty-three, was something of an unknown quantity to us. Dave and Victor had met him briefly and I had only spoken to him on the telephone, but he seemed a warm friendly person and was obviously a good climber. He had already met Harish and his friends in Delhi and assured us that if the IMF allowed us to team up with them everything would be all right. I had first heard Jim's name in 1983, when Dick and I returned from Kishtwar-Shivling to Delhi, to learn at the IMF that Chris Bonington and Jim Fotheringham had just climbed a new route on the other Shivling, in Garhwal. For Jim this had been the most recent of several successful expeditions, which had taken him to India, Pakistan, Kenya, Alaska and Baffin Island. Fast competent climbing and considerable luck with the weather had enabled him on each of these trips to climb a major route during a comparatively short holiday, before returning to his wife and children and his dental practice in the Cumbrian market town of Brampton. The fifth member of the expedition was

Henry Osmaston. At sixty-three he was not interested in attempting any diffi-cult climbing; but he was still extremely fit and very keen to take what might be a unique opportunity to do some glaciological work in the Siachen area. He had already spent two summers on geographical research in central Ladakh but had never managed to visit the northern part of the province, which had up till now been rigorously closed to foreigners. Later, during the expedition, he was to describe himself as a jack-of-all-trades who had never been much good at anything, an unduly modest self-appraisal, which did little justice to his versatile career. He was born in India, into a family of eminent colonial for-esters and surveyors, one of whom was one of the last British directors of the Survey of India. Henry's forestry studies at Oxford were interrupted by the war, after which he spent fourteen years in Uganda before returning to aca-demic life as a lecturer in Geography at Bristol University. In April he came to see me in Bath. He had all the absent-minded charm of the archetypal eccen-tric don, and looked the part, with his wild, curly grey hair, battered spectacles held together by Araldite and ancient tweed jacket; but talking over our plans, it was quite evident that he was a man of sound organisation and incisive mind. His gentle courteous manner made him immediately likeable and when the others met him in Derbyshire the following weekend they all agreed that his company would make a delightful asset to the expedition.

This was the team that finally met for the first time at Stanage Edge on Saturday 27 April 1985. The plan for Jim, Dave, Victor and me was for each of us to complete 100 rock climbs in a single day (Henry had decided on a less stren-uous programme), for which we had each been promised varying amounts of pence per climb by our sponsors. None of the climbs exceeded twelve metres in height, but it was nevertheless quite a daunting prospect, particularly for me who had done little climbing during the past year.

The others had spent the previous night at the Climbers' Club hut a few miles away. I had spent the night just below the crag, sharing the back seat of a car with a dog, while the owners slept comfortably in a tent nearby. I awoke, stiff and aching, on a cold damp morning, to see figures already at work on the escarpment above. I rushed up the hillside to discover that Jim, Dave and Victor had already completed nearly twenty routes each. After a brief intro-duction to Jim, I dashed off to start on my first climb.

In spite of the cold and the wind and the snow that began to fall later, it was an enjoyable day. The constant movement kept us warm, as we worked along the crag, ticking off the routes in the guidebook. Victor was in front, climbing as usual with great panache and scampering about between routes like some hyperactive puppy, giving a loquacious running commentary on our progress. Jim was slightly slower and made less noise. I was trying not to be too obviously competitive as I raced through the routes to catch up on the others' head start. Dave moved at his own steadier pace, oblivious of everything and everyone around him. Later in the morning Henry appeared, resplendent in breeches and a tweed jacket belted with a length of hemp rope. After about sixty-five routes, we stopped for lunch, sheltering in a small cave.

In the afternoon snow made the holds slippery and we had to warn ourselves to move carefully, particularly as we had now done about 900 metres of ascent and descent and could all too easily make a careless slip. We were climbing unroped, the only way of fitting in so many routes in one day, and had mostly chosen Very Difficults and Severes; but we also climbed quite a few Very Severes and one or two carefully selected Hard Very Severes, offering an intriguing variety of cracks, chimneys, corners, walls and slabs. Late that afternoon the clouds dispersed and while Dave climbed off into the golden sunset, Jim, Victor and I, who had completed our hundred routes, sat in the heather and talked about the forthcoming expedition, before we all adjourned to the Climbers' Club hut for a celebratory meal.

The following morning we got down to business. Henry would be travelling out to India later than us and meeting us at Base Camp, so his arrangements were largely independent; but the other four of us still had numerous details to finalise and this would be the last chance to talk together before we met in Ladakh, so after breakfast we sat round the kitchen table for our first and last 'expedition meeting'.

Dave acted as chairman, working methodically through a list of things to be done: British Airways flights to confirm – Victor; medical supplies – Jim was sorting them out with Meena Agrawal, the expedition doctor; equipment – Victor reported that Alpine Sports had promised a discount; Dave asked if anyone wanted cost-price gear from Snowdon Mouldings; stoves – Victor had two new hanging gas stoves on order; visas – I would deal with them, if everyone provided their passports, cash, photos etc; money – still an unknown, but we were assured at least £3,000 outside income and I hoped that the eventual total would be a lot higher; insurance – Jim gave us details of the premiums. Food – Jim was concerned that I, who was in charge of expedition food, had only produced carrots and celery for lunch during the previous day of cold strenuous climbing, but I assured him that the expedition supplies would be more substantial. Victor announced that his girlfriend Maggie was donating a Negroni salami to the expedition. Someone suggested that Venables, as food organiser, should do his share of the load carrying and then donate his own body in a sacrificial slaughter to provide food for the other climbers. I pointed out that I was not very meaty at the best of times and that after a few weeks' hard exercise at altitude there would be even less flesh for the taking. And so it went on, interrupted by frequent cups of tea, produced with assiduous regularity by Jim, who was proving to be a copious tea drinker.

By the end of the meeting Dave had produced a list of all the things still to be done and who was going to do them. Harish had, with characteristic efficiency, booked all the rail and air travel in India and had fixed for the whole team to meet in Ladakh's capital, Leh, on 6 June. Jim and Victor, who were pressed for time, would fly out to Delhi at the last minute and take a connecting flight to Leh. Dave and I would fly out earlier to Bombay, where we would help Harish with final preparations, before travelling overland up to Kashmir.

All the wheels were now turning to ensure that the right people arrived in the right place at the right time with the right supplies. There was, admittedly, some doubt as to what we were actually going to climb; but that element of doubt added a nice suspense to the whole operation and it was a detail which could be clarified once we arrived in India. We had been aware all along that because of the unusual nature of this expedition, and because it had been organised at such short notice, our precise objectives would probably remain in doubt right up to the last moment. Amidst all this confusion, however, we did now have a new area of the East Karakoram in mind. Having virtually settled on the junction of the massive Teram Shehr and Siachen Glaciers, Harish had recently changed his mind, when his contacts informed him that this supposedly wild, remote, romantic spot was now occupied by a large encampment of tin huts – the forward base of the Indian army's operation to control the entire Siachen Glacier. He had also discovered that a fine group of 7,000-metre peaks further east near the Siachen snout – the Rimo massif – was, contrary to earlier reports, virtually untouched. The Indian army had claimed an ascent of Rimo IV the previous summer, but Rimos I, II and III remained virgin and had never been attempted. A projected American visit to the massif had been cancelled (possibly for political reasons) and we might be able to book the area.

Looking at the Karakoram sketch map, we had already been tempted by the valley just to the south-west of the Rimo peaks, the Terong valley. We had no clue what it looked like, because no photos were available; but a glance at the map was enough to reveal three major glaciers, ringed by nearly a hundred unknown, unclimbed 6,000-metre peaks and dominated by the higher summits of the Rimo group. The Indian army had published one photo of Rimo I from the far, north-east, side, showing it to be a shapely and probably very difficult mountain. The north-eastern approach march had taken the army over ten days; we were limited for time and hoped to make the quicker south-western approach up the Terong valley, even though we knew nothing about that side of the mountain. At this stage it was all very hypothetical; but we all agreed, that Sunday, to join Harish in pressing for permission to visit the Terong valley and Rimo peaks. If the IMF agreed to our plans, and if the army commanders in Kashmir, who would inevitably have the last word, also agreed, we would be all set for an exciting journey into unknown territory.

9   Mangoes and Momoes

Bombay was waiting for the monsoon. The air was hot and saturated with moisture – dense and oppressive. Dave and I waited patiently at the back of a long queue, in the dingy airport immigration lounge. Suddenly I heard my name mentioned:

'Excuse me, are you Mr Venables?'

'Yes.'

'I have a message for Mr Venables and Mr Wilkinson, from Mr Harish Kapadia.' An airport official handed over a note from Harish and a document authorising customs clearance of the luggage. The man returned to the passport desk and a moment later beckoned to us to follow. Our passports were stamped and we escaped to the other side, leaving behind the long, slow queue. Already, Harish's uncanny ability to pull strings was becoming evident.

After collecting the luggage, I returned to Dave to find him talking to a man in his late thirties, short and stocky, with a hint of a paunch; he stood very upright, holding a folder of documents under his arm, and had a look of friendliness and quiet efficiency. Harish had managed to talk his way into the customs lounge to meet us.

He helped us push all the luggage through to the glaring heat outside. Waiting amongst the melée of shouting taxi drivers were three other expedition members. We were introduced briefly to Dhiren Toolsidas, youngest member of the team, only twenty, looking fit, handsome and enthusiastic. Muslim Contractor, only a few years older, with his wild wiry hair, preoccupied frown and thick glasses, looked the intellectual that he proved to be. Zerksis Boga, in his late thirties, was tall and thin, with the finely sculpted face of his Persian ancestors.

Loading all the luggage into two cars, we left with cries of 'chalo', the local equivalent of 'Let's go', and drove through the heat and chaos of Bombay to a quiet suburb where Muslim lived with his family in a large house shaded by bougainvillaea and flame trees. Servants helped with the luggage, an ebullient Alsatian licked and sniffed the strangers, tea was brought and various members of Muslim's extended family came and went. Harish was now more relaxed and the Indian formality vanished, as he discovered that we were not pukka sahibs, and we chatted and laughed as we discussed the shopping we still had to do, the packing, a party at Harish's flat and the press conference at Grindlays Bank. We had known for several weeks that Grindlays were going to support us but no actual sums had been disclosed in England. Now Harish, beaming like a small child longing to let out a secret, was hinting and teasing and recounting how he had suddenly been summoned to the Bombay head office, quite unaware of the overtures that had been made in London. Eventually, gleefully, he announced: 'Ninety thousand rupees! Look, I have the cheque here!'

It was a wonderful surprise: 90,000 rupees (about £6,000) was an extremely generous gift which would cover the entire cost of the expedition in India.

We spent five days in Bombay. It was a time of hard work, interspersed with frequent meals and parties. At Harish's flat near the city centre, we were refreshed with mangoes and jack fruit by Harish's beautiful wife, Geeta, and met his two sons, Sonam and Nawang, aged twelve and ten, who immediately asked us to sign their autograph books, adding our signatures to those of celebrities like Chris Bonington, Tenzing Norgay and the American mountaineer Adams Carter. One evening we returned to the flat for a party, meeting the remaining expedition member, Arun Samant, and some of the girls of the Himalayan Club. It was a convivial evening and the first of many occasions when we tasted Geeta's superb cooking.

My diary for the next day begins:

> *Wednesday 29 May. Up resentfully at 7, which still feels like 2.30 English time. Standard fried eggs and tea before leaving in the car for the St Xavier Boys School to complete food packing. It was a happy party, with Harish, Boga, Dhiren, Muslim, another helper and two of last night's beautiful girls – Hina and Parul. They gradually warmed to banter and flirtation and even asked if we were coming back to Bombay after the expedition. Most impressed by Harish's packing – not only does he persuade all his friends to come and help – he also has uniform cardboard boxes, two to a load, taped and cable bound and stitched by a professional stitcher into waterproof hessian, and then numbered and stencilled with the expedition logo. We finished, and sat in the stuffy little room, talking to the girls and Nawang and Sonam, until Harish came to drive us back to Vijay Apartment for more mangoes and cool soothing yoghurt. The afternoon was dominated by the press conference at Grindlays, near the lawcourts – a bombastic Gothic edifice, which, if it were not for the palm trees outside, leaning over the maidan, could be Manchester town hall. Inside the Grindlays office, cold neon lighting and air conditioning were a welcome relief from the heat, glare, noise and smell outside …*

Next morning driving to the airport to meet Meena past the filthy shanty-towns, I felt momentary pangs of guilt about Grindlay's generous sponsorship; amidst such hopeless poverty, there did seem something slightly immoral about all that money going to help a group of wealthy people indulge in the frivolous sport of mountaineering. However, it was only a passing moment of guilt, because, like most people who travel in India, I had cultivated a thick skin.

Some of the newspapers carried reports of our expedition, with headlines like 'Civilians to attempt Siachen Glacier'. Later The Daily published a photo of the team in front of a large banner proclaiming 'GRINDLAYS REACHES NEW HEIGHTS WITH SIACHEN INDO-BRITISH EXPEDITION'. More significantly, the papers were full of rumours about impending chaos in the Punjab. June 3rd was the first anniversary of 'Operation Bluestar', the controversial storming of the Golden Temple in Amritsar by government troops, and the Sikh separatist movements were threatening a campaign of violence to mark the anniversary. We had to travel through the Punjab to reach Kashmir, so Harish had specially booked our overland travel before 3 June; but Victor, Jim, Arun and Meena were due to fly from Delhi to Leh on 6 June. If the troubles were serious the airport might be closed, stranding half our team in Delhi. Unrest in the Punjab was not the only problem hanging over us; there was also the matter of our expedition permit. The IMF in Delhi had sent a letter confirming that we could visit the Terong valley via the Siachen; but there was still no official permit and, in spite of all our well-laid plans, it looked as though we might face considerable problems, when and if we all reached Leh.

We had known all along that an expedition to the East Karakoram would be fraught with potential difficulties for we were hoping to reach one of the most sensitive spots on India's long northern border, a vital strategic area sandwiched between China and Pakistan. Indian and Pakistani troops were still fighting over the Siachen Glacier, the latest battleground in a long dispute whose seeds were sown way back in the nineteenth century with the creation of the state of Kashmir. By the Treaty of Amritsar in 1846, the British appointed the first 'Maharaja of Jammu, Kashmir and Ladak'. He was Gulab Singh, a Dogra Hindu who had helped the British to defeat the Sikh empire. The Sikhs lost control of a large part of the Western Himalaya and the British, by creating this new semi-autonomous state, pushed their sphere of influence north to Ladakh. The terms of the treaty were extremely vague, allowing for the gradual enlargement of the state in the late nineteenth century, as obsessive Russophobia compelled the British to push their frontier further north and west to encompass the entire Karakoram range and the Muslim districts of Chilas, Yasin, Gilgit, Hunza and Baltistan.

By 1947, the year of Partition, Jammu and Kashmir was a huge sprawling state, but its northern and eastern boundaries were still marked on the map as 'undefined'. The attempt to leave such a strategic area as a self-determining independent state was probably doomed to failure. The very ambiguity of the terms of its original creation, the controversial nature of its subsequent enlargement, the lingering uncertainty about its boundaries and the mixed population of Hindus, Buddhists and Muslims – all these factors prepared the ground for a bitter dispute between India and Pakistan.

The 1948 ceasefire line left Kashmir divided. Subsequent wars in 1965 and 1971 resulted in slight alterations to the dotted line on the map, a line which was clearly defined up to a point in the lower Shyok valley on the southern edge of the Karakoram. Here the dots stopped. The ceasefire terms stipulated that they should continue to 'follow the line of the glaciers', an ambiguity open to any number of interpretations. In effect Pakistan controlled the greater part of the Karakoram while India controlled the eastern end of the range. The dividing line was somewhere on the Siachen Glacier, but exactly where it should be no one was quite sure.

India's security problems were intensified after 1950 by the Chinese invasion of Tibet and the consolidation of Chinese rule in Sinkiang (the modern name for Turkestan) to the north of the Karakoram. In 1956 Chinese troops occupied a large chunk of north-eastern Ladakh, the Aksai Chin, and in the 1962 war they extended their line of control further into Ladakh. During the 1970s growing co-operation between Pakistan and China, symbolised by the Herculean construction of the Karakoram Highway, gave the Indian government more anxiety. Chinese road construction through and around the Karakoram was matched by a massive build-up of Indian troops in Ladakh, supported by an ambitious road network. Northern Ladakh, the area around the Nubra valley and Siachen, remained strictly closed to foreigners; but Pakistan did allow some foreign mountaineering expeditions to visit the upper Siachen Glacier from their side. By the early 1980s it was quite clear that the Siachen Glacier was being treated as Pakistani territory. But India, too, was taking a more active interest in the area and the news in 1984 that a joint Pakistani-Japanese expedition was planning to attempt the Rimo peaks, right at the eastern, Indian, end of the glacier, was not well received. More alarming were rumours of a projected military occupation of the glacier by Pakistan.

Things came to a head in April 1984. Indian troops pre-empted Pakistan by advancing up the Siachen Glacier and occupying key highpoints at its head and along the south-west side. Pakistani troops counter-attacked in May but were repulsed. Later that year, Dick Renshaw and I were in Gilgit when we heard the incredible news that Indian and Pakistani troops had been fighting all summer on the Siachen, 200 kilometres further east. Reports of casualty figures varied enormously; but one thing is almost certain – that crevasses, frostbite, exposure and avalanches claimed more victims than bullets and mortars. By the autumn Indian troops retained control of the entire glacier, occupying tin huts up to altitudes of nearly seven thousand metres. For most of the long winter, when temperatures drop to −40 °C, the men were kept fully occupied surviving the bitter cold, but there was one skirmish in February when people saw casualties being flown into the military hospital in Leh.

Now, at the end of May 1985, our Siachen Indo-British Expedition was setting off for the Siachen, just as the summer fighting season was starting. If we were allowed in it would be a demonstration of the Indian army's control of the area, but at this stage we still wondered if we really would be granted access. For the time being we would press ahead with our journey and hope that under Harish's capable leadership everything would work out right.

On Friday evening we left for the north and a huge party of friends and relations congregated, in true Indian style, on the platform of Bombay Central Station, to see us off on the Frontier Mail.

I spent most of the two-day train journey sleeping. When I woke on Saturday morning we were rolling across the endless expanse of Rajasthan, passing through mile after mile of tilled fields, waiting, grey and dry, for the monsoon. After staring out of the window for a while I started to talk with a student who was travelling back to her home in Jullundher. While we talked her parents watched anxiously. Later in the mountains, on the rare occasions when conversation flagged, Harish would always resort to banter about 'The Girl from Jullundher'.

In the evening we halted at Delhi. Muslim and Boga went to the luggage van, to ensure that none of our thirty-seven loads was accidentally unloaded; Harish and Dhiren went in search of the three Bhotia porters who would be helping us for the duration of the expedition. 'Bhotia' is a generic term for the people of Tibetan origin who have settled on the south side of the Himalaya. These three men live in the mountains of Kumaon, near the Nepalese border. Two of them had worked for Harish several times before, but they had never been to Kashmir, and were excited at the prospect of visiting what to them was virtually a foreign country. Harish found them on the platform and brought them to meet us. Harsinh Senior, the eldest man, was very poised, but his unrelated namesake, Harsinh Junior, and Pratapsinh both had looks of naïve wide-eyed excitement. They had all set off from their smallholdings in Kumaon with no luggage, dressed in the motley clothes which would see them through the next few weeks. Harsinh Junior looked particularly incongruous in a thigh-length lady's tweed coat with flamboyant lapels and huge decorative buttons. Some time in the middle of the night we stopped at Jullundher and the girl said goodbye. At dawn we looked out to the fields of the Punjab. Later in the morning we travelled alongside the first forested bumps of the Greater Himalaya, passing through what had been, until the gains from Pakistan in the 1971 war, a narrow vulnerable link between India and Kashmir.

At Jammu we first witnessed Harish's impatience with Kashmiris. He seethed with anger when a surly individual insisted on the nine of us hiring an entire bus, for 1,400 rupees, to transport our loads to Srinagar. Harish seemed to regard all Kashmiris as crooks, and during the next few days many that we met certainly lived up to a reputation for devious avarice.

We drove over the first of many passes, to Batote, where Dick and I had been devoured by fleas two years earlier. Then, instead of turning east up the Chenab, we crossed the river and followed the main road north, up to the Banihal Pass. It was now dark, but on the far side of the pass the surly driver switched off the engine and the headlights, explaining that we had to be wary of a malicious ghost, taking the unlikely form of a naked woman, who roamed this road at night, waiting to molest innocent travellers; so we free-wheeled silently down the road, peering out into the moonlight and searching vainly for the naked woman. We passed unscathed through the danger zone and the parsimonious driver saved himself the cost of a few centilitres of petrol, before having to restart the engine and drive across the flat plain.

We had reached the legendary Vale of Kashmir. The moon was almost full and had risen above dark hills, to transform the flooded paddy fields into a great sheet of silver, broken only by the dark serried lines of poplars.

All the magical poetry of Kashmir was there – until we arrived at the Tourist Centre Hotel in Srinagar. It was still early in the season and the troubles in the Punjab had kept many tourists away. Even before our bus stopped, the touts leapt aboard, all shouting at once:

'Hey Sarr, you want houseboat? No houseboat – you want hotel? I have beautiful hotel. I take you shikara ride. I take your luggage? Hey, you want houseboat? Where do you stay? I have very beautiful houseboat … beautiful sister … Hey Sarr, you want hotel … houseboat … I take you in shikara – full sprung seats – we go to Mogul gardens … You want houseboat? No houseboat – you want camping? Ah – you go to Leh – very beautiful. You want trekking? I am trekking agent. So am I trekking agent – Kashmir, Gulmarg, Ladakh, Zanskar, pony trek, fishing … Hey, you see my houseboat - very cheap price …'

We fought our way off the bus into a clamorous melée of more frantic Kashmiris, who grew perplexed as Dave and I either ignored them or laughed. Harish did ask if anyone could help take the luggage to our booked rooms, but was answered with cries of 'hundred rupees', so we shouldered the loads ourselves. Fifteen minutes later the luggage was all safely under lock and key and we could go to bed.

Srinagar: Venice of the East, pleasure garden of the Mogul emperors, paradise on earth … We stayed two days, just time enough to catch a glimpse of this most clichéd of holiday spots, and to deal with vital business. On Monday we drove down avenues of majestic chinars (the famous Kashmir plane trees) to the bazaar, where a dress shop displayed a proud sign:

PARIS BEAUTIES
AVOID ALL IMITATIONS

and continued to deliver all the baggage to a warehouse, whence it would be driven under the care of the three Bhotias to one Harish Sharma, the Mr Fixit of Leh, who would store it there and arrange for transport to Nubra.

In the evening we dutifully went for a shikara ride, gliding over the oily smooth water of the Dal Lake, thinking what a pleasant way this was to acclimatise, in spite of the flotilla of approaching canoes crowding round with solemn offers of wood carvings, saris, fur hats and lotus flowers.

On Tuesday, four of us rose early to walk up to the Adi Shankaracharya temple on the hilltop above the town and gaze out over the Vale of Kashmir to the hazy snow peaks of the Pir Panjal. After breakfast we were taken by jeep to army headquarters, where guards in exotically plumed turbans saluted with an explosive stamping of feet, giving Dave the fright of his life.

This was Harish's opportunity to put our case for the Terong valley to Brigadier Malhotra, pointing it out on the relief map. The Brigadier was doubtful about our passing the army base at the Siachen snout, to reach the Terong entrance, but then decided that it could probably be arranged, provided that we only passed the army camp during the hours of darkness. He went on to explain that, contrary to IMF reports, we would have to be accompanied by an army liaison officer, but that he would be there to help us, as would the army chiefs in Leh, who would lend us a copy of the new, accurate, top secret, 1:50,000 Survey of India map. They would also transport all our luggage directly to the glacier snout, the Third Infantry Division HQ would be at our disposal, and the Brigadier's only regret was that we could not wait an extra day in Srinagar for a television press conference. It seemed that the army was bending over backwards to help us, determined to make the most of the propaganda potential of having a foreign expedition climbing under their auspices in their sector of the Karakoram.

We stayed to be introduced to Lt General Indrajit Khanna, Commander-in-Chief of the Northern Area, and then went outside for a formal photograph before being delivered back to the hotel. The protocol was complete and we could now enjoy an afternoon of relaxation.

A friend of Harish's who was stationed in Srinagar lent us his jeep and the services of his driver for a tour of the seventeenth-century Mogul Gardens. I particularly enjoyed the Nishat gardens. The actual planting – beds of tawdry flowers, with no apparent colour scheme – was disappointing; but the overall design, the brilliant mastery of light and space and perspective, had all the genius of the civilisation that produced the Taj Mahal. A series of cascades and pools, framed by the solid masses of lofty chinar trees, leads the eye down and out to the Dal Lake, silver and ethereal, with an arched bridge silhouetted above the water. Beyond the lake, the fort, massive on the hill of Hauri Parbat, rises above the poplars, dark against the distant hazy backdrop of the Pir Panjal mountains. We went on to the Shalimar (the Royal Gardens), built for Shah Jehan. Long after the Mogul empire had collapsed, Vigne described his first visit to the gardens, during the course of his historic journey of exploration in the 1830s:

> I never saw it to such perfection as upon my first visit, when Mihan Singh, the Sikh governor ... invited me to join his party there. I found him surrounded by several of his officers, wearing the gorgeous costume of the Sikhs, a single threaded shawl turban, and a Kashmirian heron's plume, sitting in state in the corridor at the side of the building, and listening to the nach-girls, who were playing and dancing before him, accompanied by their musicians, who sang and played their violins at the same time. The [governor] occasionally took a little of the strong spirit of the country, which is distilled from crushed grapes left to ferment, which is much preferred to the finest wine that Europe could produce, which would not be considered strong enough ... When he was nearly tipsy, he retired into the building to take his siesta: the nach-girls ceased their warbling at the same time.

We spent an enjoyable evening with Harish and his colonel friend Prem, drinking liberal quantities of rum and whisky, while they reminisced about the time they had met nearly twenty years earlier at a mountaineering camp in Sikkim, where the army delivered the rum in five-gallon jerry cans. Prem also talked about the 1965 war when he was one of just two survivors of a patrol of thirteen who parachuted behind Pakistani lines; and he told us about the wild, manic courage of his Gurkha soldiers. After a long evening of fascinating stories we returned to the hotel to get a little sleep before starting the journey to Ladakh.

In 1819 a veterinary surgeon called William Moorcroft, who was already in his fifties, set out on a journey which was to end over five years later with his sudden mysterious death in the badlands of north-east Afghanistan. His first destination was Ladakh, whence he hoped to cross the mountains to Chinese Turkestan. British India at this time was bound in the north-west by the Sutlej river and it had taken years of badgering for Moorcroft to persuade the East India Company to sanction the journey, the ostensible purpose of which was to buy breeding stallions from the markets of Turkestan, hundreds of miles to the north. Eventually they reluctantly agreed after he had also obtained permission from Ranjit Singh, the Sikh emperor who controlled the mountainous land to the north-west of the Sutlej, and in 1819 Moorcroft set off to cross the British frontier.

Moorcroft and his companions were the first Europeans to visit the lush forests and meadows of Kulu, and to continue over the Rohthang Pass and Baralacha La and up through the barren Zanskar range to Leh, the capital of Ladakh. Moorcroft's journals, finally published in 1841, long after his death, as *Travels in the Himalayan Provinces*, kept a meticulous record of his observations and of his admiration for the gentle Tibetan Buddhist people of Ladakh. He quickly recognised Leh's importance as a trading centre on the route between Turkestan and Kashmir, and he noted the number of Russian goods that came over from Yarkand, one of the fabled towns on the Silk Route. The Russian frontier was still far back to the west, near the Aral Sea, but already in 1820 Moorcroft believed passionately that Russia had designs on Central Asia which should be counteracted by the British:

> They [the Ladakhis] have no manufacturers and rear an inadequate supply of food. The latter can be plentifully supplied from the British provinces of India. Whether they shall be clothed with the broadcloth of Russia or of England – whether they shall be provided with domestic utensils … with hardware of every description, from Petersburg or Birmingham – is entirely in the decision of the government of British India. At present there is little doubt as to which the prize will be awarded, for enterprise and vigour mark the measures of Russia towards Central Asia, whilst ours are characterised by misplaced squeamishness and unnecessary timidity.

He also discovered that the Ladakhis resented paying tribute to the Sikhs in Lahore and suggested that, as Ladakh had in the seventeenth century paid tribute to the Mogul emperors in Delhi, they should now transfer that allegiance to the Moguls' successors – the British government, who would gain influence in Ladakh, access to the commerce of Central Asia and 'a strong outwork against an enemy from the north, should such a foe ever occur in the autocrat of the Russians'.

Moorcroft's suggestions fell on deaf ears and over twenty years were to pass before the British government made serious efforts to extend their influence northwards; but undeterred, he continued his remarkable journey. His servant, Mir Izzet Ullah, had been sent across the Karakoram Pass to Yarkand, where the Chinese, who held a rather nebulous suzerainty over Tibet and Turkestan, refused Moorcroft permission to enter the country himself. He did however, in 1821, after wintering in Leh, cross the first barrier, the Ladakh range, struggling with a yak caravan through knee-deep snow and descending to the Shyok river and its tributary, the Nubra, where he bathed in the hot springs of Panamik. He never managed to cross the next pass, the Saser La, which leads to the Karakoram Pass itself; but he was the first European to reach the Karakoram range, in the course of an extraordinarily courageous journey.

The next traveller to reach the East Karakoram and the first European to grasp the topography of the Karakoram as a whole was Godfrey Vigne, whose tracks Dick and I had already crossed in Kishtwar. Now, in the days of easy air and road travel, when a typical Himalayan expedition lasts less than three months and modem equipment cushions one against the rigours of the mountains, it is easy to forget the extraordinary courage, vision and stamina of a man who could spend five years travelling almost continuously through some of the roughest terrain in the world. After extensive explorations round the Vale of Kashmir, Vigne continued north in 1837 to Skardu, the capital of Baltistan, where the people, though of Tibetan stock and dialect, are Muslims. From Skardu he attempted unsuccessfully to reach the Hispar and Mustagh passes, but the attempt gave him some inkling of the immensity of the Karakoram range and the formidable extent of its glaciers, which no European had previously suspected. He continued east up the Indus to Leh, followed Moorcroft's steps over the Ladakh range to the Nubra valley, but was too late in the year to continue to the Karakoram Pass.

In 1838 he tried to approach the Nubra valley from the south-west, travelling up the lower Shyok river and attempting to cross the high glacier Saltoro Pass. But the sport of mountaineering had not yet been invented, Vigne had no ice axes or ropes, and his porters quite rightly refused to carry on after several days of heavy storm had covered the crevasses with fresh snow. In spite of renewed fine weather, he had to retreat. His description, in *Travels in Kashmir, Ladak and Iskardoo,* of the tantalising moment of defeat expresses poignantly the feelings which so many mountaineers have subsequently experienced: 'I looked wistfully at the glacier; it still rose gradually and majestically in advance of us, into the now blue sky, seeming to vie in height with the giant peaks on either side of it, and completely hiding all that was beyond it.'

Political pressures prevented Vigne from returning to Nubra and he never had his chance to continue over the Karakoram Pass to Yarkand. Nevertheless he had achieved a vast amount. His map, in spite of large blank areas of white, was the first to indicate the enormous length of the Karakoram range, which he labels 'Mustak' (Mustagh is the Balti word for high icy mountain), 'extended from Gilgit to Nubra'. He shows the great bend of the Shyok river, containing 'lofty snowy mountains', later identified as Saser Kangri, and he marks the 'path to Yarkand when the river is too full', the summer route from Nubra, over the Saser La, to the passable headwaters of the Shyok and the Karakoram Pass itself.

The 1840s saw the demise of the short-lived Sikh empire at the hands of the British and, at last, the extension of British influence into Kashmir and Ladakh. In 1847 Henry Strachey, Alexander Cunningham and Dr Thomas Thomson were sent on a commission to survey the eastern border, given official sanction to explore far and wide to the north and encouraged to travel to Turkestan. Cunningham's book *Ladak and the Surrounding Countries* became a standard geographical textbook. In it he mentions the first recorded crossing of the Karakoram Pass in AD 399 by a Chinese Buddhist pilgrim, Fa Hian, who called the Karakoram range the Tsung-Ling – 'Onion Mountains' – on account of the wild leeks he found growing near the pass. In 1847 the pass had still not been seen by any European and knowledge of what the crossing entailed was hazy. Dr Thomson tried that year, but by the time he arrived in Nubra, in October, the onset of winter prevented him from continuing.

He returned in 1848, approaching Ladakh from the south, over the Umasi La and the barren mountains of Zanskar. This time he continued earlier in the season from Leh, travelling north to Nubra and continuing with local guides over the Saser La, the short cut which avoids the great bend of the Shyok, impassable in summer and for many years blocked higher up by a glacier-dammed lake.

He discovered that the Saser La is a high glacier pass (5,328 metres) crossing a tremendous ridge of high peaks, but that the actual watershed lay on yet another ridge of less spectacular but incredibly barren windswept hills. After reaching the far side of the Saser La, he continued along the upper branch of the Shyok – the Chip Chap river – over the desolate Depsang Plains, following the trail of bleached pack animals' skeletons and the occasional human skull which litter the route across this stark high-altitude desert. Thomson was a frail man and by the time he reached the campsite of Daulat Beg Olde ('The Place Where Daulat Beg Died'), he was suffering from appalling altitude sickness; but he pressed doggedly on and eventually reached the Karakoram Pass, 5,570 metres above sea level. He was too ill to continue across further wild mountainous country to Yarkand; but a European had succeeded at last in reaching the crest of the elusive Karakoram Pass.

It was left to Francis Younghusband to cross the Karakoram Pass in 1889 and continue north-west along the Yarkand-Shaksgam river system. He saw the spectacular serried ice pinnacles of the glaciers which descend from the north side of the Karakoram and ascended one of these, the Urdok, in an attempt to reach the legendary Saltoro Pass, the same pass which Vigne had tried to reach from the south-west. Younghusband hoped that this pass might provide a direct route across the Karakoram from the Shaksgam to the Indus System. However, snowstorms and avalanches thwarted his attempt and the Saltoro Pass remained a mystery.

The caravans used to take twenty days to travel from Srinagar to Leh. Now a bus does the journey in two days. Nevertheless, it is a rough road, which climbs up from the Vale of Kashmir, through alpine meadows and forests to the bleak snowbound Zoji La. As we drove up towards this first pass, Harish pointed out the strategic hill posts on the left, which had been wrested from Pakistan in 1971. We stayed the night at the Muslim town of Kargil, on the far side of the Zoji La, before continuing into Buddhist country. On the second morning we stopped for breakfast at Mulbekh, where I saw Tibetan Buddhist art for the first time – a four-armed Buddha, ten metres high, carved from the red granite of a massive boulder, brilliantly etched in the sharp morning sunlight. At the foot of the boulder, trees shaded the entrance to a small temple, painted with frescoes in vivid primary colours.

The bus ground its way over a second pass then up to the final 4,094-metre pass, the Fotu La, where we stopped to look out over an arid, primeval landscape of harsh yellows, greys and browns. Younghusband, usually unashamedly romantic about mountain landscape, was not overly impressed by the landscape of Ladakh: writing of his journey over the Fotu La, en route for Leh and the Karakoram Pass, in 1889, he had this to say:

> As regards the natural scenery, it would be difficult to imagine any more dreary looking country than Ladak. Its mountains, though lofty, are not grand or rugged, but resemble a monotonous succession of cinder heaps. But the Buddhist monasteries, the fluttering prayer flags, the chortens, and the many other signs of a religion almost totally unrepresented in India, gave the country a charm which just relieved it from utter condemnation.

The man who had already, two years earlier, travelled alone across the Gobi Desert, through China to Turkestan, and continued to make the first modern crossing, without any mountaineering equipment, of the disused and heavily glaciated Mustagh Pass, could afford to be blasé. Modern travellers, arriving every day in Ladakh, by plane and bus loads, tend to be more rapturous, particularly if they have never before seen this kind of desert landscape, where the air has a dazzling clarity and, as Younghusband grudgingly admits, the bright colours and the unique architecture of Tibetan Buddhist civilisation add a special interest.

We descended the far side of the Fotu La, following merchants' trucks down dusty hairpins to the Indus. In the afternoon we approached Leh, driving past Spituk monastery and across a desolate sandy plain littered with the sprawling tents and huts of the army encampment, and then drove up towards the town, passing through a wasteland of ugly shacks. I was sadly disappointed until we suddenly turned a corner into the main bazaar and could finally see over the poplar trees to the hilltop palace-fort, which dominates the town, like a miniature but not unimpressive version of Lhasa's Potala.

The rest of the team were waiting at the Tourist Bungalow hotel. Victor was in one of his more ebullient moods, chattering excitedly about Buddhist monasteries, rock climbing, the beautiful British Airways rep in Delhi, the illegal swim he and Jim had enjoyed in the American Embassy swimming pool, Mogul restaurants, Tibetan dialects, the symbolism of chortens, the explorations of Marco Pallis … Meena sighed wearily: 'He's quite a talker, isn't he?' and went on to describe their flight from Delhi, when Victor's habitual aerophobia had prompted a manic display of verbal fireworks.

Harish interrupted to suggest a meal. For the last few days he had been salivating at the prospect of momoes – Tibetan stuffed dumplings. Now he disappeared to the kitchen and returned a few minutes later to announce that 160 momoes were on order. But first, he said, we should go and have a little snack elsewhere; so with cries of 'chalo' he herded us out to the bazaar. We walked past the mosque and the Buddhist temple, to a small dark restaurant, where we were served noodles and lemon tea by a charming woman whose bright-eyed Tibetan smile we shall always remember. Back at the hotel we demolished some mangoes, before congregating on Jim and Victor's verandah for a celebratory bottle of Famous Grouse whisky. It was the first time that the entire Indo-British team (apart from Henry who was still marking exam papers in Bristol) had met. The threatened violence in the Punjab had never really erupted so everyone had managed to get safely through to Leh and we were now all set for the final leg of the journey to the Nubra valley. As we sat round the candlelit verandah, talking, laughing and drinking whisky, there was a wonderful atmosphere of euphoria and, I think, a unanimous conviction that this was going to be a very successful expedition.

Eventually, when darkness had fallen and the last drop of whisky had been drained, the hotel manager came to tell us that the momoes were ready.

10 Beyond the Inner Line

We stayed five days in the capital of Ladakh. The plan had been to leave after two; but, in spite of all the assurances we had received in Srinagar, the various civil and military authorities in Leh conspired three times running to prevent us from driving to Nubra.

Time was short and we were anxious to reach the Karakoram. Each day's delay seemed to reduce our chances of reconnoitring and attempting to climb Rimo. However, as Jim pointed out, the time was not entirely wasted. Leh is 3,505 metres above sea level and already, resting at our hotel, we were acclimatising; and apart from such practical considerations, it was simply a delightful place to spend a few days. The dry climate, with warm days and cool nights, the brilliant light, the views out across the Indus valley to the Zanskar range, the inimitable rustle of poplars in the breeze, the good food, the immutable peace of the temple, the smiling faces of the Tibetan girls … all these things and many more turned our delay into a real holiday.

Leh is still an important trading centre, but there is no longer any traffic from Turkestan: apart from the odd truck plying the road to Nubra, all the traffic is now with the south – Spiti and Zanskar, and most importantly Kashmir. Nearly every day convoys of trucks arrive from Srinagar, with vegetables, fruit, chickens, tinned food, medicines, carpets for the tourists and Indian manufactured goods. Although the town retains its Tibetan character the presence of India is very strong. Opposite the temple the familiar blue façade of the State Bank of India is flanked by an election poster of Rajiv Gandhi. A notice hangs in one of the windows ordering 'No entry with weapons'. Below the town the plain is littered with army detritus and MIG jets roar across the valley. When the runway was first built, the flight path was blocked by a spur of rock projecting into the valley, so the Indian army had to blast away a gap. The monks of Spituk – the monastery perched on the end of this rock – were understandably upset. They insisted on compensation and were duly paid large sums of money by the Indian government for the refurbishment of their monastery.

One morning we visited Spituk. The inner temples were like dark mysterious caverns, sumptuously decorated with intricate frescoes and tankas (painted cloths), silver and gold sculptures of many-armed gods, ceremonial shawms, silver-mounted conch shells and glowing oil lamps. In one room a monk was taking a service, hazy behind luxuriant billows of incense, mumbling some monotonic chant.

We emerged from the soft darkness of the temple to dazzling clarity outside, and walked down earthen steps, winding past the unique Tibetan door and window lintels of the monks' houses. Then we left the monastery and walked across fields to swim in the Indus. Victor detests cold water, but after seeing two of us jump in, his competitive instinct got the better of him, and with much noisy protestation he joined us. Refreshed and uplifted, we returned to Leh to find out the latest news on the military front.

At first there had been no hint of delays. On our first day in Leh, Friday 7 June, we had successfully bought all our remaining food supplies. The army's promise of transport had not been realised, but Harish Sharma had arranged for a private truck to carry us to Nubra. Our liaison officer had appeared at the hotel to assure us that there were no problems. In the evening we had enjoyed a delicious dinner and countless bottles of beer and rum, with Mutup Kalon.

The Kalon family had for centuries been the hereditary chief ministers to the King of Ladakh. Now they no longer held government power, but Mutup was the owner of the successful, upmarket Lharimo Hotel, where he entertained us to a wonderful candlelit feast. It was a delightful evening with many different conversations going on at once: Zerksis the Parsee telling us about his Zoroastrian faith, Jim recounting the tale of the Croglin vampire which lurks near his home in Cumbria, Harish discussing his work as editor of the *Himalayan Journal*, Meena describing her experiences as doctor on the previous year's Indian Everest Expedition, Muslim talking about literature and politics, Mutup being reticently modest about his summit climb on the 1973 Saser Kangri expedition, and a friend of his, one of Leh's Moravian Christians, explaining the bureaucratic complexities of his work with the Save the Children Fund, one of a plethora of charities whose brightly painted jeeps throng the Leh bazaar.

On Saturday morning I was lingering over breakfast at the Tourist Bungalow, when Harish rushed into the dining room to announce that he had just met a man who had known one of the porters on Dr Visser's 1929 expedition to the Terong valley: 'He said that Rimo is a very steep mountain – sheer rocks, streaked with many colours – a painted mountain – and at the foot of the mountain there is a lake in the ice, and the lake is full of dead men's bones!' The story added an exotic touch to our imminent adventure.

Departure was fixed for Sunday morning but on Saturday evening we were informed that, 'You must wait a little longer – there is a slight problem.' On

Sunday morning there was no liaison officer. For that matter we still had no official permit from the IMF because the relevant government official in Delhi was on holiday. However, on Sunday night our liaison officer reappeared to inform us that everything was now cleared.

On Monday we left at dawn for Nubra, bumping up the rough dusty track behind the town. After eight kilometres we stopped beside a conical tent, a checkpoint on the 'Inner Line'. A policeman emerged to examine our papers. He was about to wave us on when he suddenly noticed the magic word 'Siachen'. Then he noticed four white men sitting in the truck. That was enough: on no account would he let us through. Harish and Zerksis rushed back to Leh where they woke up the Superintendent of Police and demanded an explanation. They returned three hours later with clearance, but now it was too late to cross the Khardung La, because an army convoy was coming across from the far side; so we returned to Leh.

On Tuesday, the colonels telephoned the hotel at 1.30 a.m. to announce that the LO had just had a heart attack. They were very sorry but we could not proceed to Nubra that day. At daybreak Meena and Harish went to the army hospital but were refused admission. They then started on another exhausting round of visits to the police, the secret police, the army, the India-Tibet Border Force (ITBF) and the District Commissioner. When Harish appeared for his lunchtime momoes he looked tired and harassed. Everyone was getting very depressed. Dave had started pacing, his lumbering gait heavy with gloom. No one was convinced by the LO's heart attack, particularly after Meena and Harish were refused permission to visit the supposedly stricken man. We later discovered that the mark I liaison officer had indeed suffered no heart attack; he had been prevented from joining the expedition by the sudden unexpected arrival in Leh of his wife. As Harish commented, heart throb, not heart attack, was the problem.

Two days earlier, in one office, Harish had overheard remarks about a Pakistani helicopter landing on the Siachen. This may just have been a rumour, but it was becoming increasingly obvious that there was some kind of crisis on the Siachen, which the army authorities quite naturally did not want to discuss. Later, looking at the newspapers, we saw that the summer campaign had indeed just been hotting up:

> Srinagar, 1 June: Pakistani troops have renewed their attacks on Indian positions on the Siachin [sic] Glacier, on the north of the Nubra valley of Ladakh. Srinagar, June 4: Indian and Pakistani troops exchanged fire in the 18,000 foot high Siachin Glacier area in Ladakh following violation of Indian air space by six Pakistani military jets on 29 May.

In London, on 6 June, *The Times* had also mentioned the start of the summer campaign:

> As Mr Rajiv Gandhi, the Indian prime minister, stepped off the special Air India flight which took him to Cairo, where he says he will discuss the Arab-Israeli dispute and efforts to end the Iran-Iraq War, his soldiers were manouevring on the chilly heights of the Siachin Glacier, far above the plains of India, Pakistan, Russia and China.

It was now 7 June. The crisis had presumably continued, causing the army chiefs understandable concern about the potential embarrassment of having a group of their own civilians and four foreigners accidentally shot. However, our hopes were raised again that evening when they announced that we could leave for Nubra the next day. They produced a new liaison officer, 2nd Lt Mahendra (pronounced Minder) of the Maratha Light Infantry, and, for good measure, a spare liaison officer from the ITBF who would accompany us as far as Panamik. The lack of the correct document from Delhi would not matter. The army seemed to be on our side again, and we wondered whether it might have anything to do with the fact that Harish had just discovered that a brigadier newly appointed to the area was a cousin of Geeta. The only sad news was that Henry would not be able to join us in late June as planned – in no circumstances would the authorities allow a foreigner through on his own – so we telegrammed the disappointing news to Bristol.

SORRY FINAL DECISION NO SIACHEN IGNORE FIRST TELEGRAM

That evening, we arranged once again for our long-suffering truck driver to report at two o'clock in the morning and Mahendra promised to arrive at the same time. Then we sat down to another 'last meal' at the Potala Palace restaurant. Victor woke us at the appointed hour with rambunctious singing, I had been ill the previous day, was still aching with fever, and just longed for peace and quiet; but there had been no prohibitory message from the colonels, so I had to take my place in the back of the truck.

Three kilometres outside Leh the truck spluttered and came to a halt. There was trouble with the engine.

We waited while the driver tinkered under the bonnet. We were starting to fear that this fourth attempt to leave Leh was also doomed when the engine suddenly coughed, then roared back to life and we continued up the dusty track to the checkpoint, where the over-zealous policeman now had firm instructions not to hinder the Siachen Indo-British Expedition 85. While he checked our passports, by the first dim light of dawn, Jim kindly agreed to move into the back of the truck so that I could put my aching shivering body in the warm cab next to the engine.

Kenneth Mason, in his famous Himalayan reference book *Abode of Snow*, published in 1955 a photo of yak herdsmen struggling over the Khardung La, up to their knees in soft snow. Now there is a road, completed by Indian army engineers in 1976, the highest road in the world. It is a long hard grind up from Leh to the 5,486-metre pass, where engines struggle in the thin air. We stopped on the crest of the Ladakh range to look down to the Shyok valley, 3,000 metres below on the far side. Beyond the valley the high peaks of the Karakoram were hidden in cloud.

The descent was a noisy business and we had to shout to communicate above the anguished scream of the engine and the creak of the bodywork, as our driver swung the truck confidently round hairpin after hairpin. About halfway down we reached an area of high meadows, where marmots fled shrieking, while placid yaks continued grazing. We stopped for tea at an army tent, then continued down and down into the hot Shyok valley, where the swirling grey river was hardly distinguishable from the surrounding sand and rubble. We stopped at another army base for lunch and a jawan (army private) brought a searing curry which even some of the Bombay team could not handle. In the afternoon we crossed the Shyok river and headed south-west for a few miles to the entrance of the Nubra valley. I took a turn in the back of the truck, where eight of us were flung backwards and forwards, up and down, and drenched in thick showers of dust pouring in through the back entrance.

That evening we had hot baths. One hundred and sixty-four years earlier, William Moorcroft had travelled to the hot springs at Panamik, hoping to cure the rheumatism which was plaguing him after a long cold winter in Leh. Since then the facilities have improved and the water is now channelled into a bath house, where you can sit under a luxurious hot shower, sheltered from the cold dusty wind outside. We stayed at the Dak bungalow just below the springs. On the far side of the broad valley a small monastery grew from the cliff face, remote and peaceful above the river. Further along that side a tiny village huddled among green fields, patched on to a great fan of alluvial deposit which had poured down over the millennia from a gorge above. The sun, swinging round to the north-west, pierced bright shafts through the clouds, shining down the valley and lighting the twisted silver braids of the Nubra river. It was exciting to be back in the Karakoram again. A week earlier we had been amongst the emerald ricefields and gentle wooded hills of Srinagar; now in the Nubra valley there was a feeling of wild remote immensity.

Inside the Dak bungalow, while the Bhotias prepared supper the rest of us examined for the first time the accurate modern Survey of India map of the Terong area. There was an atmosphere of excited anticipation now that we were so close to our goal. Victor was his usual irrepressible self, firing off a barrage of ideas and suggestions. I still felt ill and irritable, and eventually turned to Victor in exasperation.

'It's quite extraordinary – this sort of stream of consciousness, which comes out as a torrent of verbal dysentery!'

'You're horrible – I'm not nasty to you!' he replied, in tones of mock peevishness. It was all perfectly good-humoured but I did wonder if it might become less good-humoured at 7,000 metres. So far, however, there was a growing rapport between all the expedition members, and the Englishmen were getting to know the Indians better, finding out more about their lives and their past expeditions.

Harish was an ideal leader. In Leh his dogged perseverance and his shameless use of friends and contacts had enabled us to overcome considerable bureaucratic obstacles which on our own we would probably never have surmounted. Now that he had won the battle with the authorities he was his usual ebullient self, full of excited plans for the Terong valley, happy to be in the mountains again. During twenty years of mountaineering he never seemed to have lost his enthusiasm and now, as editor of the *Himalayan Journal*, he had a wealth of knowledge about the Greater Himalaya.

He had travelled far and wide in Ladakh, Spiti, Kumaon, Garhwal, Nepal and Sikkim, on numerous expeditions, usually with friends from Bombay. One of these expeditions had resulted in a serious accident when Harish dislocated his hip, falling into a crevasse. It had taken his friends thirteen days to carry him down, in excruciating pain, to a point where a helicopter could rescue him. After two years slow convalescence he had taken the first opportunity to return to the mountains with undimmed enthusiasm.

Zerksis Boga, usually called 'Boga', worked for a German drug company in Bombay. He too was in his late thirties, had been climbing for many years and had witnessed Harish's accident on Devtoli. As one of the older members, he did occasionally, like Harish, seem just slightly autocratic with the two younger Indians; but there was no antagonism and to the English climbers he always showed a warm unaffected friendliness.

Arun Samant seemed more reserved, but perhaps that was because there was less time to get to know him. We had only met briefly in Bombay, he had not been in the overland party and he was one of the first to leave at the end of the expedition, hurrying back to Bombay, where he lives with his wife and young son. His father is a well-known opposition politician and Arun too is involved in politics as well as working as a civil engineer in the family firm. I remember him best for his white-toothed grin and his passion for P. G. Wodehouse.[1]

---

1 Arun Samant died in 1999 on Gyasumpa, a peak in eastern Ladakh, close to the Tibetan border.

We had already met Meena in London, where she had been working long hard hours at the St Mary Children's Hospital, saving up every moment of holiday for the expedition. She, too, had been climbing for many years, had been the leader of one of India's first all women expeditions and had, in 1984, climbed to 7,500 metres on Everest. She came on this expedition as a member of the Bombay Mountaineers and the Alpine Club. She was also a member of the IMF. Although she has settled as a successful paediatric surgeon in London she retains very strong ties with her family in Bombay and remains devoted to India. This was brought home on the occasion when we were stopped by the policeman outside Leh. Exasperated by Indian bureaucracy, I exclaimed with deliberate contempt: 'This country amazes me!' Meena responded immediately: 'If you were Indian and you had fought three wars to defend the border, you'd understand.'

Dhiren had at the age of twenty already been on three Himalayan expeditions during university holidays. (He was now a third year engineering student.) Like Harish, he is a Gujarati Hindu and he also shared our leader's passion for cricket. He was probably the fittest and most agile of the Indian members, a good natural climber and strong at altitude. Very much Harish's blue-eyed boy, he was entrusted with much of the expedition organisation and was expedition treasurer, a position he filled with diligence and efficiency, meticulously recording every rupee and keeping all the receipts for the auditors. This caused a slight problem on our return to Leh, when Dhiren asked a hotel manager for a receipt for 240 rupees' worth (about £14) of beer. The manager did not want to incriminate himself for illegal selling of beer, so wrote 'Siachen Expedition – Coca-Cola: 240 rupees' – the price of at least fifty bottles.

Muslim, the second youngest member of the team, moved more cautiously and was quite slow (perhaps because, like me, his daily attempts to give up smoking were unsuccessful); but he shared Dhiren's enthusiasm and was full of perseverance. His family are involved in the Bohra Muslim reform movement, but Muslim himself, in spite of his name, professes atheism. He had studied chemical engineering at Bombay University and was now working in his family's ink manufacturing firm – a job for which he exhibited no obvious enthusiasm. In Bombay we had heard Beethoven's Ninth blasting from his bedroom and during the expedition his wide knowledge of European music and literature became increasingly apparent. His incisive wit was a constant source of delight and although, like the others, he was passionately fond of his country and would never question the seriousness of her security problems, he was engagingly cynical about some of India's most revered institutions. Later I was to read some of his book reviews in the *Himalayan Journal* which exhibited the same sharp sense of humour.

On Thursday 13 June, we left Panamik and continued up the left (north) bank of the Nubra river. The truck lurched across boulder fields, negotiating river beds and winding between thickets of rose bushes. At Sasoma the ever-hospitable army showed us into a dugout built from empty jerry cans and lined with an old parachute, where we were served sweet cloying tea. We drove on, passing the improbable entrance to the Saser La on our right. We could just make out a faint track, zigzagging up steep scree and skirting round a spectacular gash in the massive granite cliffs. This was the centuries-old trade route, mapped by Vigne and crossed by Thomson, which crosses the northern Karakoram axis to the desolate Depsang plains of the Chip Chap river and the final, cruel Karakoram Pass. Now the Karakoram Pass itself is a sealed frontier, patrolled by the ITBF; but the Saser La is still used to supply bases on the Chip Chap river and every summer, from July onward, the men of Nubra provide mule and yak transport across this glacier pass. We, however, continued north-west up the Nubra valley.

We stopped in the last major village to stock up with paraffin. The last settlement of all, Warshi, boasts just three inhabitants, but this village had a sizeable population and a large crowd of people gathered round the gleaming whitewashed chortens to inspect us. After trying the local chang, Victor and I went to visit the village school, where a young man presided over about thirty children, ranging from five years old to fifteen. They all sat in order of size on the school verandah, with Urdu books in front of them. While the teacher ticked off the register, they suddenly erupted into song – a discordant outburst, accompanied by a small girl beating a stick violently and unrhythmically on the blackboard. The children were delightful but that strident din brought back my grimmest memories of school teaching and when Dave came to fetch us I felt relieved to be leaving the children in someone else's care.

I fell asleep in the back of the truck for the last stage of our journey, wedged among piles of luggage, and only woke after it stopped. Someone was handing loads to shouting people outside. After much yawning, I climbed down and blinked in the harsh light. The truck was parked in a plain of dazzling pale sand, enclosed by steep walls. High above the walls, towers and pinnacles were silhouetted like cardboard cut-outs against an intense blue sky. The river was hidden in a dip and at first I was completely disorientated. Then I noticed the Siachen snout, about four kilometres away, an innocuous-looking dirty heap of rubble. No wonder Henry Strachey never guessed that in what he called the Saichar Glacier he had discovered in 1848 the snout of an immense glacier around seventy kilometres long.

It was Dr Thomas Longstaff whose 1909 journey filled in two of the most important missing pieces in the jigsaw of exploration – the position of the Saltoro Pass and the extent of the Siachen Glacier. In his quest for the elusive direct route across the Karakoram, Longstaff had come to suspect that the

1892 Survey of India map was wrong in locating the passes noted by Vigne and Younghusband as one and the same. From a study of their latitude recordings, they should be nearly thirty kilometres apart. Younghusband himself suspected that this was the case. Now he was the resident governor of Kashmir and, entertaining Longstaff en route for the Karakoram, he gave the younger man every encouragement to solve the mystery.

Longstaff was an experienced mountaineer (he had already in 1907 made the first ascent of Trisul, in Garhwal) and, unlike Vigne seventy-one years earlier, was suitably equipped to climb up the Bilafond Glacier and cross the Saltoro Pass (now called Bilafond La). Descending the glacier on the far side, he was thrilled to discover not the arid valleys of Turkestan, but another vast glacier three kilometres wide, streaked with the dark parallel lines of medial moraines. Looking up the glacier to huge snowfields of arctic dimensions, he saw far away in the top north-east corner a prominent snow saddle, the pass which Younghusband had nearly reached from the far side in 1889. Immediately opposite and nearer was a massif of high peaks which he correctly estimated to be well over seven thousand metres high and which he called Teram Kangri, because his Balti porters had spoken of legendary mountains of Teram. (Kangri, like Mustagh, is a generic term for high icy mountains.) These mountains were part of the northern axis of the Karakoram – the main watershed and quite separate from the Saltoro ridge.

Longstaff had discovered the largest glacier in the Karakoram, whose extent had until that time hardly been suspected. However, he still did not have definitive proof of where it flowed out; so he retraced his steps south, back over the Saltoro Pass, to travel south-east up the Shyok river, then back north-west, wading back and forth across the Nubra river to the snout of Strachey's 'Saichar' Glacier. Unlike Strachey, he followed the glacier round a sharp curve, to see a great river of ice stretching ahead. He continued for several kilometres and, rounding another larger bend, arrived at the same upper glacier which he had reached a few weeks earlier. The outstanding riddle of the Karakoram had been solved and a huge blank in the map filled – filled by a mighty glacier over seventy kilometres long, which Longstaff correctly called 'Siachen', a Ladakhi name which refers to the profusion of wild roses (seia) in the area and can be translated either as Place of Roses or Having Roses.

Now, in 1985, the glacier snout was guarded by yet another military camp, almost completely hidden among boulders and bushes. We were shown to a distant campsite where we could not be accused of spying on the army base. However, the camp commanders were extremely hospitable and while we were shifting the luggage a khaki truck rumbled across the sand to deliver a huge lunch of rice, potatoes, vegetables, curry and yoghurt.

We pitched our tents and took shelter while clouds smothered the mountains and a malignant wind whipped sand and dust, then rain, down the valley.

In the evening a jeep came bouncing across the sandy plain and drew to a halt outside our tents. I was reminded of old newsreels of Montgomery visiting the chaps at Alamein, but the style was not quite right; the two officers who emerged from the jeep were too immaculately uniformed. We all rushed to our feet, hastily shuffling into sandals and flip-flops and assembled in a semi-circle to shake hands with Colonel Gupte. He spoke the impeccable, precise English of the pukka army officer, was affable and welcoming and conscien-tiously bland on the subject of Indo-Pakistani hostilities, merely hinting that 'those chaps over there', nodding in the direction of the Bilafond La, 'are being a bit of a nuisance', but behind the nonchalance there was an obvious pride in his work and an uncharacteristic enthusiasm for the bleak landscape of the Karakoram. His companion was even more enthusiastic about the mountains. He was a pilot, and had flown the length and breadth of the Siachen and Rimo glaciers; he told us about the snow leopard he had spotted, running across the snow of the Saser La.

Harish got down to business, discussing our approach to the Terong Glacier. We had only managed to find nine men in the Nubra valley to porter for us. The Bhotias brought the number up to twelve, but we had over forty loads. Colonel Gupte promised that we could borrow some of the men who had been carrying loads up the Siachen for the army; they could only be spared for one day but that would be some help. They would arrive at 2 a.m., so that we could pass the army base before daybreak and avoid seeing any military secrets. He thought that the eighteen-kilometre approach to our proposed Base Camp above the snout of the Terong Glacier could be done in a single ten-hour march. I was sceptical about this at first, but was soon carried along in the general mood of optimism. Everything seemed too good to be true.

Only a few extra porters were available, and only for one day, so we would have to do two or three ferries. For the moment Harish, Dhiren and Boga would remain in the Nubra valley, Harish wanted an English volunteer to stay with them. I was still feeling ill, so I agreed to stay down.

We were all lying quietly in bed that night when another jeep suddenly roared towards us out of the darkness. An officer asked urgently: 'Excuse me – have you been flashing torches? Has anyone been outside the tents? We have seen lights – are they yours?' Various sleepy voices answered 'No' and he left. We didn't think much more about the incident until Jim was told later that Pakistani paratroopers had dropped that night into the Nubra valley, some-where below our camp.

At 2 a.m. I was woken by pandemonium. The Tower of Babel had nothing on this scene: outside the tent, thirty people were shouting at each other in Ladakhi, Gujarati, Kumaoni, Hindi and English, trying to resolve a situation of total chaos. The army porters, spoilt by months of secure employment, announced that they would only carry twenty-kilo loads, instead of the normal twenty-five kilos. For an hour everyone struggled noisily in the darkness to re-sort our beautifully packed loads. Eventually the cacophony died down and they all left for the Siachen Glacier.

Harish, Boga, Dhiren and I returned thankfully to bed. Later in the morning we rose to rationalise the chaos of the remaining loads. I was feeling ill again and struggled weakly to help, before escaping to shelter inside a tent from the merciless sun, plugging into my Walkman cassette player and enveloping myself in the bitter-sweet nostalgia of Richard Strauss's Four Last Songs.

Harish and Dhiren left the following morning with the next ferry of loads. News had come down that not all was well in the Terong valley. The army porters had dumped their loads at the valley entrance and left. The other Ladakhis had continued reluctantly to a campsite just inside the valley. Base Camp was, at this rate, another two marches away, and the Terong river was, as I had suspected, complicating matters. In the course of its meandering journey down the valley it abutted against impassable cliffs, first on one side, then on the other. Setting off from the camp on the left bank, Arun, Jim, Dave, Muslim and Victor had to wade the icy water to the right bank, before they could continue up the valley to explore the route on to the Terong Glacier. Returning that evening, they found the river dangerously swollen with the afternoon's glacial meltwater. Jim, our thirteen-stone gentle giant, attempted to wade back across, was swept off his feet, and ended up doing an ice axe brake on the boulder bed of the river, in a frantic bid to save himself from a turbulent death by drowning. He just managed to escape back to the right bank.

Five members of the Siachen Indo-British Expedition were now stranded on the wrong side of the river, as night was falling, without bivouac equipment. Muslim and Arun repaired to a cave, hoping that it was not the lair of snow leopards or bears. Dave and Victor built a stone wall shelter and stuffed their clothes with dead dry grass for insulation. Jim (now also known as 'Crog' after his local Croglin vampire) went for a brisk run to try to get dry, before making his own shelter in another clump of dead grass. Thereafter, no one ever tried again to cross the river in the evening, and on our frequent journeys up and down the valley, the Crog's nest was to become a familiar landmark, reminding us of the dangers of Karakoram rivers.

Meanwhile our nine Ladakhis, helped by our Bhotias, Pratap and the Harsinhs, were relaying loads up from the Siachen snout to the first camp in the Terong valley. Harish and Dhiren left before dawn on the second day. I remained with Boga, feeling lousy. In the afternoon Meena came down to mother the invalid and announced that I had a temperature of 103. It seemed that I was destined to start every expedition with a debilitating bout of flu.

In the evening an army truck drove us and the remaining loads to a different campsite right under the Siachen snout. We bounced through the darkness, past a small town of tents and Nissen huts. Most of the resident soldiers were at the camp cinema, but there were sentries on duty to check our papers. Apparently, another group of sentries had not been warned of our shift of camp, and we heard the next day that while we were pitching our tents they had trained their guns on our suspicious torchlights. They were officially supposed to shoot suspicious strangers on sight, but luckily they consulted a senior officer, who told them not to pull the trigger.

On the third day I started to feel better. In the afternoon I was frightened by an enormous bang and for several minutes the valley reverberated with the din of heavy artillery firing at some invisible target on the far side of the glacier. In the evening Colonel Gupte dropped in to see how I was doing. He seemed anxious that we should all move up to the Terong valley, because beside the army base we were sitting targets for any possible Pakistani attack – potential catalysts for a highly embarrassing international incident. I assured him that I would be well enough in the morning to leave.

When Longstaff made his historic journey up the Siachen Glacier in 1909, he walked past the entrance to the Terong valley, and was struck by the unusual sight of a tributary valley devoid of ice. From where he stood, the ice of the Siachen had bulged out sideways, spilling down about two hundred metres on to the valley floor, where a large river flowing down from above disappeared under the ice. Looking up this valley, he saw only the river, in its flat bed of sand and boulders, disappearing round a bend between steep granite walls.

The glacier whence it flowed had retreated far from its original confluence with the Siachen. He did not have time to explore this valley, intent as he was on solving the immediate problem of the Siachen itself; but he realised that the Terong valley would be an interesting objective and suggested: 'When it is desired to survey this unknown corner, will the party please proceed five miles up the glacier and take the first turning on the right.'

In 1929, the Dutch explorer Dr Ph. C. Visser did just that, accompanied by his wife Jenny, a Dr Wyss, the Indian surveyor Khan Afraz Gul Khan and the famous Swiss mountain guide Franz Lochmatter. Now, fifty-six years later we were following in their footsteps. Harish had only discovered about the Visser expedition just before our departure, and none of us had read the report. We knew that they had carried out a limited survey of the basin, but that was about all. We had seen no photos and were in a state of blissful ignorance about what lay ahead, having only the map and the old man from Leh's story about the Lake of Bones to go on.

Walking up with Meena on Monday 17 June, I felt all the excitement of discovery as we approached the entrance to the valley. We left at dawn to climb up on to the Siachen snout and follow a well-beaten path over rubble-strewn hummocks, past marker posts and trailing telephone wires. After a mile or two we passed a group of jawans on their way down from one of the higher camps.

Helicopters passed overhead. We left the main track, veering right along another path, beaten down by our porters during the last three days. Magnificent spiked towers of red granite reared up on the far side of the glacier. Somewhere beyond them lay the Gyong La, one of the strategic passes controlled by the army. We continued, and as the glacier curved round to the right a great vista unfolded – the vista which Strachey had failed to reach in 1848 – of the huge Siachen valley flanked by high snow peaks. We arrived on a crest at the edge of the glacier to look right to another less extensive vista: for the first time I stared down into the Terong valley, curving away out of sight, tempting with the allure of the unknown. (The name Terong probably comes from the Ladakhi words (g)ter = hidden and rong = narrow gorge.) We ran down to the floor of the valley, where the river roared into a monstrous cavern, swallowed up under fractured walls of blue ice. It was an oppressive place and I was glad to turn my back on the Siachen, to walk across sandy flats, past clumps of golden grass and aromatic herbs and thickets of scrub willow, to the first camp.

Only Muslim was there, surrounded by the debris of breakfast. All the porters were ferrying from Nubra, and the other climbers were at the river crossing. They returned later for a lunch of vegetable stew in the makeshift kitchen, under a large overhanging boulder. In the afternoon we sheltered in our tents from the wind-blown dust. We had called this camp Gyazgo, meaning Gateway, but the name which stuck was 'Dust Camp'. We were now finally established in our valley, safely out of the army's way, but we had not covered much ground. The porters were proving to be a belligerent lot and Harish was growing tired of the constant negotiating. After the repacking in Nubra, we now had nearly sixty loads, with only nine Ladakhis and three Bhotias to help carry them. From here they would carry only as far as the Terong Glacier snout in the next stage, and it would take a third stage to reach Base Camp.

Rimo still seemed very distant, but it was good just to be in the Terong valley, free at last from military and bureaucratic complications, and one consolation for all the delays was that everyone was becoming very fit with all the load-ferrying. It seemed quite a contented crowd of people that gathered in the evening round a blazing fire of dead juniper, talking, reading and eating an enormous supper cooked by Pratap and the Harsinhs, while Harish sat on a boulder with his ear glued to a transistor radio, following assiduously every move of the England v Australia test match at Headingley, relayed to him by the BBC World Service.

11　To the Lake of Bones

Wednesday 19 June. An enjoyable carry to the river crossing, on my own, in the early morning cool; then back to Dust Camp for omelette breakfast before final departure. The river crossing was painfully cold. I did three carries across before Meena told me to stop: 'If you get cold your flu will come back – don't be so obstinate.' So I stopped being obstinate and lay in the sun.

We were on our way to the second camp at the snout of the Terong Glacier. The previous day we had ferried all the loads to the river crossing and now we were carrying them across. Already at this hour of the morning, when the water did not even reach your knees, you could feel the strong tug of the current, and I was glad of the rope handrail which was now fixed in place. Harish, after protracted negotiations and the promise of a pay rise from seventy to eighty rupees a day, had persuaded the Ladakhis to continue working for us and carry as far as Base Camp. Dave, Jim and Boga had gone ahead the previous day to look for a suitable site for this on the Terong Glacier.

The fierce heat slowed us down on the next stretch. Feet dragged on the sandy floor of the valley as we carried our loads up the right bank. On our left, ancient juniper trees clung to towering cliffs of ice-sculpted granite. Their isolated contorted shapes reminded Victor of Japanese landscape paintings. On the far side of the valley there were vestiges of grass meadow, high above the cliffs, inaccessible to shepherds and hunters, safe for roaming ibex. On the valley floor there were just isolated clumps of last year's golden grass, tamarisk and rose bushes, and a copious supply of dead juniper firewood – a luxury in the Karakoram, where so many high valleys have been exploited for centuries by hunters and shepherds, and more recently by mountaineering expeditions. Now that we had rounded the river's bend we could see the glacier snout ahead, a monstrous slag heap pouring down between dark rock walls.

Snout Camp was on a shelf of sand right at the foot of the glacier, where its tongue licked the floor of the valley. With our stone-walled kitchen, the Ladakhis' shelter, several brightly coloured tents and over twenty people milling around, it looked like a small village. The Ladakhis had built a round, dry-stone-walled enclosure, like a sheep pen, where they sat on their blankets, playing cards, cooking on a juniper fire and, later in the evening, placing some hot coals on a boulder and sprinkling them with tsampa (roast barley) as an offering to the gods. They seemed happy and cheerful and it looked as though they would stay to help carry all the loads to Base Camp. The following day, however, a bizarre misunderstanding nearly brought them all out on strike.

It was the second of two improbable incidents that enlivened the day. We all did two load ferries from the river dump to Snout Camp. I set off later than the others on the second carry and missed the first incident. The others arrived at the river dump to find ten jawans, replete with sub-machine guns, inspecting our pile of luggage. They had only just been posted to the Siachen battle zone, had never seen a glacier in their lives before and apparently knew very little about map reading. Instructed to march up to the army's first camp on the Siachen, they had inadvertently followed our tracks into the Terong valley and had continued right up to and across the river, to be informed by the Siachen Indo-British Expedition that they were in the wrong valley and would not find any action here.

After lunch I set off on my own to do my second carry. The nine Ladakhis were also doing their second carry and had set off about ten minutes before me. I followed a slightly different route, approaching the luggage dump from behind a bank of boulders. I saw the Ladakhis starting back up with their loads and I waved to them, but they didn't seem to notice. I filled my rucksack with climbing equipment and set off in pursuit, striding back towards the Terong snout which was dark and ugly in the distance, beneath lowering clouds. As I neared the Ladakhis, one or two of the men turned round and noticed me. A moment later they had all disappeared.

I continued walking. Suddenly a face appeared from behind a boulder. Then, one by one, they all popped up – a row of quizzical Tibetan faces. It was the first time that expedition porters had ever played hide and seek with me, and I burst out laughing. Some of them laughed back, but Norbu, a man who had already given Harish a good deal of trouble, looked angry. They crowded round, jabbering at me in Ladakhi, while I smiled back in incomprehension. Some of them were laughing again and repeating the word 'Pakistani'; so, keen to join in the joke, I mimed a little act of reaching into my rucksack for a gun. Some of the men smiled, but Norbu looked even crosser, pointing to my green ex-army trousers and eyeing me with dark suspicion.

The porters returned to Snout Camp just before me. When I arrived there was a tremendous row going on, with all the Ladakhis crowding round Harish and shouting. Harish explained: 'They were very frightened: they thought you were a Pakistani spy.'

'*I* was a spy? I thought they were the ones playing at spies!'

'No – they said you followed them secretly.'

'Well, what's all the fuss about? Now they know it was just me they've got nothing to be frightened about.'

But unfortunately it was not as simple as that. They had never seen me coming down the valley, hence their alarm on the way back up when they suddenly noticed a lone figure in military trousers (and, I might add, a thoroughly unmilitary British Airways T-shirt) following them back up the valley. Once they realised it was me, not a Pakistani agent, they assumed that I had been sent by Harish to spy on them. They had worked faithfully for a week – but now he was spying on them – he didn't trust them with our loads – they had been wrongly accused of dishonesty – now they knew that Harish did not trust them they were not going to work for him. The dispute raged for three hours. Harish, Boga and Meena struggled to convince the porters that there had been a mistake. Norbu, the self-appointed shop steward, shouted and stabbed the air with his finger, eyes blazing with paranoid fury. I tried to offer apologies and Jim told me to keep out of the way.

By the evening we were all friends again. Thanks mainly to Meena's gentle diplomacy, Norbu had been pacified and the nine men, tempted by yet another pay rise, had agreed to stay for the final three days of load-carrying to Base Camp, before they returned to their villages to start work on the first caravan over the Saser La. During the next three days, whenever any of us approached the Ladakhis on the route up the glacier, we always made a point of standing on top of a suitably prominent hummock to wave our arms and shout at the tops of our voices, to indicate our presence and make it quite clear that we were not secret agents in the employ of the Pakistan army or Harish Kapadia.

Anyone who has travelled amongst the great glaciers of the Karakoram knows that in their lower reaches they usually present a hideous turmoil of ice hummocks littered with rock debris, gouged and scoured from the mountains above. If you are lucky, the lateral moraine will have developed a solid crest, with perhaps a gentle grassy ablation valley between it and the mountainside, forming a perfect path up the side of the glacier. The Terong Glacier had only an apology for a moraine, a crumbly conglomerate of mud and boulders, squeezed up against the valley walls, with no accommodating ablation valley; so we had to stumble up the debris of the glacier itself, weaving a line up and down and in between wave after wave of heaped slates.

Jim, Victor and I set off from Snout Camp soon after dawn, on Friday 21 June. The others would be following later after a more leisurely breakfast. Jim quickly disappeared, while Victor and I followed at a steadier pace. It was an immaculate morning and when we stopped after about an hour to look back west, down over the level bed of the Terong valley, the snow peaks on the far side of the Siachen were already flat white in the bright morning sunshine. We continued slowly up the slag heaps, skirting round walls of black gritty ice, zigzagging from one hummock to the next. On the right we could see the broad valley of the South Terong Glacier stretching many miles to the south-east; but ahead of us the main North Terong Glacier reared up to curve round out of sight between enclosing walls of dark slate.

Jim was waiting at Base Camp. As yet there were no tents, just a small pile of loads dumped on a terrace of slates beside a pool of dark sludge. Harish, in poetic vein (and perhaps inspired by Victor's orientalism) had described this spot as a Japanese rock garden. Rubble tips blocked the view down the glacier and out to the South Terong; the near side of the glacier was a wall of conglomerate, piled up against the slate mountainside; above us, the upper glacier was blocked from view by a great bulge, but there the monotony was at least relieved by decorative pinnacles of white ice.

Siab Chushku was the official ethnic name given to this bleak spot. Chushku means camp, Siab the meeting place of three waters. The 'three waters' were the three main glaciers of the Terong basin – the main North Terong Glacier, joined near here by a river from the receded South Terong Glacier, and, flowing in between these two valleys, the icefall of the Shelkar Chorten Glacier. Siab Chushku was the official name but the name I remember is 'Mud Camp'. The tents were pitched on terraces of shingle and dust, beside a small pool of mud, thick and dark, with the smooth consistency of chocolate mousse. During one of their rare rest days, Jim and Victor, both respectably married, professional men in their mid-thirties, spent many happy hours lobbing stones into the slurry, competing to see who could make the biggest splatter.

Today, however, on our arrival at Mud Camp they were content to sit in the sun and enjoy a bar of chocolate and several mugs of tea (as well as mud, there was a stream of moderately clear water) before continuing on their long plod up the glacier. Harish had asked them to go ahead and select a suitable site for Advance Base, somewhere near the Lake of Bones, at about five thousand metres. The rest of us would remain below, helping the porters to ferry all the loads to Base Camp, which would effectively be a staging post, with Advance Base as our real home for the main part of the expedition. Because we had the luxury of three permanent Bhotia porters, we would only have to do two carries to Advance Base. After that, the Bhotias would keep it supplied, while we investigated the Rimo massif. Later we would return to Mud Camp for our exploration of the Shelkar Chorten and South Terong glaciers.

For the first time in my life I was on an expedition with a leader. It felt strange to have someone issuing instructions (however courteous and diplomatic) and I felt slightly resentful about staying below, while Jim and Victor had the excitement of pushing ahead towards Rimo. However, my envy was qualified when Victor reluctantly shouldered his thirty-kilo rucksack to continue up the glacier in the enervating heat of mid-morning.

I said goodbye, put on my empty rucksack and set off back to Snout Camp. Halfway down I met Meena and Dave on their way up. Dave was stopping every few metres to mark the route with cairns. I recognised the style – neat tapered columns of small stones – from his compulsive cairn building on the Kunyang Glacier four years earlier. I added one or two landmarks of my own, extravagant Gothic fantasies in slate and granite. (Victor, the architect, later extended the line of cairns right down into the valley, producing some fine studies in elegant Bauhaus simplicity.)

Back at Snout Camp, I sheltered under the kitchen tarpaulin from the fierce sun and ate an enormous plate of idli with mayonnaise, prepared by Bogas' wife in Bombay.

Saturday 22 June. Another ferry up and down. Just Meena, Mahendra, Pratap, Harsinh Junior and me left at Snout Camp in the evening, for baked potatoes. Jim and Victor were on the upper glacier. The other climbers, apart from Meena and I, were at Mud Camp. The Ladakhis had done a double carry that day and had now, with great relief and with their pockets bulging with rupees, departed for Nubra.

On Sunday morning we packed the tents and carried up the remaining five loads. We had all finally reached Base Camp, completing what was probably the slowest approach march in the history of Himalayan mountaineering: it had taken ten days to travel a mere eighteen kilometres from the army base in the Nubra valley!

Victor and Jim returned to Mud Camp at midday, beaming and bubbling with excitement: 'It's wonderful … red granite … yes, a great plug of granite, rising above all the black shale … terrifying … steep buttresses – as steep as the Walker Spur … ice couloirs … a "chandelle" like the Frêney Pillar … it looks really hard … '

Jim summed it up solemnly: 'It must be one of the hardest unclimbed 7,000-metre peaks in the world.' They had only been allowed brief, tantalising glimpses of Rimo I, and for most of the time it had been hidden in swirling cloud. Jim compared their reconnaissance to the opening chapters of Salman Rushdie's *Midnight's Children*, when Dr Aziz is summoned repeatedly, on the pretext of spurious ailments, to visit the coy adoring girl whom he eventually marries. In the interests of modesty she is always hidden behind a large sheet, but there is a tiny peephole in the sheet and each time he visits her the hole is moved to reveal a different, supposedly ailing, part of her body.

Victor and Jim had found the Lake of Bones. There had been no bones, but the gleaming ice pinnacles surrounding the lake gave credence to the name. There were actually two pools, separated by an isthmus of reasonably flat rubble-strewn ice, where we could pitch our tents. At about 5,000 metres, it was a 700-metre climb from Mud Camp.

We spent the afternoon sorting out food rations and equipment, organising a priority of loads for transport to Advance Base. Everyone was happy except our LA, Mahendra. He was sad that the borrowed army radio, which he had so looked forward to operating, was not working. He was sad that even the long-suffering Jim had grown tired of listening to his repetitive jokes. He was sad because Meena was not impressed by the story of his single-handed fight with a leopard. (In the officers' mess there was some disagreement as to whether Mahendra or the leopard had been the more frightened.) Now he was upset because his brand new white plastic Kastinger climbing boots were missing. He strutted round the camp in a pair of jet-set ski goggles that would have graced the slopes of Verbier, searching for the equally modish boots; but they were nowhere to be seen and in the evening he insisted on going down to search for them, dragging with him Harsinh Junior, who was to be his personal bearer. He returned with his boots two days later, having descended all the way to the army base to find them. Apparently, the jawans who came up the Terong valley a few days earlier had walked off with them. Why they had taken them and how Mahendra retrieved them were never disclosed, and the boot affair, like the missing bottle of rum, remained one of the many mysteries surrounding our enigmatic expedition clown.

The rest of us gathered in the kitchen. Victor asked Harish what the Indian mountaineering establishment thought of drinking in the hills.

'Oh, no; they don't approve.'

'So the IMF don't like people drinking?'

'Oh, no,' Harish reiterated, breaking into one of his high-pitched chuckles. Then, with a solemn frown and lowered voice, he continued: 'It is in the IMF book of Do's and Don't's: Do not drink alcohol in the mountains!'

There were roars of laughter as Victor gleefully poured out mugs of Famous Grouse. We drank a toast to the IMF and passed round a plate of peanuts, donated to Harish by a Gujarati farmer. Pratap and Harsinh swigged their whisky and chattered in Kumaoni as they cooked supper over two roaring primuses. They giggled in astonishment when the three smoking sahibs scrounged three of their bidis, the Indian poor man's cigarette, made from a single rolled tobacco leaf. They were even more amused when I said 'Thank you', unable to affect the master-servant relationship which was perfectly natural to the Bombay climbers, who, like all middle-class Indians, had always had servants in their homes. We were very lucky to have the Bhotias with us. It was rather like the famous 1930s expeditions of Tilman and Shipton, who had always taken with them three or four trusted Sherpas. Harish had a similar arrangement with these men from Kumaon, who worked tirelessly and cheerfully throughout the expedition, carrying heavy loads all day and worked through the evening to cook for all the hungry climbers.

On Monday Victor and Jim rested at Mud Camp, drinking tea and playing their splattering game, while the rest of us did a carry up the glacier. We left the dead rubble landscape of the lower glacier and climbed up through avenues of fantastic ice pinnacles, through which we could glimpse, on the right, the narrow entrance to the Shelkar Chorten Glacier.

I never found the Lake of Bones that day. I seemed now to have recovered fully from the flu and I drew ahead of the others, walking alone past Jim's and Victor's cairns, perched improbably on top of boulders and ice pinnacles. I passed several side glaciers, white between walls of black shale, disappearing up into clouds. After a few miles the cairns stopped. Victor had said something about a streambed and a big buttress. There were glacial streams flowing all over the place, but there was one very definite buttress far ahead on the right, a great whaleback of granite rearing up into the clouds, so I plodded on across the great expanse of ice, heading for the buttress. I stopped for ever-more frequent rests, sitting down on stranded boulders to get the dragging weight of the rucksack off my shoulders. The air was damp and my light trekking boots were sodden from surface meltwater. Higher up there was a covering of sodden snow and I found some footprints, but there were no cairns to be seen. Looking back down the glacier I could see no sign of the others on the vast expanse of ice.

I drew level with the buttress, which was now almost completely hidden in cloud. There was no sign of a lake, so I continued towards the next buttress. I knew that I must now be right at the foot of Rimo. I had been walking for over six hours and they had said it was a four-and-a-half-hour walk. I was tired and cold and becoming increasingly frightened of possible concealed crevasses; so I stopped, unpacked my rucksack and left the load on a prominent boulder.

Three and a half hours later, after an interminable, cold walk down the glacier, through desultory drizzle, I arrived back at Mud Camp. The others had long since returned. Dave and Victor pounced on me to ask where I had been.

'Why didn't you follow the cairns?' Victor asked.

'I did; then they stopped.'

'Didn't you see the funny one?'

'You mean the one with two legs?'

'Yes – it's an Inuit-style cairn – the Eskimos build them like that because they show up better – they think it probably came from Tibet originally … er, you know – just as you see Tibetan characteristics in other parts of the American continent … have you seen those hats they wear in Bolivia? … and … er, yes … Tibetan – maybe there are Tibetan-style cairns in Baltistan, like the Balti dialect … I think there's something about it in Marco Pallis – he describes – '

'Yes, Victor. What am I supposed to do at this Inuit or Tibetan cairn?'

He returned to practicalities with a vengeance: 'I *told* you that's where you have to turn left and head up another stream bed to the big buttress.' He was enjoying himself immensely and Dave was interjecting schoolmasterly admonishments: 'Typical Venables – you never listen, do you? Always in too much of a hurry!' Harish was chortling with amusement as I questioned Victor about the exact site of Advance Base.

'But I *told* you,' he repeated, 'You just head for the huge buttress. It's only about forty-five minutes from the Inuit cairn.'

'Right down there … where the glacier divides?'

'Yes, I told you the lake is right at the foot of the buttress dividing the two glacier branches.'

'You call that a buttress – that sprawling slag heap? I thought you were supposed to be an architect!'

I did at least have the dubious distinction of having travelled further up the North Terong Glacier than any other human being. (Jim and Victor had explored as far as the footprints that I passed.) Once I had changed into warm dry clothes and settled in the kitchen with a large mug of tea and a cigarette I could shrug off my mistake with equanimity.

Harish was once again glued to his radio. The English had just beaten the Australians at Edgbaston. On a less happy note, an Air India passenger plane had been blown up over the Atlantic.

The next day I stuck with Victor on the walk to Advance Base. Jim presented that most depressing of expedition sights – a rapidly diminishing dot, striding ever further ahead into the distance, while we followed at our own pace. Dave came later at an even slower pace with Harish and co.

We passed all the pinnacles and continued across a honeycomb zone, formed by sun-warmed pebbles sinking into the ice. At the two-legged cairn we turned left into falling snow, crossing to another trough, where a crystal stream dashed down a channel of translucent ice between granite boulders. The Lake of Bones, a pool full of icebergs, nestled in the fork of the two glacier branches below Victor's 'buttress'. There was another small pool, fed by a surface stream, on the right of Advance Base that consisted so far of a single bivouac dome tent. Jim was sitting on a boulder outside, heating some soup on the gas stove.

The snowfall stopped. We relaxed over a lunch of soup, oatcakes, Samsoe cheese and Bündnerfleisch – Swiss dried beef, donated to the expedition by a friend from Basel. Victor talked about his schooldays at Gordonstoun, where he had failed to live up to expectations of rugged manliness. His subsequent career of masochistic alpine winter climbing and Himalayan expeditions seemed to have compensated amply for any shortcomings at school. In the afternoon he heroically accompanied me up the sodden snow of the upper glacier, to help retrieve my misplaced gear dump of the previous afternoon.

When we returned to Advance Base, Jim was putting the finishing touches to a stone-walled kitchen. All the climbers had arrived and several tents were dotted around the isthmus, perched at odd angles amongst the boulders. The Bhotias had returned to Mud Camp for the next day's loads, so, in their absence, I supervised the cooking of a large meal of soup, noodles and idli.

During our two days of load carrying from Mud Camp, we had seen no summits and Rimo had remained hidden resolutely in the clouds. Now, as we all settled into our new home at the Lake of Bones, the clouds began to lift and the afternoon sun broke through to light up the icefall of the western glacier branch on our left; but Rimo, six kilometres away, above the broad sweep of the main glacier on our right, still lurked invisible under cloud. It was only later, at dusk, that the clouds lifted briefly, coyly, to reveal soaring rock buttresses plastered white with new snow. It looked steep, cold and hostile. The speed of the clouds, swirling round the ridges, showed that there was a vicious wind up there. We could see the crest of what Jim and Victor had called 'the shoulder'. Then the clouds lifted a little further to give us a momentary, tantalising peep at higher snowfields; but the actual summit remained hidden and the clouds soon descended again.

Lying in bed that night, listening to the soft thud of snowflakes falling on the tent roof, I felt excited and disturbed by our brief vision of Rimo. As Victor and Jim had said, it looked difficult and frightening. The granite buttresses were horribly plastered with new snow. It was going to be a hard climb.

12   Exploration

In the morning we saw Rimo again. When I woke at dawn the tent roof was sagging with the weight of fresh snow and still more was falling. But later it stopped and when I went outside the fresh powder was sparkling in sunshine. While I was lighting the primus stove for breakfast, Victor appeared, sent by Jim to fetch his morning tea. The Crog's 'bed chai' was a sacred ritual that had to be observed punctiliously.

While the water was heating, we examined Rimo. Now we could see both peaks, Rimo I and Rimo III, dominating the valley. Rimo III, on the left, was a steep pyramid, obviously very difficult from this side but, according to the map, easier on the far side. Rimo II was not really a peak at all, just a shoulder on the North Ridge of Rimo I. The wind was whipping tatters of cloud and snow plumes from the top of Rimo I, which I now saw for the first time. It was a massive mountain, with the summit sitting above long sprawling ridges, flanked by steep buttresses, gullies and ice fields. On the right we could see the gash of the 'Ibex Col', the name given to the pass by which Harish hoped to cross to the remote South Rimo Glacier on the far side. Just this side of the col were the rock pillars which had inspired Jim and Victor to such flights of rhetoric and which we had seen fleetingly the previous evening. Now they were plastered even more heavily with new snow, and the whole mountain had about it a look of cold inviolability.

One by one the others emerged from their tents, to enjoy the brief moments of sunshine, before the clouds closed in again to hide Rimo for another thirty hours.

The Bombay team toyed unenthusiastically with some porridge until Harish rummaged among the food supplies to find something less British. While we ate our various breakfasts we discussed plans. Harish had made it clear all along that once we reached Advance Base everyone should split up into small teams to attempt as many objectives as possible. Although there was a growing friendship between English and Indian climbers, he recognised that, when it came to actual climbing, we had different aspirations and different ways of doing things. It was obvious that any route on Rimo I was going to involve some difficult technical climbing. The Indians had little experience of that sort of thing and most of them, certainly Harish, were enviably free of ambition. Ideally, we would have climbed together on small peaks, getting to know each other's abilities, before making joint attempts on some of the higher peaks. However, time was short, we wanted to climb at least one of the Rimo peaks and Harish was doubtful whether any of his team were up to a quick alpine-style attempt on Rimo I; so he suggested magnanimously that we should attempt Rimo I, while the Indians if possible made a long circuitous approach via the Ibex Col to the far side of the Rimo massif, to attempt an easier but dramatically isolated route on Rimo III. For the time being we would all make the Ibex Col our first objective. At 6,200 metres it would be ideal for acclimatising, before going to 7,000 metres. If it proved to be a practical pass it would provide Harish with his route to Rimo III. The approach to the col, up a side branch of the North Terong Glacier, would give us a chance to examine possible routes on to the South-West Ridge of Rimo I. But right now bad weather and the avalanche hazard of fresh snow confined us to Advance Base.

Wednesday 26 June was domestic. During intermittent snow showers we sheltered in our tents and under the kitchen tarpaulin. Victor and I cut out foam insoles to insulate our boots. Dave pottered about making the beer. Harish snooped and pried with his telephoto lens, photographing all the team. I taught Meena the art of high-altitude bread making. Victor and Jim, in the absence of a mud bath, played a game of bowls on the ice of the smaller lake.

While we were cooking lunch, Jim won a competition to see who could stand longest barefoot in the snow. In the afternoon the Bhotias arrived with more loads. They were supervised by Mahendra, who carried an enormous empty packframe and wore his successfully retrieved boots. The ski goggles were still perched jauntily on top of his army woollen hat. We unpacked the large dome and worked for an hour to clear a platform on the ice, levelling it with gravel before pitching the tent.

On Thursday the sky remained overcast. In the afternoon Dave, Victor and I walked up the glacier, towards the cwm below the Ibex Col, and on past my 'buttress' of three days earlier, to the foot of the next cwm where we watched the clouds lifting to reveal the great North-West Face of Rimo I. Victor pointed out a possible mixed route to the left of huge rock walls. I wondered about avalanches. A moment later there was a loud roar and we gawped at billowing clouds of snow dust plunging down the face and sweeping across the cwm at its foot.

We walked back down the North Terong Glacier and stopped to look up the South-West Cwm. The sky was clearing and we could now see a route up the cwm to a steep snow slope just below the Ibex Col.

Sitting in the kitchen that evening, the four Englishmen discussed tactics. Victor wanted to head straight up to the Ibex Col the next day; Jim, Dave and I were more cautious, anxious about possible avalanche danger after the heavy snowfall.

'Anyway, Victor,' I said, 'if we go right up the cwm tomorrow, we'll be going very slowly and we'll end up on the steep snow slope during the heat of the day. 'Jim pointed out that we needed anyway to establish a dump of food and equipment. For the first day at least we could make this part of the way up the cwm, well clear of any threatening snow slopes higher up.

We walked up the glacier by torchlight and at dawn roped up to continue into the snow-covered cwm. The altitude suddenly hit me with that awful helpless sensation of leaden legs and gasping lungs. Dave and Victor were going a little better, but couldn't manage Jim's pace. Every time we started after a rest, he would go striding effortlessly ahead, jerking us all forward on the rope, and in the end we sent Dave in front to set a steadier rhythm.

We stopped well short of the big snow slopes on Rimo and pitched the tent in a hollow on the glacier. Although the glacier was easy, I was wearing my new crampons to try them out. Now, one of the brand-new razor-sharp spikes tore a tiny nick in the tent. Dave screamed at me: 'Look what you've done, Venables – you clumsy idiot!'

'Oh shut up, you old woman.'

'I'm not an old woman,' he shouted back, his voice shooting up an octave. 'You're the old woman, wearing crampons when you don't need them.'

Feeling better for this little outburst, Dave resumed his normal placid demeanour. We packed all the food and gear into the tent, then set off down with empty rucksacks. The Bombay team were now on their way up. They had been loth to get out of bed before dawn, and were now struggling to climb up sticky slushy snow in the glaring heat of the day.

In the afternoon, everyone rested at Advance Base. Now that the day's climbing was over, we could enjoy the hot sun. Every half hour or so Jim would announce 'Tea gentlemen!' and remind us that high-altitude dehydration was an evil to be avoided rigorously.

Everyone had his views about how the noble brew should be prepared. Harish favoured Indian-style tea, insisting that the strong mixture of milk powder, sugar and tea (with perhaps a dash of ginger) should be brought to the boil, removed from the heat and then boiled once more. When the Bhotias were in residence and we were making an early start, this hideous concoction would be brought to our tents at two o'clock in the morning and 'bed chai' was guaranteed to shake awake the most sleepy idler. Now, however, on that Friday afternoon, I insisted on an effete suffusion of Lapsang Suchong and fresh lemon juice.

The weather remained fine and we sorted out final loads for carrying up to the cwm the next day. We hoped to remain there for several days and perhaps, if the weather allowed, make an attempt on the South-West Ridge of Rimo I.

Saturday 29 June – afternoon – a bowl of glaring heat at our high camp (about 5,600m), at the start of our proposed route. Feeling very lazy after two nights with only four hours' sleep and, today, one carry all the way here from Advance Base and two more carries from yesterday's dump lower on the glacier. A beautiful, peaceful spot underneath a great russet wall of granite, tents sheltered by snow-block walls, peace only disturbed by Victor's incessant chatter and the not-so-distant boom of heavy artillery. The usual endless discussions about tactics, with Victor as impatient as ever, reminding us how he spent thirteen days of bad weather on Bojohaghur and insisting that he has never had such good weather and that we must use it immediately to start the route. Dave, predictably, favours more 'pratting about at 6,000 metres' to get acclimatised. The issue is complicated by Dave having badly sprained his finger, falling into a hole this morning. We all hope that it will cure rapidly. The ideal would be to make tomorrow a complete rest day, then 'go for it'. More pedestrian would be to go to the Ibex Col tomorrow for wonderful views and a spot more acclimatisation (6,200m), rest the following day and finally leave for Rimo on Tuesday.

My diary perhaps gave undue emphasis to our disagreements. We were in fact very happy to be camping in such wonderful scenery, exploring the approaches to a major peak which had never been attempted. It was just frustrating to be so pressed for time.

After all the delays of the approach, we now had only two weeks before Jim and Victor were due to leave for home, and Victor was understandably anxious to get to grips with the mountain. We should ideally have carried out a thorough reconnaissance, including a trip to the far side; but because we were so short of time and because the Indian army photo had shown no obviously straightforward route on that side, we had decided to try our luck on the Terong side of the mountain. Victor and Jim, with limited holiday allowance, would probably only get one chance.

That evening a fan of high cirrus clouds spread across the sky from the south-west. Then hazy mackerel stripes of cirro-stratus confirmed the approach of a front. On Sunday morning we woke to falling snow.

We dozed till about nine o'clock, when Dave unzipped our tent porch to collect the lump of crusty snow that he had left ready for the breakfast brew. There was an anguished, petulant cry of 'Saunders – have you stolen my snow briquette?' In the other tent, a few feet away, Victor chortled smugly as he nursed a litre of melted snow, now starting to simmer on the gas stove, ready for the Crog's morning tea.

After breakfast we heard voices outside and I pulled myself half out of my sleeping bag, to sit up and look out. It took a few moments to recognise the goggled, hooded faces in the mist outside. Boga was there, with Dhiren. Pratap had come with them to carry an extra load and Mahendra for once had his ski goggles put to their proper use, pulled down over his eyes. They left, to establish a camp a short way across the glacier and I sank back into my sleeping bag to read another chapter of Graham Greene.

Snow continued to fall, but it was only a very light shower, so Jim, Victor and I decided to go outside for some exercise, while Dave stayed in bed to nurse his finger. After a few hundred metres we stopped to look up at the South-West Ridge, on our left. The upper part was lost in cloud but lower down the features that we had examined and debated endlessly during the last few days were dimly visible through the falling snow. Unless we found a suitable route from the Ibex Col, there were three choices. Near the head of the cwm a rock spur rose steeply to 'the shoulder', high on the South-West Ridge. This route, which Jim had originally favoured, was christened the Crog Spur. Dave, who has an aversion to high-altitude rock climbing, had pressed for an 800-metre icefield, further down the flank of the ridge. This route would provide quicker climbing on to the crest of the ridge, but we would reach the crest lower down, at the foot of the 'Pinnacles' – an abrupt step in the ridge which met the Crog Spur at the summit of the shoulder. The third option was a gentler angled snowfield, to the left of the ice field, which would lead us to a lower point on the crenelated crest of the ridge. I had an aversion to hard ice and, fearing that dark glassy streaks on the ice field might give us trouble, I favoured a route up the gentler snow slope, followed by some horizontal climbing along the ridge crest to the foot of the Pinnacles.

Victor was getting keen on the third choice: 'We'll be able to solo most of it. We can leave really early and climb most of it in the dark. Look, the only hard bit is the rock narrows near the top – maybe two pitches of roped climbing.'

'I'm all for getting on to the crest as soon as possible,' I agreed.

'Once we're up there, there'll be places to camp.' Jim, too, thought that the crest of the ridge would be easy, as far as the Pinnacles:

'You know, we might even reach the foot of the Pinnacles in a day. Then another day to the top of the Pinnacles. Then get as near to the summit as we can on the third day.'

'Yes,' Victor enthused. 'If we get close enough to the top, we can leave everything at the bivouac – just go really light to the summit and back on the fourth day – perhaps just take one rope for the four of us -'

'And head torches!' I interrupted.

It was brave optimistic talk. We had come a long way from the first feelings of awe about the mountain. Now that we had broken it down into manageable sections, it all seemed more feasible; and we had the advantage of starting high: the high camp was at about 5,600 metres; the summit of Rimo I was, at 7,388 metres, less than 2,000 metres above the start of the route. Of course, there were still many unknowns: parts of the upper snow ridge, above the Pinnacles, were hidden, and we didn't know what the snow conditions would be like – there might be dangerous windslabs up there. The rest of the ridge had some little towers and turrets which might give us problems. And there were the Pinnacles, a major obstacle, which might give us some very hard technical climbing. But these were the doubts that are part of any big climb.

Today, however, the weather was bad, and we contented ourselves with the more straightforward climb to the Ibex Col. We continued up the frozen crust of the cwm and stopped to put on crampons for the last steep rise. In spite of the cloud cover the air was now becoming warm, making the snow slope avalanche-prone, so we climbed up islands of shattered rock on the right.

There was no wonderful view, just a saddle of bare ice and rock, swept clear of snow by the wind funnelled through the gap. On the left, steep cold repellent cliffs reared up into swirling clouds. There was little hope there for an ascent of Rimo I and we were confirmed in our choice of the snowfield route, lower down the cwm.

However, our time had not been wasted. We had climbed to 6,200 metres and it was reassuring to see that it had not been particularly tiring: after all the delays of the approach we were very well acclimatised. And we saw that there was a route down the far side of the col, a steep but feasible snow gully, curving down between rock walls. The South Rimo Glacier was lost in the clouds, but as far as we could see there was a route down to it.

No one had ever been to the Ibex Col before. Two members of Dr Visser's expedition had reached the Lake of Bones in 1919; Filippo de Filippi had explored the South Rimo Glacier and the Indian army Rimo IV expedition had been there in 1984; but we were the first people ever to visit this high pass linking the two glacier basins. Our only regret was that Harish might be upset about our beating the Bombay Mountaineers to the col. However, if he was upset he never showed it, and in any case the first actual crossing of the pass was done by Meena and Boga a week later.

Two days later, while waiting for the weather to improve above, we made a quick descent to Advance Base to reprovision. In a few days the glacier had transformed dramatically and crevasses gaped everywhere. Victor went first on the rope. He had adopted the American euphemism for crevasse and shepherded us down with cries of: 'I've just trodden in a slot' and 'Mind the slot, please!' and 'Here's a Crog-sized slot.' The snow was hideously slushy and there was much stumbling and jerking on the rope as we lurched our way down. Tempers were a little strained after long debates at the high camp and everyone was relieved when we reached the main glacier, where there were no concealed crevasses and we could safely unrope, to make our separate ways down to Advance Base.

The weather inevitably improved as soon as we started down. By the time we reached Advance Base, the clouds had almost vanished and Harish told us that the barometer had started rising at four o'clock. It was still rising and everyone was excited at the prospect of a spell of fine weather and the chance, at last, to get some real climbing done. Although we now knew that there was a route over the Ibex Col, it was not suitable for the Bhotia porters, and Harish was having doubts about the logistical problems of the long circuitous approach to the back of Rimo III without porters. It looked as though most of the Bombay climbers were going to stick instead to peaks nearer home, in the North Terong basin.

The movement of the ice had almost destroyed Jim's kitchen; Pratap and the Harsinhs had built a new, bigger shelter, where we all gathered, wrapped in duvet jackets, to enjoy what proved to be the last evening when the entire team was together. The Bhotias, as usual, were slaving over the primuses, cooking a vast meal of rice and dahl. Mahendra was talking conspiratorially to Dave, confiding that he wouldn't be joining the Bombay team on any of their climbs, because he couldn't be bothered with 6,000-metre peaks. (He was still in cloud-cuckoo-land, and fondly imagined that, although he had no climbing experience whatsoever, he might be able to join us on Rimo I and notch up another 7,000-metre first ascent for the glory of the army. Dave tactfully put him right.) Harish was poring over the map, making plans for our visits to the Shelkar Chorten and South Terong Glaciers – the second phase of the expedition, when half the team would have gone home to their jobs. First, however, we had work to do on the North Terong Glacier. Before dawn we would all be setting off again: Meena, Boga, Harish and Dhiren for the glacier branch behind the Lake of Bones; Muslim and Arun for Safina, a peak opposite Advance Base, on the far side of the main glacier; Dave, Jim, Victor and I for Rimo.

The moon was full that night. We had seen the last full moon reflected in the Dal Lake, at Srinagar. Now, a month later, the whole Terong cirque was flooded in white light. Every detail of our proposed route on Rimo, six kilometres away, was clear, and above the summit snowfields only the faintest wisp of cloud lingered in the sky.

On the evening of Wednesday 3 July, everything was ready. The four of us had returned to the high camp with fresh supplies early that morning. We had sheltered in the tents from the worst heat of the day, then, when the air cooled, had emerged to pack rucksacks. Victor and Jim, Dave and I would be operating as two teams, each team carrying its own tent, stove, six days' food and fuel and two ropes. The rest of tie climbing gear – pegs, nuts, karabiners, ice screws and slings – would be shared between the four of us on the difficult sections and during the abseil descent. Jim's suggestion that we might reach the Pinnacles in a day seemed unduly optimistic but we hoped to make reasonable progress, climbing most of the snowfield in the dark and perhaps climbing some of the horizontal ridge crest by the afternoon.

We ate well that evening and drank copious mugs of soup, tea and coffee, in preparation for the long dehydrating day ahead. The sky was a deep blue and the mountains of the Terong basin, which were now familiar friends, had a new sharp clarity. Dave was still doubtful about his finger, but he had to admit that the weather really looked set fine for our attempt.

As the light faded and the temperature dropped dramatically, we crawled back into the tiny dome tents for a short rest, and perhaps some sleep. The alarm was set for 11.30 p.m.

13 Seven Days on Rimo I

Right foot kick – breathe – left foot kick – breathe – right foot kick – breathe – left foot kick – breathe – right foot kick – breathe – left foot kick – breathe – right foot …

The snow was crisply frozen. The sky was full of stars and the moonlight almost made our head-torches redundant. Victor was above me; Jim and Dave were a short way below. Each of us trailed a rope, reducing slightly the weight in our rucksacks. We moved independently, each man choosing his own pace and rhythm.

Higher up the face we started to lose the rhythm. By daybreak the snow was softer and steps were starting to collapse. By the time we reached the Narrows, rock was starting to show through as the slope steepened to well over fifty degrees. We stopped to rope together. From this point it was 200 metres at the most to the crest of the ridge; but this last stretch took eight hours – eight hours of exhausting excavation, struggling to make progress up ever-mushier snow, plastered loosely to friable granite. The Crog, at thirteen stone, fared worst. Dave and I did little better, and it was finally left to Victor to lead us all out on to the crest of the ridge. His extreme lightness and his delicacy of touch, perfected over many weekends on some of England's most disintegrating sea cliffs, came to our rescue in an inspired, determined performance.

Sixteen hours after leaving the South-West Cwm, four weary demoralised climbers finally arrived on the crest of the ridge. Our easy snow slope had been a depressing struggle and the ridge offered no relief, for its narrow crest of crumbling granite was liberally festooned with bulging snow cornices and the southern flanks were, as we had already discovered, plastered with snow that varied in consistency from caster sugar to congealed porridge. We all felt utterly spent but there was still work to do and it was nearly dark by the time we had excavated two small platforms, ten metres apart, where we perched the tents precariously just below the fracture line of the cornices, roping them in to ice screws and rock belays. Finally everything was secure and we could all crawl into bed to drink the first of many well earned brews of tea.

The following morning there was a crisis. I was hard at work on the ridge, working across difficult rock slabs just below the crest. We had deliberately left late in the morning, giving ourselves the chance to rest well from the previous day's exertions. I felt a renewed enthusiasm, intensified by the brilliant weather and the spectacular views. Now that we were on the crest of the ridge at about 6,400 metres, we could see far out to the north-west, and I had just realised that the monolithic pyramid in the distance, sixty miles away, was of course K2. Dave seemed rather gloomy, but Victor was full of enthusiasm for the hard climbing. Jim was not giving much away but seemed content enough. I had led the first pitch. Dave had continued a short way and now I was leading again, happily absorbed in poking and scraping at the snow, excavating little nicks in the rock underneath for hand and footholds. The rope was clipped reassuringly into a sling a few metres back and I was searching for a second runner placement, pecking at the shattered rock with my ice axe. It was slow work, but I was in control and there was no longer that feeling of helpless exhaustion which had dogged us in the enervating heat of the previous afternoon. The ridge ahead was blocked by a steep tower but we could deal with that problem when we came to it; for the time being I was happily absorbed in the present.

I could hear the murmur of Dave's and Jim's voices a short way back. Then I heard Jim shouting across to me: 'Can you hang on a minute?'

'What's wrong?'

There was more murmuring, then another shout: 'You'd better come back here. Dave thinks we should go down.'

'What!'

'Look, just come back to the belay and we'll talk about it.'

They pulled the rope in as I traversed back and up to the belay on the crest of the ridge. Victor had arrived from below and looked upset. Dave was silent and Jim explained that both he and Dave thought we should go down: 'It's just hopeless. At this rate it's going to take at least two days to reach the Pinnacles!'

'Yes, I know it is,' I remonstrated. 'But the weather's fine … we can take it slowly and go easy on the food.'

'But it's ridiculous – that tower looks desperate … the snow's appalling and the rock's really shitty … and look at those cornices!'

I was bitterly disappointed and argued that we could keep well below the cornices. As for the rock, it was not very good, but amidst all the debris we could find sufficient secure belays and runners to make the route safe. Victor agreed that we could climb the route safely, but Dave now reinforced Jim's argument: 'It'll be like this all the way – lousy snow on cruddy rock. Okay, maybe you'll get runners, but they'll be a long way apart and sooner or later someone's going to go for a big swing and hurt himself. It's just too dangerous.'

'But I was just starting to enjoy myself,' I insisted. 'I really want to climb Rimo!'

'I also want to climb Rimo,' Dave retorted. 'But one thing I want more is to stay alive!'

Dave and Jim were adamant about abandoning the route. Victor and I were now in a quandary, half wanting to carry on and half tempted to follow the others' decision. We all traversed back to the bivouac site and repitched the tents for an afternoon of agonising. Dave made his position clearer. He had seemed unusually subdued and preoccupied since the previous afternoon. Now he explained that as well as his misgivings about the route, he was concerned about the state of his body: his finger was still very delicate and would be a real liability on prolonged technical climbing, and he was worried about a worsening cough, which was now producing spectacular green sputum, indicating a chest infection.

I felt empty and depressed. We had put such high hopes on this route and had already invested a day of extremely hard work. Now that we had reached the crest of the ridge, I was loth to go down and start all over again on some other route. Like Victor, I thought Dave and Jim were exaggerating the dangers and difficulties; but it was impossible not to be influenced by two very experienced mountaineers whose opinions I respected. Perhaps they were right; perhaps if we carried on we would have some ghastly accident?

I sat in the tent entrance, with my feet hanging over the drop in the ridge. Victor was in the other tent a few metres below. He now definitely wanted to carry on, if I would come with him. I was not sure what to do and said that I would decide before the evening. We pondered over what to do if we all descended. Should we try the Crog Spur? Would it be any better? Wouldn't it just be the same desperate snow on rock? Should we try the ice field – that would get us straight up to the foot of the Pinnacles, but by the time we had done that we could have reached them from here. Should we try the other side of the mountain … or try Rimo III … or abandon the whole Rimo idea and go for something smaller? The only certain answer was that whatever we did we would only have a short time to do it in, for Jim and Victor were supposed to be leaving in about eight days' time.

I agonised for two or three hours. Eventually I decided to go on with Victor and shouted down to the other tent: 'Let's give it a try.'

'Are you really sure?' Victor replied. 'I don't want you to come just to make me happy.'

'Don't worry,' I assured him, 'That's the least of my considerations! No, seriously, I'd like to try the route.'

'Okay, we'll just take it really steady and you've got to be careful. We'll just see how far we can get. If it's hopeless we can abseil back down to the glacier.'

I felt much happier once the decision had been made, and immediately busied myself sorting out food for the climb. Now that Dave and Jim were going down, we could each take a full six days worth of food from here, and enough gas to spin out for nine or ten days if necessary. We could take the bulk of the climbing gear to cope with what was going to be a harder route than we had expected. While I sorted the food into day rations, Dave and I talked about past climbs in the Alps … skiing in the Chamonix valley, the Eiger, and a route we had done in Bolivia which had been very similar to this ridge, but much easier because of sound rock and excellent snow conditions. I felt sad not to be continuing this climb as a team of four, as we had intended. On the other hand, two people could move more efficiently than four on this precarious terrain. Climbing with Victor, I could be sure that if we were unsuccessful it would not be for lack of trying. In the valley he could at times be a little exasperating – impulsive and hard to pin down (his London friends didn't call him 'Slippery' for nothing); but on the mountain, faced with the immediate challenge of technical problems, he was all concentrated purpose and skill, and when it came to difficult climbing on steep, loose, mixed terrain, he was one of the most talented people around.

The sun was sinking. I leaned out of the tent door to look down the ridge to the other tent, poised improbably above the 800-metre drop. Looking out to the west, we could see the upper basin of the North Terong Glacier. The wall on its far side was a massive barrier of ice cliffs, which sent frequent avalanches roaring down on to the glacier. Above the ice cliffs, shadows were lengthening across the velvet surface of a vast plateau, the Teram Shehr Plateau. Jim called it the Football Pitch, but you could have fitted several Wembleys between its retaining walls. This plateau lies at the head of the southern branch of the Teram Shehr Glacier. The branch flows away from Terong to the north-west, to join the main flow of the Teram Shehr into the Siachen; but it also has an overspill right at its head – the ice cliffs which tumble over into the North Terong Glacier. It was a dramatic spectacle probably unique in the Greater Himalaya. After the days of enclosure in the Nubra valley and on our way up the Terong valley, it was exhilarating to climb at last above the valleys and experience for the first time the full arctic immensity of the East Karakoram. Now that we were here and were committed to continuing, I hoped desperately that the weather would allow Victor and me to remain on the crest of the ridge, and watch this extraordinary view grow even more immense as we climbed higher on Rimo.

We left at dawn. I was cold and clumsy … apprehensive, momentarily envious of Dave and Jim setting off down … nervous, anxious about the clouds drifting ominously round the Ibex Col. But the therapy of action quickly changed all that as I became absorbed in the climbing – the challenge of hard strenuous work and the fascination of scraping, brushing, excavating, prying through the sugary snow to the granite of the mountain, searching out cracks and rugosities, unearthing finger holds and little nicks for teetering crampon points.

The clouds vanished. The sky was blue. I realised that I was actually enjoying myself. I was nearing the end of the third pitch. Victor had shouted words of encouragement as I traversed into a chimney that breached the rock face of what we had named the Fortress. Now, bridging up the chimney, reaching up with gloved hands to flakes of granite, I was revelling in the rhythm of movement and the thrill of solving problems.

I paused beneath an overhang, forcing myself to wait and place a secure nut and slow my violent breathing, before stepping out wide with crampons and reaching up with outstretched ice axe to hook a wedged block, then pull and swing round on to a sloping ledge, where I tied on to a huge spike and thankfully removed the dragging weight of the rucksack from my shoulders, clipping it safely into the belay.

Victor continued up the Fortress, the tower which everyone had been so apprehensive about the previous day. He disappeared above. While I belayed him, Jim and Dave appeared from behind a rock spur far below us, two small figures hurrying down the snow slopes that we had toiled up two days earlier. Victor was still moving slowly up steep ground above. There was a sharp clatter of falling rock and a sudden stab of pain in my shoulder.

'Aaouaouw! Watch what you're bloody doing!'

'Sorry.'

When my turn came to follow this pitch I marvelled at Victor's superlative skill: on a steep wall of atrociously loose rock, which disintegrated under my crampons, collapsing in a cascade of granite blocks, he had knocked off just one small stone, which had done no serious harm to my shoulder.

Above the Fortress I climbed deep sun-softened snow for a few metres to a resting point, where we stopped for a tea break, suspending the wonderful new hanging stove from a peg. Then there was more snow, some hard brittle ice and more scraping at snow-covered rock. I led the final, seventh, pitch up a steep rock wall, slanting right, calling occasionally for tension on the rope as I leaned across to reach wide for another granite flake or finger crack, testing it before swinging across to more holds.

We stopped that afternoon in a notch below a spectacular rock tower, and worked hard to dig a ledge from the snow, building up its outside edge with a dry-stone wall. It was a little narrow and one side of the tent overhung the edge by a few inches, but there was just room to squeeze inside for a reasonable, if over-intimate, night's sleep.

Sunday 7 July, six weeks since I had left England. Now Victor and I were spending our fourth day on Rimo. We left just after five, and continued slowly, laboriously, hating the weight of our rucksacks. All the time we were following the southern, right-hand flank of the ridge, staying well clear of lethal cornices that jutted out over the abyss on the left. For most of the morning we were shaded by the bulk of the mountain above us, but the cwm below was dazzling white in the sunlight and we could just see the minute pencil shadows of four figures moving up the glacier. Then we saw two shadows coming back down again, heading back for Advance Base. Later we discovered that it was Mahendra and one of the Bhotias we had seen, helping Meena and Boga carry loads up to the Ibex Col, before returning and leaving Meena and Boga to descend the far side and spend several days exploring the peaks round the South Rimo Glacier.

Victor and I stopped at midday, right at the foot of the Pinnacles. We had only done six pitches since leaving the notch, but they had been a tiring struggle with deep snow, and now we wanted to rest well before tackling the crux of the route: the Pinnacles. We passed a contented domestic afternoon. The tent was pitched on a spacious excavated ledge and was tied safely into an overhanging rock wall above. Our boots and mittens were hanging up outside to dry in the sun, while we relaxed in the dome. The arrangement was that Victor would deal with breakfast if I looked after the afternoon and evening brewing; so while he dozed in his sleeping bag, I spooned snow into the hanging stove and thought how luxurious it was to bivouac in a real tent where things could not be dropped and the stove was suspended securely from the apex of the dome, safe from accidental spillage. I roused Victor periodically, to hand him a mug of tea, oat biscuits spread with Danish butter and cheese, a slice of the lovely Maggie's salami, a bowl of noodles, chunks of Yorkie bar … We talked, but I cannot remember what we talked about. Now that we were at about 6,600 metres (above 21,000 feet), our speech was slower and was punctuated by gasps for breath. Victor was more subdued and seemed more relaxed, now that he was free to get on with the job of climbing. Our progress had been, as Jim predicted, ludicrously slow, but it had not been dangerous. We had never felt out of control. Victor and I had never before done any serious climbing together, but now we seemed to be working as a good team, enjoying our slow journey along the ridge.

The Pinnacles were the biggest question mark on the route. We had spent hours at Advance Base staring through binoculars, weaving a hypothetical line up snowy ramps and chimneys, which we hoped would lead us up the left side of the steep jagged buttress. Now, on our fifth day on the mountain, we prepared to investigate this line. We packed up in the dark so that Victor was ready to leave at the first glimmer of daylight. To reach the start of the chimneys he had to climb down and round, across the top of the big ice field. While he led this first pitch I watched the Karakoram come to life.

K2, second highest mountain in the world, caught the first rays of sunlight. Sixty miles away it suddenly glowed peach coloured above the surrounding blue mountains. Then the Gasherbrums were lit up, the greatest concentration of high mountains in the world. Closer to us, the peaks on the far side of the Siachen were lurid purple, yellow and orange. Saltoro Kangri and K12 looked menacing amongst massive clouds building up from the south-west. Further round to the south-east, isolated fins of snow were lit pale yellow against dark purple clouds, which diffused a sea of distant, unknown, unnamed peaks beyond the Nubra valley. I looked back to the north-west, where the sky was clear and K2 was now bright white. It was exciting to see the great pyramid again. I had seen it in previous years from a greater distance, from the south-west and the north-west; but now looking from the south-east I could see the famous Abruzzi Spur and, profiled on the right, the North-East Ridge, the route which the Poles so nearly succeeded on in 1976 and which was later climbed by the Americans. I wondered who was up there now and whether they were anxious about the clouds massing in the south.

For the time being the weather over Rimo remained fine. I followed Victor round the corner and joined him fifteen metres up an icy runnel. I continued up an obvious gully line to struggle with collapsing snow. Higher up it became more enjoyable as I pulled over a rocky bulge and reached for large rock flakes to pull up to the belay. Victor followed the obvious continuation of the gully, showering me with snow as he dug a trench up into a corner. Then the climbing changed, with smears of ice providing purchase for picks. On the fourth pitch I veered right into another chimney, climbing between overhanging rock walls, bridging up with my crampon points scraping the granite each side. There was an exhilarating strenuous heave round an overhang and again the line unfolded round the corner, where I teetered up a steep ramp, scraping through the thin snow to search for holds and spending an age prising off shattered rock to find sound cracks for a peg belay. Victor led some enjoyable rock climbing and we found ourselves on the crest of the ridge, weaving between tottering pinnacles. The clouds had finally advanced across the Siachen and now swirling mist and snowflakes heightened the drama of our plunging view down the Pinnacles to the twisting white ribbon of cornices on the lower ridge. After a short tea break, I led a tension traverse across a shattered wall, then flailed up a snow-choked chimney, scraping, thrusting, pushing, with ice axes, knees and elbows, while Victor spurred me on with shouts of 'Well done – you're climbing really well!'

Victor led the eighth pitch, which took us back again on to the crest of the ridge. When my turn came to follow on a tight rope, I could not work out how he had managed to win the battle with gravity. The snow was atrocious and was lying at a ridiculously steep angle on top of more loose rock. It was the only pitch on the route that was really dangerous, having virtually no protection. I was supposed to continue to what we hoped would be the top of the Pinnacles. However, after poking half-heartedly at the start of the pitch I decided to stop. For over eleven hours we had been coping with sustained, strenuous climbing above 6,600 metres. The next pitch looked long and hard, it would soon be dark, it was starting to snow again and I had had enough. So we lowered ourselves ten metres from the belay to the only available camping spot, a huge blob of snow, stuck to the crest of the ridge. We shovelled, kicked and stamped out a platform in driving wind and snow and laboured with numb fingers to erect the dome, feeding the sprung poles through the sleeves in the frozen fabric. Then we clung firmly to our precious home while Victor threw in a rucksack to hold it down in the wind. He crawled inside to get organised, while I secured the outside, staking down the comers with ice axes and clipping the apex into the ropes that hung down from the belay ten metres above. We fed a sling through a slit in the roof, so that we could clip directly into the ropes from the inside. (One end of the tent was resting on the lip of a cornice, hanging out over the South-West Cwm; if by any chance the cornice were to collapse during the night we wanted to be firmly tied on.)

When Victor was ready, I handed in my sleeping bag, karrimat, down vest, bivouac socks, spare mittens, mug, spoon, food bag and the stove. Then I checked everything outside, before backing into the tent porch, to sit in the doorway and unzip gaiters, unlace boots, brush off all the clogging snow and hand them back into the safety of the tent. Victor was impressed by my unto-ward carefulness: 'I don't know how you can hang around in the cold so long.'

'It's best to get everything organised before getting into bed,' I replied.

'I know, but I just felt completely knackered.'

'Well, you did just lead that eighth pitch – anyone would feel knackered after that.'

'It was horrible … really insecure … it was all right where there was that solid ice, but the bit above … horrendous snow and rubble … '

'Yes, it was desperate,' I agreed, joining enthusiastically in the game of mutual admiration. 'Even with a tight rope it was exhausting … do you remember that huge block half-way up?'

'It took ages – '

'Well, the lousy thing just came away. I hooked it with my axe and pulled up and this great boulder just came away from the mountain!'

We rested, cocooned in goose down and sheltered from the wind by the dome of stretched Gore-Tex. I handed Victor his rations – half a slice of salami, a sliver of cheese, soup thickened with only a sprinkling of potato powder, sug-arless coffee … We had to conserve our food. Already we had left one day's rations wedged in a crack at the bottom of the Pinnacles, intended for our descent, but now we realised that it would be virtually impossible to reverse the slanting, flanking chimneys and ramps of the Pinnacles. We would have instead to drop directly down the south flank of the ridge. If the weather remained unsettled we would probably be heading down soon. However, if there was a full-scale storm, we might be stuck here for several days. On the other hand, if this wind and snow proved to be only a temporary flurry and the weather improved again, we would be continuing and might well be on the mountain for another five or six days. Whichever way it went, there would not be a lot to eat.

We slept well, oblivious of the spectacular drop beneath our feet. On the morning of our sixth day on the mountain, the tent was still buffeted by wind and snow, so we enjoyed the luxury of a lie-in.

At seven o'clock I finally unzipped the inner door, stuck my head into a shower of frosted condensation in the porch, unzipped the outer door and looked out.

'The weather's perfect – we'll have to go climbing,' I informed Victor. The clouds had vanished and the mountains had a surreal clarity, dazzling white against an immaculate blue sky. The snow which had been beating on the tent was just wind-blasted spindrift.

The cold was intense (that morning Meena recorded –20 °C at a lower altitude on the South Rimo Glacier) and the wind was still fierce, but it came from the north, promising continued fine weather.

At 9.30 we emerged from the tent. The sun was still blocked by Rimo's summit and it was slow cold work packing our rucksacks. As usual Victor took the tent, an unwieldy bundle of frosted Gore-Tex. I took the tent poles, some of the food rations and the gas stove, packing them with all my personal bivouac gear into my sack. I had ambivalent feelings about this rucksack. It had always been an unwelcome dragging weight on my back, detracting from the pleasure of climbing; but it had done its job well as a trusted companion on Kunyang Kish and Shivling, in Peru and Bolivia. It had been twice up the Karakoram Highway and had hitch-hiked across Germany … it had sat in untold dingy hotel rooms … it had been lashed to the roofs of countless buses … it had been sat on in the backs of trucks. It had skied the glaciers of the Alps, had crossed rivers and had been hauled over ice cliffs … and now it was still doing good service, carrying our vital survival equipment up the South-West Ridge of Rimo I, on the sixth day of a wonderful climb.

We pulled ourselves back up the ropes to the belay and I set off on the first pitch. Again we had to outflank the tottering towers of the crest. I edged round to the left, hammered in a peg runner, then placed a sling runner higher up on a rounded block. It looked a little dubious, so I lowered myself tentatively, testing it before tensioning across a vertical wall of shattered crockery. I leaned out and across, stretching, reaching for holds. Suddenly I swung and dropped in a clatter of rock.

'Aouaouw!'

'Are you all right?' Victor shouted.

'Aouw – yes – Aargh shit! – The bloody sling came off!'

I had only fallen a few feet before the rope came tight on the peg runner. The pain of a bruised knee was trifling and after a few moments' rest I continued, now traversing a lower line on the shattered wall, then wading into a snow gully. Then the old game of Venables-versus-Gravity started again – digging, scraping, nicking up fissile granite buried under vertical piles of snow. Crampons scraped, ice axe picks hooked blindly, numb fingers clawed at cracks, knees and elbows pushed at collapsing snowdrifts. I found a sling runner, stood in it and reached up to hammer in a peg, heaved on that with my left hand, while my legs thrashed wildly to push higher, right arm stretched up a flailing ice axe and lungs gasped at the thin air.

It was wonderful. I was enjoying the heat of battle.

After about forty metres I belayed to a secure block of granite. The sun was now stroking the ridge with warmth and the wind had died right away. I sat contentedly at the belay while Victor came up. There was some complicated business with the ropes as he tensioned across the shattered wall, but not too complicated to stop me from glancing out to the north-west, over the Football Pitch, to K2 and the Gasherbrums again and further left, the immaculate white roof of Chogolisa, Conway's 'Bride Peak'; somewhere in the gap a great rocky monolith – the Mustagh Tower perhaps? – and further round towards the Shyok valley, the massive bulk of Masherbrum.

'Tight rope!'

'Sorry – is that better?'

'Thanks,' Victor shouted back, between panting gasps. 'This is desperate – ' more gasps – 'brilliant lead ... just like the hard ... bits ... on the Eiger ... in winter ... ' I basked in the sun of approval. Victor continued his struggle below. 'Tight now ... really tight!' He hammered out one of the pegs. There was more scratching and scraping and gasping exclamation: 'Desperate ... how ... did you ... do it?'

When he arrived at the belay he asked: 'What about the pegs – did you pull on them?'

'Of course I used them. I had to get up it somehow!'

'No wonder I found it so hard! Why didn't you tell me?'

'You never asked.'

Victor continued up a chimney and disappeared from sight. The rope snaked out quickly: it was easier, he must be there. I followed, and emerged on to the crest of the ridge. Beyond Victor I could see the easy snow slopes leading up to the shoulder. We had cracked the Pinnacles and the crux of the route was behind us.

For two pitches we weaved round enormous cornices, descending seventy degrees snow and ice on the north flank, then climbing back up and over a knife-edge crest. Then the climbing became easier, I led out a full rope-length up the snow ramp, kicking slow steps. It was hard work, but at least there was no shattered rock to contend with, just deep snow with an even consistency, where it was possible to establish some kind of rhythm. While Victor led the sixth pitch, I leaned back at the belay, enjoying the fantastic sensation of height and space. Evening shadows were streaking the distant snowfields of the Bilafond La. Somewhere over there Indian soldiers were manning their gun-posts, but we had heard no shooting for a few days. We could now look over the North Ridge of our mountain to the upper Rimo Glacier and the arctic expanse of the Col Italia. For the first time we could see the bleak rounded hills separating the Rimo Glacier from the deserts of Turkestan. Looking back south, down the curve of our North Terong Glacier, past previously unsuspected turquoise pools to the junction of Advance Base, I wondered who was in camp? What were Jim and Dave up to? Could anyone see us, up on this fantastic ridge? This expedition had started as a large sociable party, but now there were just two of us, isolated and committed, high on the mountain, just as Dick and I had been on Kishtwar-Shivling.

It was growing cold, so I reached into the rucksack clipped in beside me to pull out my quilted anorak. After a while Victor shouted to me to come up, so I shouldered the rucksack, removed the belay and started up the next fifty-metre stretch. Victor had found no bivouac spot, so I had to continue. Now we were at about 6,850 metres. It was hard work: plunge in ice axe – step up high and kick deep in the soft snow – take two deep breaths in and out – plunge in the other axe – step up … But there was a rhythm, a slow steady movement. The weather remained perfect and for the first time since we had left Dave and Jim, I dared to hope that we might just reach the summit of this mountain. There was a long way to go and it would take another two days, but if the weather held and if the hidden gap below the summit held no insurmountable obstacles, we would probably make it.

As I led out the last few feet of rope, I reached a slight levelling on the broad ridge crest. On my left the ramp dropped away towards rocky outcrops. Between them and the dark shadows of the North-West Cwm, there were a thousand metres of unseen steep and overhanging rock. I stopped to dig out a platform. First, I had to remove the restricting weight of my rucksack. I planned the sequence of actions very carefully, acutely aware that I was tired and prone to mistakes after a day's hard work at altitude. First, I plunged my ice axe deep in the snow. Then I heaved the rucksack off my back and rested it on the snow. I held the straps firmly with my left hand, while I reached out with my right hand for the safety sling, grasped its karabiner and reached up to clip it into the wrist loop of the ice axe. The karabiner clicked. The ice axe was still attached to my body with a shoulder sling, and before removing that I wanted to make quite sure that the axe was secure; so I started to pull in the remaining slack in the rope, to tie a loop and attach that to the axe, just in case it should pull out of the snow. As I pulled on the heavy dragging rope, I swung slightly to the left. Then I turned back to the right.

The rucksack was moving. I reached out, but it had gone – sliding, accelerating, then wheeling, bouncing, somersaulting and bursting open as it flew over the edge, to disappear into the dark depths of the North-West Cwm.

One green bag of food rations remained, slung on a rock fifty metres below, right on the brink of the abyss. Everything else had gone. The ice axe was still in the snow beside me, with the wrist loop hanging down, unmoved. Apparently, in a moment of tired double vision, I had not actually clipped the karabiner into the wrist loop. It had clicked on nothing.

At first I was perfectly calm. I kicked back down the snow to a point where I could see Victor and shouted: 'We've got to go down.'

'What do you mean?'

'We'll have to go down. I've dropped my rucksack.' Then the calm vanished as I stormed down the ramp, blinded by tears of rage and misery. Victor took charge: 'Look, for God's sake pull yourself together. I don't want to die. You can do all the worrying you like when we get down, but now you've got to concentrate. This is very serious. You must concentrate on the job of getting down alive.'

I slithered down pitch six on a top rope. I waited at the belay for Victor. He arrived to find a howling madman. Later, at Base Camp, he entertained the others with a brilliant re-enactment of my hysteria. But now, high on Rimo, he was a paragon of restraint, uttering not a word of reproach and treating me with quite undeserved sympathy: 'Don't worry. Everyone drops things … it's happened to so many people … at least it was the sack and not you … anyway we've climbed the crux of the route – we've had six days of fantastic climbing … that's what counts – the summit isn't everything … '

He didn't believe a word of it and nor did I, but it was some comfort. One thing was certain: carrying on without a stove or my bivouac equipment was out of the question.

We abseiled down pitch five and left the ropes in place to secure our bivouac. The temperature was dropping sharply and the night wind was starting to whip snow in the air, but the sky was still clear and the Football Pitch was bronze in the lingering light of a cruelly beautiful sunset, which seemed a deliberate mockery of my incompetence. We dug out a platform and suspended the pole-less tent as best we could from the ropes. Then we settled inside for a miserable night. Victor gave me his spare half-length of karrimat, his Gore-Tex outer sleeping bag and his down jacket, to wrap round my feet. I vowed never, ever again, to write rude things about him in my diary. We had enough clothing to survive, but not enough to stop us shivering violently. It was bitterly cold, and all night long the tent fabric was flapped by the wind against our faces, showering us with frozen condensation and inducing in me a breathless claustrophobia. We huddled together, shivering with cold and sucking lumps of ice and boiled sweets, trying to relieve nagging thirsts. For me, there was a horrible sense of *déja vu*.

If we had been on our way down from a successful summit climb the discomfort would have been quite acceptable, even exhilarating; but the sensation of humiliating defeat made it almost unbearable. As Victor said, it was one thing to be forced back by bad weather or unacceptable dangers, but quite another to have to abandon a route because of one irrevocable human mistake. He had to face the double agony of being forced down by someone else's mistake. I was quieter now, almost resigned, but every few minutes I would be stabbed by the same horrible memory of a tumbling rucksack, dark blue against the brilliant snow slope. It was the silence that had been so awful; the sack had burst open without a sound, like some ghastly never-forgotten vision in a nightmare.

Our morning departure was simplified by having no stove: instead of the usual slow breakfast we just packed up to leave. It was again bitterly cold, well below –20 °C, and after the shivering night with inadequate clothing and no warm drinks, we fumbled clumsily. There was only room for one of us to get ready at a time. Victor went first, then waited outside while I struggled to warm numb toes and encase them in double boots. By the time I was ready Victor had lost all sensation in his feet and hands and was worried about frost-bite, so he came back into the draped tent to take off boots and mittens for a rewarming session.

At daybreak we were ready. It was a beautiful morning. As the night wind died down, the arctic landscape around us started to glow pink with a clarity that promised continuing perfect weather.

If only, if only, if only … but there was no question of going on.

We had to go down.

We made eight abseils, straight down vertical and overhanging rock walls on the south flank of the ridge. After the rucksack fiasco, I had the dubious satis-faction of working efficiently, fixing up a faultless series of abseils which took us quickly down on to the ice field. Then we unroped and downclimbed – down, down, down the great sweep of the ice field, kicking steps in perfect frozen snow. The streaks of hard ice were few and far between, and I realised that we should have come up this way, as Victor had originally suggested. Already I was thinking of a second attempt, hoping that Victor might be per-suaded to extend his holiday and give the route another try. If I managed to retrieve my bivouac gear from the North-West Cwm, and if the weather remained fine, we could climb straight up this ice field to the foot of the Pinnacles, reaching them in one day instead of three.

We continued down and down, 600 metres to the glacier of the South-West Cwm. As we neared the bottom of the ice field I drew ahead of Victor. Suddenly I was frightened by the sound of something rushing down towards me. My heart jolted at the thought of Victor falling or an avalanche sweeping down the face; but as I looked up I saw that it was just Victor's rucksack cartwheeling down the slope, to run out harmlessly on the smooth glacier below. Tired of its merciless weight, he had decided to emulate me and send it down the quick way.

Eight hours after leaving the vicious cold of the bivouac we reached the camp in the cwm. The snow was like porridge and the whole cwm was a fur-nace of white heat, but there was now a surface trickle of water and for the first time in thirty hours we could drink. We rested for three hours, collapsed in the enervating heat, then carried on down, taking it in turns to carry our one rucksack.

The glacier was alive with running water. Where there had been snow, there was now bare ice, split by crevasses. At the main glacier we unroped. It was Victor's turn to carry the sack again and I drew ahead on the final walk down to Advance Base. It was an exquisite twilit evening as I approached the Lake of Bones. Just before the camp I saw someone pottering around on the glacier. He was dressed in baggy clothes and walked with a slight stoop. It looked like Dave, out for one of his habitual evening strolls, but something was wrong – he looked somehow aged, and wasn't the beard grey? Suddenly I realised who it was:

'Henry!'

'Hello, how are you? Have you seen an ice axe lying around anywhere? I seem to have mislaid mine.' It was a delightful surprise to find Henry Osmaston there. He had ignored our telegram and, against all odds, had charmed his way past the various bureaucratic and military defences to the Nubra valley and on up to the North Terong Glacier, where he was now in residence, happily employed with his ice drills, thermometers, measuring sticks and notebooks.

I gave Henry a brief account of the rucksack fiasco, then left him searching for his ice axe. A few minutes later Victor, walking alone down the glacier, stumbled on an ancient wooden-shafted Aschenbrenner ice axe and wondered if he had found a relic of Dr Visser's 1929 expedition. He turned it over and found written along the shaft the words 'Henry OSMASTON'. A moment later he too found the owner.

Meanwhile, I had arrived at Advance Base. I met Jim first, then the others appeared in twos and threes. Only Muslim hung back and a few moments passed before his worried frown dissolved into a smile of welcome. Afterwards he explained that, seeing me coming down alone with no rucksack, he had feared the worst. My animated talk and the others' laughter soon made it clear that Victor was not dead, and a few minutes later the long-suffering man himself appeared, accompanied by Henry.

Everyone apart from Meena and Boga was there that evening.

We demolished the last bottle of Famous Grouse and enjoyed our first supper together for eight days.

Harish told us what everyone had been up to, filled us in on the latest news of the test matches and told us that a seventeen-year-old German had just won Wimbledon. Henry told us how, like me on my first carry up the glacier over two weeks earlier, he had walked straight past Advance Base and given up hope of finding the expedition. It was only after setting off back down again that he accidentally bumped into a group of Indian gentlemen in the middle of the glacier and asked them if by any chance they were anything to do with the

Indo-British expedition. After the strain of six and a half days' strenuous climbing above 6,000 metres, it was good to relax with all these friends again, and for a while I was able to forget the biggest disappointment of my life and think how wonderful it was just to be alive.

The expedition was by no means over. The Bombay team was leaving in the morning for more climbs. Henry was busy with his research. Victor and I had to rest, but already Victor was talking of extending his leave and giving our route on Rimo I another try. Jim too had decided to delay his departure for a few days. He had been waiting for Dave to recover from his chest infection. But now Dave felt better, and they were packed and ready to leave before dawn, to cross the Ibex Col and try their luck on the far side of Rimo.

In the following chapter Jim takes up their story from the moment when they descended from Rimo I.

14 The Far Side of Rimo
by Jim Fotheringham

Dave and I descended abseil after abseil down that now-familiar insecure snow. To our left the morning sun had triggered off the first of the avalanches that threatened the lower part of our descent. The changes in the terrain after only two days were dramatic. In many places our upward tracks had been obliterated by the runnels of the snow slides. Summer was coming to the Karakoram.

Maximum speed without achieving terminal velocity was the day's order. The furrow left by Victor and Stephen was now far above us. Their ridge was in dangerous condition, the major difficulties were still days away and we were concerned about their chances of success or survival.

Dave and I were both veterans of lightweight expeditions and were not used to the luxury of retreating to a manned camp, so it felt unreal to relax back in the organised security of Advance Base. Harish's anxious question, 'Where are the others?' nagged at the back of my mind. In truth I did not know. I fetched the binoculars from the tent, rested them on a rock and focused them on to the line of footprints on the now distant ridge. At the end of the thin line drawn in the snow were two dots, almost imperceptibly moving. How slowly the expedition's shock troops moved.

We feasted as Pratap and Harsinh prepared good meals and, more importantly as far as I was concerned, the two-gallon teapot was put on. Time was against Dave and me, but the expedition as a whole was advancing towards its various goals. Harish, Meena, Boga, Muslim and Pratap had been up the badly crevassed western branch of the glacier, but had failed to find a route on to the Teram Shehr Plateau, but Arun and Muslim had climbed Safina and plans were now afoot for Meena and Boga to cross the Ibex Col and explore peaks on the South Rimo Glacier.

Dave was putting up stoically with an extremely bad cough, broken finger (which we still thought was only sprained) and a recently sprained ankle. He chose wisely to rest and recuperate, and I joined the Indians for a reconnaissance to find an alternative route from the cul-de-sac of the main North Terong Glacier up on to the Teram Shehr Plateau, a thousand metres above, which would give access to a host of peaks. In the event, Muslim and I found a route, but the objective danger ruled out any protracted attempt on the plateau, so the others decided to stick to the peaks directly above the glacier.

At this stage of the trip I was becoming really well acclimatised. The days at altitude were having no adverse effect but I was becoming increasingly worried about Victor and Stephen, because from this northerly viewpoint the true character of the upper ridge on Rimo I could be seen. It was a lot longer and steeper than any of us had realised. This trip of mine was a reconnaissance that we should have done before the attempt. Hindsight is a wonderful thing.

When we reached camp again three days later I was alarmed to hear that they were still not back and had not been seen through the binoculars for two days. We did not know that they were hidden from view in the Pinnacles and Harish was becoming quite concerned; but when he asked Dave what was to be done about Stephen and Victor, Dave replied with affected sangfroid: 'It's their problem.' In fact, Dave was just as concerned as I was and we resolved on a plan: we would wait one more day, then go up to the South-West Cwm and try to see what was happening; if they did return, but had been unsuccessful, we would cross over the South Rimo Glacier and attempt Rimo I or Rimo III from there.

While we waited, we packed for our journey. Dave felt better, and after the weeks of delays and false starts it now 'felt right' to be setting off. It 'felt righter' when a weary-looking Stephen appeared on the glacier, still supported by his two ski sticks without which he never appeared able to walk. My immediate question – 'Where's Victor?' – got the great answer, 'Just coming.'

They had obviously had a hard time and conditions on the ridge had never really improved. The rucksack incident ended their climb but I sometimes wonder, having seen that top ridge in profile and knowing how committed they were, whether there was good luck in the accident. Nothing else would have turned them back and they really were out on one hell of a limb. But what a fantastic try, a truly bold attempt.

The last bottle of whisky was cracked and Dave and I made final preparations for our attempt on the far side of Rimo. At 4 a.m., 11 July, Pratap brought the chai that cheers up even a predawn start. Then we left, feet crunching up the familiar glacier and into the South-West Cwm. The easy pace allowed for inner reflection and doubts to surface in the predawn blackness. It is ironic that the best time to start a high mountain day is the hour when the human spirit is at its lowest ebb. However, as we reached the high camp the sunlight broke across the Ibex Col and turned the grey ice to white crystal, a magic transformation that never fails to thrill.

We retrieved our cached climbing gear and continued climbing towards the col.

Ten days earlier on the first climb to the col we had seen nothing. But now the weather was fine and our effort was rewarded with a view east to a great white highway between black peaks that stretched back into the pastel pinks and browns of the Turkestan hinterland.

Now we had to descend to that highway. Meena and Boga had crossed the col four days earlier and left a fixed rope to safeguard the descent of (and eventual retreat back up) the poor snow of this east-facing wall. We abseiled down the fixed rope, tied on to our own rope to continue to the bottom of the couloir and on to the South Rimo Glacier. We were wearing 'raquettes' – light snowshoes popular for alpine winter climbing. Made from a light wooden frame strung with nylon, they were the answer to glacier travel on the soft snow in the tropical daytime heat, and without them we could not have done this crossing in one day. As it was, we only travelled slowly across the glacier and the snowshoes did not stop us occasionally breaking through into crevasses, which were a monumental struggle to get back out of.

Gradually the scene unfolded. Massive, grand and terrible was this world of black rock, white snow and burning sun. We rounded the East Ridge of Rimo I and saw for the first time the staggering far side of the whole Rimo cirque. We snowshoed down and across to a band of moraine gravel on the glacier, where we stopped late that afternoon to camp. Exhaustion demanded tea, tea and more tea. Later, rehydrated, we could take stock of our situation.

Rimo I looked impossible from this side. Although relatively easy climbing would get us two-thirds of the way up, the summit was defended by a final wall of steep rock and amazingly fluted snow formations, quite out of the question for a quick attempt with minimal gear. Rimo III, however, looked very different from this side, a great round-shouldered giant. Although we could not from here see a complete route, we could see that a branch of the glacier led up into a great cwm between Rimo III and IV, and we could see the top part of an eminently climbable ridge leading south-west up to the summit of Rimo III.

We thought and talked about it and decided to go all out for Rimo III. On alpine-style ascents it is almost impossible to carry more than about six days' food and fuel, without seriously slowing down the ascent. 'Lightweight' is more than a fashionable name tag: it is a dire necessity at altitude, for the increased speed from travelling light is the safety factor. With this in mind, Dave and I drastically cut down our loads. We resolved to climb on one rope and take just six slings, ten karabiners, two rock pegs, two ice pegs, snowshoes and ski sticks, plus food and fuel for five days.

The sun was disappearing and Rimo's shadow crept towards us. I felt very lonely. We were contemplating an ascent of an unknown mountain by an unknown route, with no support and with a retreat that would involve a 1,200 metre climb back up to the Ibex Col. Nevertheless, it still 'felt right'

We slept the sleep of the exhausted.

12 July – our third day out from Advance Base. Woken only by the paling eastern sky at 4 a.m., we were off to a late start at five. The day's ascent looked straightforward, but once again we under-estimated the Karakoram. A series of turbulent streams were only crossed with great difficulty, before we could

continue up the steepening glacier. The previous twelve-hour day was beginning to make itself felt and I started to think Dave had been right to suggest a rest day. But the die was cast. The sun rose on this east-facing glacier with malevolent speed and soon we were ploughing deep furrows through softening snow, struggling in the insidious heat, as we climbed up into the great glacier cwm enclosed by the Rimo peaks. High on Rimo II two massive bands of ice cliffs had collapsed, smashed down on to the glacier and surged right across and up the far side, triggering in turn another massive avalanche which had blasted back down on to the glacier. We had to clamber over debris ten feet deep for about half a mile, to reach the upper glacier.

We passed the danger zone and at midday stopped to camp, too exhausted to go any further that day. Now that we could see the whole of our route on Rimo III, we realised that it was more difficult than we had first suspected. I was clearly not going to get back to Advance Base in time to join the first party back to Leh and I was going to be late home. Up to now I had been enveloped in the timelessness of the big hills, but now my worries about being late suddenly induced a flood of guilty feelings about unreliability and thoughtlessness. I was in a sort of panic – not about the mountain, but about home.

The following morning all doubts were forgotten as we left at 3 a.m., to wind our way up through labyrinthine crevasses and ice cliffs towards the foot of Rimo III. The peak loomed above us, with its summit guarded by white cowls of corniced snow. The route was now obvious; a mixed buttress led up to the ridge. The buttress separated steep slopes of poor snow and bare ice. Although not easy, it would at least provide security and an abseil descent, in contrast to the treacherous-looking slopes flanking it.

We contoured across towards the bergschrund at the foot of the buttress, where we stopped for a reviving brew. We had no altimeter, but estimated our height to be about 5,800 metres. High above us on the crest of the ridge coils of wind-blasted spindrift sparkled in the sunlight. It was a wonderful sight, but did the wind herald a change in the weather?

Dave starts up the buttress, traversing above the bergschrund. I follow through, up and across a runnel of ice to reach a solid belay on good granite. Dave leads up floury snow for fifty metres, then I take to the rock. It's probably harder but the rock gives a feeling of solid security which I miss on the unpredictable consistency of Himalayan snow. Dave swings into the lead again, hurrying up loose snow and bombarding me with fragments. The climbing is hard, harder than we anticipated, uncomfortably hard for our lightweight selection of gear, and the thought of abseiling back down this terrain with only one rope is mildly alarming. I lead again, up beautiful rough brown granite that is actually warm to touch. The mountains are crystal under the blue sky, as we climb up our untouched peak. This is why we climb.

Dave, the iceman, scratches past and sets to on an ice pitch. It is the very worst stuff, loose wet snow layered thickly over brittle splintering ice, the sort of climbing that I find most frightening at altitude and, as I lead on past Dave, each step is a lurch from one set of collapsing holds to another, but I eventually reach the haven of a good rock belay. Now we have climbed about four hundred metres from the bergschrund and the wind-driven plumes of snow on the ridge are not far above. But it turns out to be another six pitches before the angle eases slightly, and we find a small depression just below the ridge, where we decide to camp.

What a place! We cut a platform as fast as we can, for the wind is gusting violently across the ridge. Dave decides to excavate an emergency snowhole as well, in case the wind presages a drastic change in the weather. The view is magnificent. Now we can see over to the north, across the Col Italia to the mountains of China. Our path of ascent up the South Rimo Glacier looks incredibly long and above it is the impressive bulk of Rimo I. This is our altitude gauge, for Rimo I is just 150 metres higher than the 7,233-metre summit of our Rimo III. We still have a long way to go – about 800 metres.

We take turns at digging the snowhole. It is hard work at this altitude and at the end of a long day. Eventually we cut a hole big enough for all the gear and a shelter wall for the tent. Dave's karrimat is lost in the rising wind, which tries to take the tent as well, plucking and snatching at the loose nylon, until we secure all the corners and, for additional safety, rope the tent down through the ice to embedded snow stakes.

Oh, what a lovely home a tent can be! Zipped up inside the green nylon we can revel in a false security; like budgies with a bag over their cage, we can rest and sleep. We're happy with our progress but unhappy with the weather. Low cloud is boiling up from the valley and higher clouds are winding shrouds round the peaks. The question is, 'How long have we got?' As always our safety lies in speed, so we decide to go for the summit in one push without any bivouac gear.

I am worried about Dave. His prolonged racking fits of coughing are keeping me awake – or is that just pre-summit nerves? Suddenly in the middle of the night he starts vomiting. I avoid having to make a decision myself by asking Dave how he feels about going on the next day. His answer leaves no room for doubt: cough and broken finger notwithstanding, we are starting at 4 a.m.

Cold and dark, the gusting wind slaps at the tent. Dave, bless his cotton socks, has got a brew going. I linger in my sleeping bag, savouring every last calorie of warmth. There is a method to starting in these unpleasant conditions in the middle of the night.

The main thing is to accomplish as much of the preparing and packing as possible without leaving your sleeping bag, and most certainly without leaving the tent. It is horribly constricted but it does allow the necessary retention of heat and it avoids catastrophes like dropped boots or gloves.

Dave must be feeling weak after his sleepless night, but he doesn't complain. When everything is ready, we go outside and struggle to dismantle the tent and stash it in the snowhole. If left pitched, it would not survive this wind. Cold and stiff, we start to move up. The sky above us is clear and stars twinkle in some sort of cosmic code, trying to tell us what, I wonder. But below us there is a silent billowing sea of cloud, pierced by the dark islands of high peaks. When dawn comes it will be spectacular.

Up we go, moving together on deep snow and across a little overhang on to the crest of the ridge. Up here it feels like flying while standing still, a euphoria compounded of sheer elation, an unreal position and oxygen starvation. The sun breaks through and a shocking breathtaking panorama unfolds. The clouds below are white and gold and we seem higher than the few peaks that pierce them. Dave and I could be the only people in the world and it is impossible to conceive of normal life and normal people doing normal things, while we tread our way up to the very edge of existence.

We reach a small platform and rest. The way ahead looks intimidating as a narrow corniced ridge stretches westward to a huge rock tower. I lead off while Dave belays. I move from rock to rock, ploughing through the deep snow on the windward side of the cornice, and tie on to a solid belay. Dave is left to force his way along and over an extraordinary snow mushroom sprouting from the ridge. It is an insecure and exposed pitch, 'vertical on one side and overhanging on the other', as the Victorian pioneers would have said.

Later we pass the rock tower, and the ridge becomes broader and less steep. Now we can safely move together, zigzagging up the slope. But each breath is hard and each step harder. Rhythm is vital, slow and steady, breathing synchronised with movement. Step by step we crawl slowly up the great whaleback. False summits come and go, the mist swirls in and steals our view, the only sounds are the wind blasting across the ridge and the swish of ice fragments sheared off by the rope, down into the swirling void below.

We know that the summit must be near, but the way is blocked by a steep wall of snow. I struggle to surmount this final twenty-metre pitch with a high-altitude butterfly stroke and dig my way to the top. Then there is nothing more and I sit on the top of a dome of snow. Whooping with joy, I bring Dave up and as he nears me I see his cracked bearded face light up. We've done it!

The wind whips clouds over our summit and spoils the view. But no matter; there's nothing for us here anyway. We just have one task to do: Dave produces a little packet of blue flowers that Harish's son Nawang gave him to place on the summit as an offering to the gods. We bury them in the snow, then set off down at 11a.m. It has taken us seven hours to reach the summit.

The descent to the top camp was easy. It is amazing how quickly one can descend ground at altitude that takes so long to climb. The weather was worsening, though mercifully it was doing it slowly. But it was still going to be a hard descent. We did not have enough gear for the dozen or so abseils we would have to make down the buttress, so Dave spent the evening untying slings from ice axes and cutting nylon tape off his rucksack. Even so we were forced the next morning to downclimb between abseils. Some of the abseil anchors were memorable – a rucksack strap on a spike, an ice screw driven into rock … Finally a desperate tension traverse took us on to the steep snow above the bergschrund. When we reached our cached ski sticks we collapsed, exhausted by the nervous tension of the last few days. But we had to get up and continue down the steep snow to the glacier bowl, where we put on snowshoes and headed straight on down for the moraine camp. It was an arduous trek, but the monotony was broken by finding Dave's karrimat about a mile from where he dropped it. We ploughed on down through soft snow, slush and water. I inadvertently led us into a maze of crevasses. We extricated ourselves with difficulty and finally plodded, sodden-footed, on to the moraine, our rocky oasis in the middle of the hostile ice desert. Dave was so weary that he dumped his sack and snowshoes by the Ibex Col Glacier turning, ready for the morning, and did the last few hundred metres to the moraine unburdened.

About fifteen pints of Lapsang Suchong later, we started to feel better. I stared up at the huge wall of Rimo I opposite. I could see now what the people in Leh must have meant when they talked of Rimo as 'the painted mountain'. The great bands of ebony dark rock looked brushed on to the wall by some giant hand.

Next morning we crossed the Ibex Col in wind and snow and descended to the South-West Cwm. Since our journey up six days earlier there had been a massive sérac fall across the route.

Further down, the glacier was now a tortured surface of bare ice and rock, riven by huge crevasses and rushing water, and it was impossible to recognise our line of ascent. We fell greedily on the food cache, picking out favourite items, devouring chocolate and condensed milk, brewing tea.

Then we continued down, stumbling wearily back to the familiar North Terong Glacier and finally returning to the Lake of Bones. Our journey was over.

In the final chapter Stephen resumes the story of the other expedition members.

15 The Double-Humped Camel and Mahendra's Bridge

After the rucksack fiasco on Rimo I, Victor and I had to rest. On Thursday, 11 July, our first day back at the Lake of Bones, we sat in the sun and endured the agony of seeing Rimo etched with brilliant clarity on an ultramarine sky and thinking 'we might have been up on that summit snowfield today'. I apologised again and again to Victor and tried to console myself with thoughts of all the distinguished mountaineers who had dropped things: Boysen's crampon on Everest, Zawada's crampon on Mandaras, Shipton's sack full of precious food supplies into the Rishi gorge, Herzog's glove on Annapurna, Bonington's gloves on Annapurna, Chris Watts' boot on Bojohaghur, Chris Watts' rucksack on Everest, Ned Gillette's rucksack on Conway's Saddle, Joe Brown's rucksack on Thalay Sagar ... but the knowledge that I was in good company did not alter the fact that my mistake had ended what might have been a successful ascent of one of the highest, most challenging unclimbed peaks in the world.

The sun shone and the mountains kept their surreal clarity and the nights were fiercely cold as the extraordinary spell of fine weather continued, teasing us with the possibility of another attempt. In the dazzling afternoon heat the glacier was loud with water cascading down blue-green sluices towards the Terong river, the Nubra, the Shyok, the Indus, the Indian Ocean. Days of intense radiation had transformed parts of the glacier surface into a shimmering skin of wafer-thin ice, which tinkled like shattered crystal under our feet. The Pinnacles by the Lake of Bones had grown. The big dome tent was perched on a metre-high pedestal of ice, shaded from the melting rays of the sun. The lake had forced its way out through a sub-glacial borehole, sinking to a fraction of its former volume and leaving a huge iceberg stranded like some beached white-spiked leviathan.

After a day's rest Victor and I climbed up with Henry to the North-West Cwm, where we found the rucksack and most of its shattered contents sprawled in the snow. On the way back I walked ahead, leaving the other two ambling down discussing glaciology – an incongruous pair, with Henry's tousled beard and billowing patched cotton trousers and Victor looking dapper in his favourite red dancing tights. Base Camp was deserted. Everyone was away climbing and Mahendra had volunteered to go down to the valley, cross the river and continue to the army base to arrange for our departure. I was enjoying the peaceful afternoon when Victor and Henry returned. I was about to offer them tea when there was a frantic shout from nearby:

'Quick … quick … camera! You must take a photo!'

Ski goggles appeared from behind a hummock and Mahendra rushed into camp, with Harsinh-Junior in breathless pursuit.

'Quick, you must take a photo. I have just escaped from the jaws of death!'

Mahendra, the leopard-wrestler, had narrowly escaped drowning in the Terong river, attempting to wade it that morning. The fixed rope had been swept away, but he had told Harsinh to belay him with another rope. His knowledge of belaying techniques was hazy, and he had not actually tied Harsinh to anything on the bank. Instead he had left Harsinh unattached and had instructed him to pay the rope out through his bare hands, saying in Hindi 'If I am swept away and you think you are going to be pulled in, LET GO OF THE ROPE – I SHALL DIE FOR THE EXPEDITION.'

The river had now been swollen by the meltwater of ten days' fine weather to at least twice its original volume. Even at six in the morning, after a hard night's frost on the glacier, the current was far too strong and Mahendra was quickly swept off his feet. Harsinh had ignored his instructions, had held on grimly and saved Mahendra's life; but that was enough of heroics and he made it quite clear that crossing the river was now out of the question.

The Siachen Indo-British Expedition 1985 was trapped in the Terong valley.

Mahendra asked us what we were going to do about it. Henry's joking solution was simple: we might find a way out over a high pass but the easiest thing would be to stay put until either the water went down or Colonel Gupte sent in a helicopter. But Victor had a more highly developed sense of team responsibility. Climbers were due back at work and he persuaded me that we would have to descend to the river and attempt to fix ropes across the cliffs on the right bank, enabling the others to exit from the valley the moment they returned from their climbs. I reluctantly agreed to leave the next morning and before going to bed we scraped together all the available ropes, pitons, nuts and karabiners at Advance Base.

The following day we walked down past Mud Camp and Snout Camp to the old river crossing, which was now a deadly torrent of crashing water, thick with the sediment of pulverised granite and awash with ice blocks torn down from the glacier. Mahendra was a brave man.

We carried on down the right bank to the point where the river abutted against cliffs. A first outcrop was quite easy to cross; then the river veered away from the valley wall and we waded the icy current of four side braids before starting work on the main cliff, where the river pounded against smooth boilerplates of granite. At dusk our work was still incomplete, so we had to return the next morning to continue difficult climbing across the cliff. Our 300 metres of rope just sufficed to reach the end of the cliff, where the river again veered to the left and it would be possible to walk down the valley floor to the Siachen Glacier. After tightening the ropes and checking all the anchor pitons we plodded back to the Terong Glacier and at Mud Camp we met Arnn and Boga, who were hurrying down on their way home. We assured them that the exit from the valley was now fixed. Meena was with them and told us about her successful trip with Boga to the South Rimo Glacier. After crossing the Ibex Col they had climbed two points on a ridge before setting off by moonlight early one morning to make the first ascent of 6,070-metre Lharimo: the holy mountain.

The next morning Victor and I were back at Advance Base, where Harish and Dhiren were packing up to leave. Dhiren and Arun had been up the spectacular icefall into the cwm on the far side of the glacier, to climb two beautiful snow peaks. Harish had with him a list of suitable names and he called these two peaks Sundbrar and Sondhi, explaining that the names come from nearby Baltistan: Kashmiri Brahmins and Hindus used to gather each summer on a certain date at Sundbrar ('beautiful place') to worship the goddess Lakshmi. They would wait and pray for the special moment when a basin would suddenly fill with water. This sudden beautiful appearance was called 'Sondhi'. As Harish observed, Baltistan is a Muslim province, but this Hindu ritual had survived from an era which stretched back many hundreds of years before the Indian subcontinent was hit by the surge of Islam.

Finally in the afternoon, Muslim and Harsinh Senior returned from their ascent of Doab, the 6,045-metre peak just behind Advance Base. Harsinh grinned happily, for this was the first time he had been to a summit. The Indians all left for Mud Camp and in the evening there were just Victor, Henry and me left at the Lake of Bones. Victor and I had packed our rucksacks and were ready to leave for Rimo if the weather in the morning should be fine. But we knew that the chances were slim: for two days now the sun had been filtered through haze and high cirrus had been spreading from the south-west. Rain started to fall in the morning. Later it changed to snow and Henry packed to leave for Leh, where he would continue his researches around the Indus valley. We were sad to see him go, for his gentle humour and detachment had been a welcome foil to our fretting ambition. We stayed on gloomily, wondering about Dave and Jim, who had been hidden from view for five days.

Jim appeared in the afternoon. His smile gave everything away and we only had to ask *which* mountain they had climbed. Half an hour later, as Jim was starting on his first bucket of tea and telling us all about Rimo III, Dave arrived, exhausted and happy. After the disappointments of previous years in the Karakoram he had now climbed a major peak by a remote committing route. I felt twinges of envy mingled with relief at seeing them both safely back on the Terong side of the mountain and satisfaction that the expedition had successfully climbed one of the Rimo peaks.

That night Victor and I again set the alarm for 3 a.m. – 'just in case'; but in the morning it was snowing again. We were not to get a second chance.

It was still dank and grey when Jim and Victor packed to leave. Jim would almost certainly be late home, and half the population of Brampton would be waiting to have their teeth fixed, but when they heard why he was late they would understand. A couple of weeks earlier he had said that he didn't think he would be likely to reach any major summits this time, but that it had been such an extraordinarily enjoyable trip anyway that he would not mind. Now he had completed an outstanding climb at the last possible moment, turning his expedition into an unqualified success. Victor, too, had enjoyed the trip but he had to leave without the extra bonus of a summit. I was luckier, for I could stay another week in the mountains. If the weather improved again I could join the others in exploring the South Terong and Shelkar Chorten Glaciers and perhaps even reach a summit.

Four days of rain and snow came to an end. On Saturday, 20 July, we set off on our final journey of exploration. After breakfast Dave left Mud Camp with Harish, Dhiren, Muslim, Harsinh Junior and Pratap for the South Terong Glacier, while I climbed up into the narrow entrance of the parallel Shelkar Chorten Glacier. We had five days before we were due to leave for Nubra.

It was exciting to break into new terrain again. Dave and the Indians were probably the first people ever to struggle up the rubble river gorge to the snout of the South Terong and climb up on to its vast motorway surface, striped by the dark parallel lines of medial moraines – the ordered debris of its many side branches. Harish was in his element, covering wide areas, sending Muslim and Harsinh to inspect the Warshi La on the south side of the glacier, while he and Dhiren explored one of the northern arms to yet another previously untrodden pass, the Terong Col, a broad snow saddle from which they looked down to the great white expanse of the South Rimo Glacier. This pass, much easier than the Ibex Col, could provide in conjunction with the Warshi Col an easy route across the main Karakoram axis – an alternative to the traditional Saser La route, linking the Nubra valley to the Chip Chap river and Karakoram Pass.

Meanwhile, I climbed slowly up the Shelkar Chorten Glacier. Later I was to read Dr Visser's account of the 1929 expedition and discover that while his colleagues mapped the North Terong he struggled up the hideous icefall of the Shelkar Chorten, squeezed between walls of rubble, which sent a rock avalanche crashing down within feet of his porters. But at the time I was unaware of Visser's earlier visit, as I zigzagged laboriously up through a labyrinth of ice towers leading to a weary succession of false horizons. It was only on the second day that I emerged on to the immense upper snowfield, shimmering white and oppressively silent. Dr Visser must have come less far, for his map (on which my sketch map was based) showed the Shelkar Chorten extending much further east than is actually the case. As I plodded up the snowfield, a low ridge slowly rose into view and by midday I stood on its crest, surprised to find that I had reached the head of the Shelkar Chorten. Beyond lay the encircling arms of the much bigger South Terong, covering a large area that had been assigned to the Shelkar Chorten.

I camped just below the ridge and rose at dawn on Monday to climb a 6,050-metre peak above, which we later christened Chorten Peak. After the slow struggle on Rimo it was exhilarating to move quickly up an easy peak. From the summit I planned my route down to the South Terong and across to a distant double-summitted peak on its far side. Unknown to me at the time, I narrowly missed bumping into the others on the South Terong and it was only afterwards that I could tell them about the elegant compelling arête on the peak with two summits. Harish suggested a Ladakhi name, Ngabong Terong – the Double-Humped Camel of Terong.

Early on Tuesday morning I climbed up a fifty-degree snow and ice face on to the arete. Already by 8.30 in the morning the snow was becoming dangerously soft, so I stopped to camp in the shade of a crevasse. At dawn on Wednesday I continued, revelling in the freedom of climbing unladen, crampons biting perfectly on the frozen arête which glowed pink in a soft blue sky. The furthest hump proved to be the highest and I had to make a long detour across a nasty slope of sugar-coated ice and a connecting ridge before I could stop on the true summit to enjoy my last view out over the icy wilds of the Eastern Karakoram. Then it was time to return to the crevasse. Dangerously sticky snow forbade a descent to the valley that day, so I settled down for another long lonely vigil in the ice grotto, whose lambent blue walls now seemed dank and joyless. I had no book, my food was finished and the tobacco supplies had long since run out. I fantasised painfully about brown bread and Stilton and smoked bacon, but most of all I longed to be back with the others. It had been moving to spend five days utterly alone and this journey over two glaciers and two summits had been some consolation for the disappointment on Rimo. But now I had had enough of solitude.

The weather broke again and on Thursday I trudged down through falling drizzle, taking ten hours to reach Mud Camp, which was dismal and deserted. I was a day late and the others had left, so I settled down for another lonely evening. There was plenty of food left but I had looked forward so much to the sound of human voices. They had gone but I did have surrogate company in the form of cassette tapes, so I sat in my sleeping bag under the tarpaulin, sheltering from the grey drizzle, lost amongst desolate slag heaps, and switched on the Walkman. If one had to select a human voice out of the blue after six days' solitude, one could do worse than choose Ellie Ameling's exquisite soprano singing of Schumann songs. The following morning I returned to the valley. The landscape had changed again. The rock and earth debris lying on the glacier ice was spangled pink with the new blooms of willow herb. Down by the river the old golden grass of the Crag's nest was interleaved with new green shoots. The tamarisks were showers of coral and the roses – the sia – had burst into flower with an exuberant display of pink intensity.

As I passed the old river crossing I saw the rest of the team, distant dark figures wading the icy braids between the cliffs. I rushed on as fast as my loathsome thirty-five-kilo sack would allow and scrabbled up the first cliff, along the traverse and down the rope at the far end, then waded across the first river braid, where Pratap and the Harsinhs were waiting, welcoming me with their big boyish grins. One of the most rewarding things about this expedition had been the growing friendship with these delightful men, and now I was incredibly touched when Harsinh Junior pulled out of his pocket a crumpled packet containing his last stained, flattened cigarette, which we shared, sitting on the boulders, surrounded by the roaring waters and dashing ice blocks of the Terong river.

I found the rest of the team further on and after lunch we started on the main cliff. That afternoon we did four carries along the ropes: first the river-level traverse, sliding along with a karabiner, hanging above the pounding waves, then a jumar ascent to the start of the high traverse, where we tensioned across boilerplate slabs, then a short descent along a ledge, then another jumar followed by a final ledge across to the platform overlooking the drop at the far end of the cliff. From there we lowered the loads on a rope to the flat valley floor, before returning across the fixed ropes to do it all again.

That night we camped on the far side of the cliff. We lit a fire of dead juniper and sat around the huge orange blaze, talking about our different journeys of the past few days. Everyone seemed to agree that it had been an unusually enjoyable expedition. Nearly a month had passed since we set off on our attempt on Rimo I and the moon was again high in the sky, inspiring Harish to thoughts of romance. He told me about his 'open-heart sessions' with Dave: 'Oh, yes, we are very close now. Dave has told me everything. You know he was deeply in love with the German girl on the bus from Srinagar. He is going to look for her when we return to Leh.' I suddenly remembered the girl with soft brown eyes and I remembered Dave's wistful look when she had left the bus at Lamayuru to go walking off into the desert with her chaperone. Harish talked for a while with his Bombay friends and they all burbled in a rapid mixture of Gujarati and Hindi, punctuated by the occasional incongruous English word and frequent acknowledging grunts of 'achar'. Dhiren and Muslim burst out laughing and Meena exclaimed 'achar … really?!' Harish chuckled and turned to me to ask: 'And what about you Steve-sahib – are you visiting Jullundher on the way home?'

Saturday, 27 July, our last day in the Terong valley, was blessed with brilliant sunshine. Dave, Dhiren, Muslim and I did four more ferries across the cliff, to fetch the rest of the luggage, while Harish, Meena and the Bhotias started to carry loads down the valley towards the Siachen.

It was hard repetitive work, but I enjoyed the sensation of hot sun on bare arms and the spectacle of the glittering braids of silver, twisting along the valley floor below. I wished that we could stay for a few days to climb further up this magnificent cliff of warm granite, but Colonel Gupte was expecting us for dinner in the officers' mess that night, and had already sent his emissary, 2nd Lt Mahendra, to hurry us on our way back to Nubra.

I had almost forgotten about Mahendra – our Mahendra, the debonair leopard-wrestler, the apprehender of boot-thieves, the man who had braved the icy waters of the Terong. Ten days earlier he had accompanied Arun and Boga across the ropes to the outlet of the Terong valley, back up on to the Siachen and down to the army base, where he had remained ever since. He had arranged with Victor to meet any returning climbers at a certain army signpost on the glacier, to escort them safely down to the base, but when Victor arrived at the signpost with Jim and Henry three days later, there was no Mahendra. They were most anxious to get down that night, but were worried that, with no official army escort, they might be mistaken for alien spies and shot. They decided to set off down but as a precaution Henry and Victor stopped on the crest of every hummock to bellow at the tops of their voices and wave their arms while Jim looked on in embarrassment. As they neared the glacier snout they decided to rig up a white handkerchief on the end of Henry's ice axe but were not sure who should go in front with the flag. (It was now dusk and the handkerchief was in any case a dirty shadow of its former white glory; the sentries could easily fail to notice it.) The three of them were about to draw lots, when Henry said in his softest most gentlemanly tones: 'Look, why don't I go first? I'm quite a bit older than you two and I probably have fewer years to lose.' And with that noble speech of self-sacrifice, he strode off down the glacier with the dirty handkerchief held aloft.

Their precautions proved unnecessary. They descended on to the valley floor, crossed the Nubra bridge and walked straight into the base without seeing a single sentry. The Crog's instinctive nose quickly sniffed out the aroma of brewing chai and it was only after the three Englishmen had settled down in the canteen with steaming mugs of tea that anyone thought of asking what they were doing there.

Mahendra eventually appeared to arrange transport to Leh for the three climbers. Once that was done, he had a few days free before meeting the rest of us. After one failed rendez-vous, he was determined now to do better. Not only was he going to meet the rest of the team in the Terong valley; he was also going to bring with him ten jawans, released kindly by Colonel Gupte, to help with our baggage. We were extremely grateful for this assistance and Mahendra was delighted with the opportunity to display his leadership qualities. Unfortunately, that was not enough for him. Since his narrow escape from drowning, he had been nursing a secret desire to take his revenge on the

Terong river. Now that Victor and I had fixed the cliff traverse along the right bank, there was no need for anyone to get wet; but that did not deter Mahendra, who was now a man with a mission: obsessed by a fanatical determination to cross the river.

On Friday, 19 July, while I was walking down from Mud Camp and the others were load-ferrying down the right bank of the river, Mahendra was there on the opposite bank, with his obedient jawans, who were struggling to position two lengths of aluminium ladder across the water. The ladder barely reached the middle and the jawans had to give up the struggle. Mahendra tried to communicate across the river with much gesticulating and shouting, which was obliterated by the roaring water. Eventually, he realised that the Siachen Indo-British Expedition '85 was not going to reach the end of the valley that day, neither by crossing the river nor by the laborious cliff traverse. He also realised that Harish could not hear a word of his shouting; so he wrote a note, tied it to a stone (along with a generous gift of some cigarettes) and hurled it across the river. Harish read the note:

> Meet you by Siachen with ten jawans in morning. Dinner at officers' mess – 7 p.m. tomorrow. LONG LIVE S.I.B.E. '85!

On Saturday morning Mahendra appeared again, as we were starting on the final load-ferries across the cliff. This time I was present to witness his frantic attempts to shout above the deafening roar of the torrent. Not a word reached our side but his gesticulations made it clear that we were to meet him further down the valley right at the point where the Terong river is swallowed up under the Siachen Glacier and it is possible to climb directly out from the right bank on to the glacier.

We had a long hot morning of load-ferrying and midday had passed by the time everyone and all the luggage had arrived at the appointed spot. Mahendra had finally triumphed, choosing the narrowest point of the entire river, where the torrent was funnelled past a giant boulder. This boulder was on the far bank. Ten jawans sat on top of it, clustered round their leader. At the water's edge on our side a platform of smaller rocks had been built up. The two sections of aluminium ladder were stretched across from this platform to the giant boulder, poised above the crashing waves which poured down to disappear with an apocalyptic roar into the ice cavern of the Siachen a short way downstream.

The three Bhotias had crossed the bridge earlier that morning but now the water had risen and it looked dangerous. Harish announced that he was walking round over the hummocks of the glacier, but agreed that it would be worth sending the loads across the bridge to save the jawans walking round. After all the luggage had been pulled across the Indians set off to walk over the glacier.

Out of politeness and perhaps curiosity, Dave and I stayed to try Mahendra's Bridge. Dave went first, tied to the middle of a rope, belayed by me on the near side and fourteen men on the far bank. As he reached the middle, the ladder sagged right into the water and was tossed and pummelled by the furious waves. Dave clung grimly to the rungs as the ladder bucked wildly. I tried to support him with the rope, bracing myself against a small boulder to which the ladder was tied. Then I felt it ripping from the earth – so much for Mahendra's belay. The near end of the ladder started to rock wildly on its platform. I watched helpless and terrified as Dave clawed his way along the ladder, desperately trying to keep his head out of the water. The jawans hauled on the rope and Dave heaved up the rungs, just reaching the outstretched hands on the far bank as my end of the ladder finally slid off its perch and swung round into the waves. The jawans heaved him up on to the large boulder and he collapsed in a sodden spluttering heap on the safe sun-baked granite.

I took the slightly longer route over the glacier.

Late that night we arrived at the officers' mess for dinner. We were all lined up in seats along one side of the tent. The officers sat facing us on the other side, with Colonel Gupte at the centre of the line. A huge stove, with a chimney disappearing up out of the roof, separated the two teams.

Orderlies brought whisky. Colonel Gupte congratulated us on our successful expedition and Harish thanked him for all his help. More drinks were brought. Muslim and I breathed a sigh of grateful relief when the cigarettes appeared. We told the colonel about our adventures at the river and he turned to Mahendra and said: 'You are about to attend a mountaineering training camp, aren't you? You will be able to teach them all about bridge building!' He turned back to us and said: 'You know he fought with a leopard? Let's have a look Mahendra … ah, yes, you can just see – there is a scar under his beard.' All the officers laughed at their favourite old story. More drinks were brought. Dave enthused on the excellent quality of the Indian whisky. Meena hissed: 'Psssst – Dave – we're drinking brandy now.' My taste buds were insensitive to such distinctions, as an orderly filled my glass yet again. Muslim reached for another cigarette. The colonel told us that transport to Leh would have to wait for another day, but that tomorrow we could stay at the main base and he would arrange a special late-night showing of the recent Hindi blockbuster *Silsila*, at the camp cinema.

The food finally appeared, dishes piled high with rice, vegetables, chickpeas and cheese, dhal, chapattis, boondi raita and mutton. Dave excelled himself and for months afterwards the officers of the Maratha regiment would speak in tones of awe about the Englishman who never said no, but kept on eating, devouring kilo after kilo of mutton, licking his fingers between helpings and mumbling through his beard: 'Yes please, I'll have more – this is delicious,' before embarking on another gargantuan plateful of hot curried meat, eating his way relentlessly through the night, oblivious of the sweat and tears pouring down his face.

It was an inspired performance which none of us, not even Harish, could hope to emulate. Dave finally stopped eating and our admiring incredulous hosts could order pudding. Later, after a long round of handshakings, signings of the visitors' book and profuse thanks to our hosts who had done so much to help us after the initial hiccups in Leh, we returned to our VIP quarters to fall drunkenly asleep.

Postlude

One evening about three weeks later some of us gathered at Harish's flat in Bombay. Muslim and Dhiren were there. Boga dropped in on his way back from work. Arun was meeting us later. Victor, Jim and Dave had long since returned to England. Meena, too, was back at work in London. Henry was still in Ladakh. Pratap and the Harsinhs had returned to their village in Kumaon. Mahendra was at his mountaineering training camp. It was my last evening in India.

Already the Karakoram and the Siachen battlefield seemed very remote. So much had happened since our dinner at the officers' mess. There had been the jolting drive back to Leh with an army convoy. We shared the back of a truck with some happy excited jawans, who were on leave and just starting the long dusty journey back from the Siachen Glacier to the Punjab. In Leh we met Henry and Mutup Kalon for a celebratory meal at the Potala Palace. Harish made one last pilgrimage to the momo restaurant. Harish Sharma, our inscrutable Mr Fixit, jumped us forty places up the waiting list for a flight to Delhi and we all boarded the plane, to return south at ridiculous speed, over the Himalaya, passing somewhere near the mountains of Kishtwar before flying over green forests and descending into a hot damp wodge of monsoon cloud, piled up against the southern side of the range.

For two weeks now I had been back in the plains. Muslim's family had again been extremely hospitable. Harish and Geeta had taken me on a tour of Bombay's restaurants. I had spent a few days on Mount Abu in Rajasthan, living in a bungalow in the forest, isolated amongst swirling mists and the jungle noises of monkeys and peacocks. Twice I had visited the intricately carved marble temples at Delwara, before returning on the slow rumbling train to Bombay. Then I had joined Harish, Geeta and other members of the Himalayan Club on a long weekend in the Western Ghats, the range of hills near Bombay. We walked through warm soft rain and waded swollen rivers that had none of the destructive power of the Terong river. We slid up and down muddy paths, winding across fields, over hills and through forests of wild banana trees, festooned with jasmine. The air was filled with the sound of birdsong and everything was green with a vivid luminosity that delighted the eye after the stark ochres of the Karakoram.

Now, on my last evening, we met at Vijay Apartment to see the first batch of slides which had just returned from Kodak. Harish's parents sat on the sofa. Some of the other people found chairs. I sat on the floor with Sonam and Nawang, who had just finished their homework and could enjoy the slide-show with a clear conscience. Muslim switched out the light and Harish projected the slides on to the white wall. The noise outside of taxis and rickshaws was soon drowned by laughter and excited exclamations, as we saw Spituk monastery, the Nubra river, Victor's dancing tights, the Lake of Bones, Dhiren in his red duvet camping near the Terong La, Jim nursing a mug of tea at Advance Base, the vast white snowfields of the South Rimo Glacier, Sundbrar, Rimo III, the two humps of Ngabong Terong, the wild roses brilliant against brown granite, the cliff crossing with Dhiren and Muslim hanging high above the swirling water, and, of course, Mahendra's bridge – the final tragi-comic denouement of the expedition.

'Chalo-we must go to eat!' Harish hustled everyone down to the street and we drove to the home of Geeta's mother. She had been persuaded by her son-in-law to cook a last farewell meal, and had dutifully prepared a great array of prawns, lobster, pomfret and crab, fresh from the Indian Ocean. It was a delicious feast and made a wonderful conclusion to my stay with these delightful hospitable people. While we ate our way through second, third and fourth helpings, Dhiren and Harish took turns to press their ears to the over-used transistor radio. Harish neglected to finish his fifth helping of prawns and his face was puckered with concentration as he lost himself in the last moments of England bowling their way to victory in the fifth test, at Edgbaston.

The following week David Gower scored his double century in the final triumphant match of the series. Harish was attending a cloth dealers' conference in Goa, but I am sure that between meetings (and most probably during meetings) he found time to switch on his radio and follow the drama at The Oval. I was back in England. The Karakoram now seemed even more remote, but I still had the photos and the memories of a very special adventure.

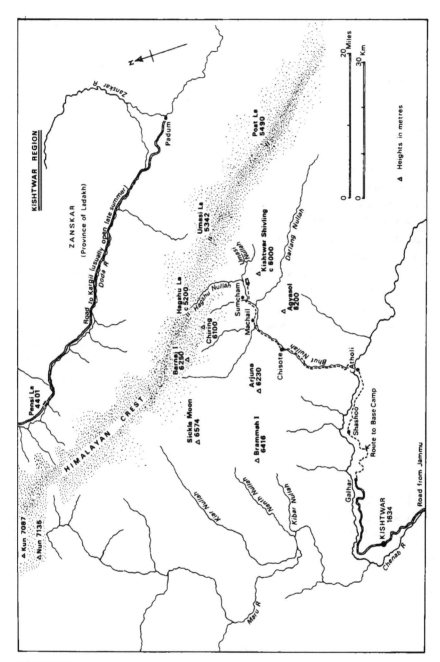

Kishtwar region

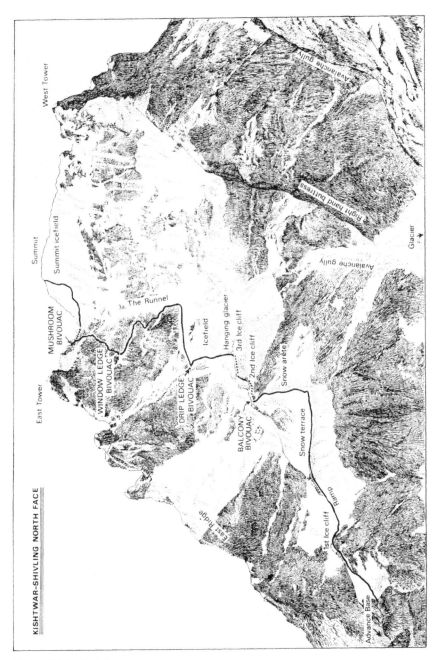

Kishtwar-Shivling North Face

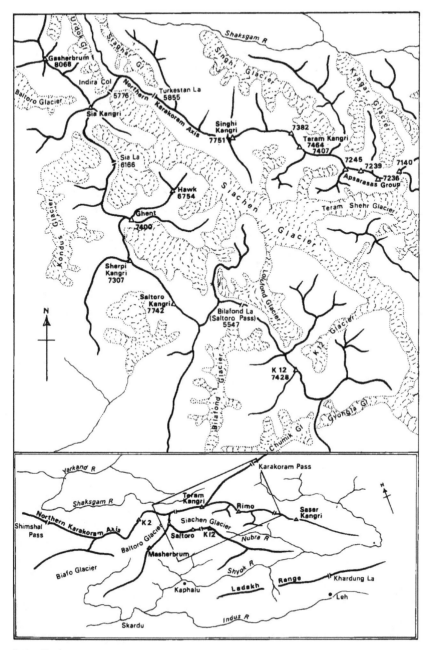

Eastern Karakoram

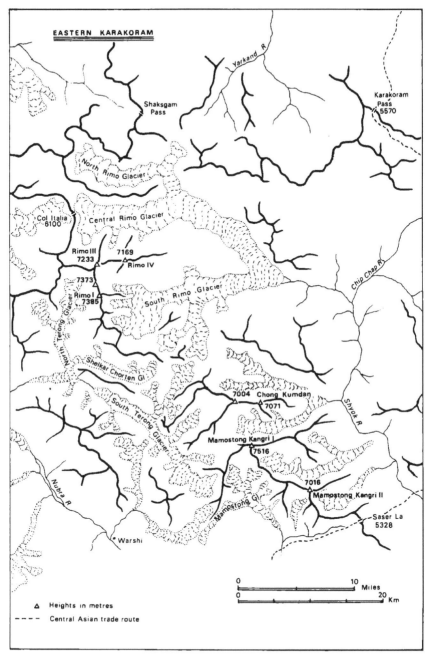

Eastern Karakoram

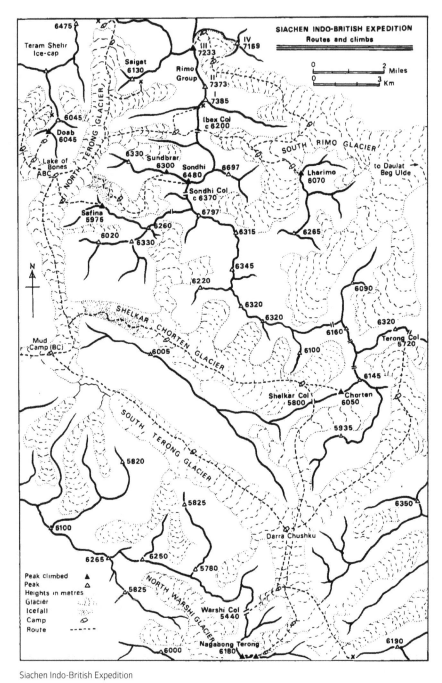

SIACHEN INDO-BRITISH EXPEDITION
Routes and climbs

6475

Teram Shehr
Ice-cap

III 7233
IV 7159

Saiget
6130

Rimo
Group

II 7373
I 7385

6045

Doab
6045

Ibex Col
c 6200

SOUTH RIMO GLACIER

to Daulat
Beg Ulde

Lake of
Bones
ABC

NORTH TERONG GLACIER

6330

Sundbrar
6300

Sondhi
6480

6697

Lharimo
6070

Sondhi Col
c 6370

Safina
5976

6797

6260

6315

6265

6020

6330

6345

6220

6090

6320

SHELKAR CHORTEN GLACIER

6320

6320

6160

Terong Col
5720

Mud
Camp (BC)

6005

6100

6145

Shelkar Col
5800

Chorten
6050

SOUTH TERONG GLACIER

5935

5820

5825

6350

6100

Darra Chushku

6265

6250

5780

Peak climbed ▲
Peak △
Heights in metres
Glacier
Icefall
Camp
Route

5825

NORTH WARSHI GLACIER

Warshi Col
5440

6000

Nagabong Terong
6180

6190

N

0 ——— 2 Miles
0 ——— 3 Km

Siachen Indo-British Expedition

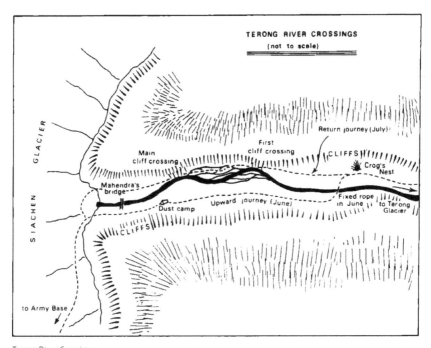

Terong River Crossings

Appendix 1   Expedition Diary: Kishtwar-Shivling, 1983

5 August	Stephen and Dick fly London-Delhi
6–9 August	Preparations in Delhi
10 August	Stephen, Dick and Patial arrive in Jammu
11–13 August	Bus to Kishtwar. Landslide delays
15-19 August	Walk-in from Galhar to Base Camp
21 August	Dick's reconnaissance to the col
23–24 August	Walk to Umasi La and back
25–28 August	Bad weather at Base Camp
29 August	Carry supplies to Advance Base
30 August	Abortive recce above Advance Base. Return to Base Camp
1 September	Climb back up to Advance Base
2–3 September	Bad weather at Advance Base
4 September	Climb to snow towers and return to Advance Base Camp
5 September	Final preparations at Advance Base
6 September	Climb to the Balcony
7 September	Climb to Drip Ledge
8 September	Climb to Window Ledge
9 September	Climb to the Mushroom
10 September	Climb to summit and return to the Mushroom
11 September	Descend to Drip Ledge
12 September	Descend to Base Camp
13–14 September	Packing at Base Camp
15–18 September	Return to Kishtwar
20 September	Return to Jammu
21 September	Return to Delhi
22–25 September	Stay at Guest Keen Williams guesthouse in Delhi
26 September	Fly back to London

Appendix 2   Mountaineering in the Kishtwar Himalaya, 1947–1985

In the interests of space and simplicity, each expedition is listed under the name of a single organiser or correspondent, regardless of his prominence in the actual climbing. There is some doubt over the precise locations and heights of many Kishtwar peaks and many of them lack accepted local names, hence the profusion of unofficial names given by visiting expeditions – e.g. Flat Top, Doda Peak, Delusion Peak and Chiring Peak. To aid research, references are given for articles in the *Himalayan Journal* (HJ) and *Alpine Journal* (AJ) and summary notes in *Iwa-to-Yuki* (ITY). Further information can be found in *Mountain*, other national journals and, at least for the British expeditions, in individual expedition reports available in the Alpine Club and Royal Geographical Society libraries.

1947   F. Kolb | Austrian | HJ 14
        Exploration of eastern approaches to Sickle Moon. First ascents of Dreikant and Solstice Peak. Exploration of Muni La and Poat La.

1965   C. Clarke | Cambridge University
        Attempt on Brammah I. Exploration of Brammah Glacier.

1969   C. Clarke | British | HJ 30
        Further exploration of Brammah Glacier and Kiar Nullah. First ascent of Crooked Finger.

1970   N. Clough | British
        Exploration in Brammah area.

1971   C. Clarke | British | HJ 31
        Attempt on SE Ridge of Brammah I reached within 100 metres of summit.

1973   C. Bonington |Indo-British | HJ 33
        First ascent of Brammah I by SE Ridge.

1975   R. Collister |British | HJ 34

Attempts on Brammah II from Donali Glacier and Kijai Nullah.

(First Westerners to penetrate this difficult nullah). First ascent of Consolation Peak.

K. Keiryo |Sapporo Alpine Club (Japanese) | HJ 35
First ascent of Brammah II from Brammah Glacier.

F. Yuki | Japanese Defence Army
Attempt on Sickle Moon.

Col D.N. Tanka | Indian High Altitude Warfare School
First ascent of Sickle Moon.

1976   J. Cant |University of St Andrews
Attempt on Arjuna. First ascents of Sher Khan, Taragiri and Sundar Pahar.

C. Bonington |British
Attempt on Katori.

Japanese | ITY 55
First ascent of P.6,550 metres (Doda Peak) above Durung Drung Glacier, approached from Abring in Doda valley.

1976   A. Judkowski | Loughborough University
Attempt on Cathedral.

Japanese Alpine Instruction Technique Club
Attempt on Barnaj II. First ascent of P.5,310 metres nearby.

K. Ohtaki | Japanese
Attempt on Sickle Moon.

1977   C. Torrans | Irish Mountaineering Club
Attempts on Eiger and Cathedral.

S. Hepburn | Carlisle Mountaineering Club
Attempt on Sickle Moon. First ascent of p.6392 in Kiar Nullah.

N. Kubo | Japanese

*Attempt on Barnaj II. First ascents of P.6,150 (central) and P. 6,17 (south) summits of Barnaj II.

G. Tier | British | AJ 84
*Attempt on Barnaj II defeated by appalling weather.

Maj. A. G. Roy | Indian Army Signals
First ascent of Gharol.

R. Collister | British AJ83 (Asia notes) & HJ 42
First ascent of Viewpoint Peak (c.5600m) from Durung Drung Glacier and crossing to Prul Glacier to make first ascent of Delusion Peak. (Ascensionists doubted the height of 6560m given on Japanese sketch map, hence name. However, later visitors think the peak may in fact be this high.)

1978   A. Wheaton | Brunel University | HJ 36
Second ascent of Brammah I

R. Rutland | British
Attempt on Arjuna.

C. Graham | British
First ascent of Brahmasar.

L. Griffin | North of England Himalayan Expedition
Attempts on Barnaj I* and P.6000m to west of B.I. First ascent of P. 5,750 (south of Barnaj III). First ascents of three aiguilles in Chiring Nullah.

1979   K. Denda | Japanese Alpine Club
Second ascent of Sickle Moon. Third ascent of Brammah I.

J. V. Anthoine | British
Attempts on Brammah II and Flat Top.

J. Curran | British
Second ascent of Barnaj II S. summit.

W. Fiut | Polish
First ascent of Brammah's Wife, by NW Ridge from Nanth Nullah.

A. Wheaton | British
Ascent of Brammah's Wife by W Ridge. Attempt on Eiger.

R. Urbanck | Polish
Ascent of Brammah's Wife.

M. Kokaj | Polish
First ascent of P.6,013 (east of Eiger).

1980   Maj. R. Wilson | British
First ascent of Flat Top.

A. Bergamaschi | Italian | HJ 37, 42
Ascents of six peaks in Durung Drung range.

Y. Kubota | Tokyo College of Pharmacy Alpine Club
Repeat of 1977 route on Barnaj II to S. summit, but failed to reach central or main summits.

Kingston Polytechnic
Attempt on Agyasol.

R. Rutland | British
Attempt on Sickle Moon.

E. Schmutz | French
Fourth ascent of Brammah I, by new route on North Ridge.

K. Lozinski | Polish
First P.6,013 from Kijai Nullah.

D. Hillebrandt | British Padar Expedition
Several ascents and attempts around the Hagshu and Umasi Nullahs. Ascent of Khagayu Dost. Almost successful attempt on Chiring Peak abandoned when C. Lloyd was killed falling from summit ridge.

1980   L. Hughes |British | HJ 38
Inspected approaches to Kishtwar-Shivling, quoting an alternative local name, Talanganna, before continuing over Umasi La to peaks in Zanskar.

1981 B. R. Sarkar | Climbers Circle Calcutta
Attempt on P. 5,594 in Kiar Nullah.

S. Richardson | Oxford University | HJ 39
First ascent of Agyasol and Spear Peak from Kaban Nullah.

W. Otreba |Polish
First ascent of Arjuna South from Kijai Nullah. Connecting ridge to main summit abandoned due to shortage of time.

M. C. Boerlage | Dutch
Second ascent of Brammah II by new route on South-West Face.

G. Agostino | Italian
Ascent of Z3 from Durung Drung Glacier.

1982 R. Collister | Eagles Ski Club | AJ87 (Asia notes)
April ski tour – the first trip of its kind in Kishtwar. Nordic skis found indispensable for crossing deep snow from Bhazun Nullah to Kiar Nullah, climbing Consolation Peak en route (probably second ascent).

1983 S. Venables | British
First ascent of Kishtwar-Shivling by North Face.

M. Kendall |American
Attempt on Brammah I.

H. Komamiya | Japanese
Attempt on South Face of Eiger.

B. Slarno | Polish
First ascent of Arjuna main summit from Kijai Nullah.

B. Dass | Indian
Third ascent of Brammah II.

P. Finklaire | British
Attempt on North Face of P.5,861 from Kibar Nullah. The team intended originally to attempt Hagshu Peak, but were deterred by reports of a destroyed bridge on the approach.

D. Walsh | British | AJ 89
First crossing of Chobani La from Barnai Nullah. First ascent of
P.6,240 metres (just SW of Doda Peak) before descending north to
Doda river.

Edinburgh University
Second ascent of Doda Peak and ascents of P.6,000 and P. 5,600.

J-P. Chassagne | French
First ascent of La Shal (6,135 metres) (Hagshu Peak or Chiring Peak?)
from Hagshu Nullah.

1984   S. Richardson | British
Attempt on NE buttress of Mardi Phabrang (incorrectly marked as
Gharol on most maps) from Kaban Nullah. First ascent of Tuperdo II
and crossing of new col (mistaken for Kaban La) near E Ridge of
Agyasol.

J. Lynam | Irish | HJ 42
Second ascent of Z8 from glacier north and parallel to Durung Drung
Glacier.

1985   J. Thackray | American
Attempt on Chiring Peak from north.

M. Rosser | British
Attempt on Hagshu Peak from Hagshu Nullah. Failed at c. 5,400 metres
due to bad weather and altitude sickness.

* There is some confusion over the labelling of the Barnaj peaks and it is still
not clear exactly which summits have been climbed.

Appendix 3   Siachen Indo-British Expedition, 1985

Climbers

Meena Agrawal (42)	Paediatric surgeon (expedition doctor)
Zerksis Boga (39)	Medical representative
Muslim Contractor (26)	Chemical engineer
Jim Fotheringham (33)	Dentist
Harish Kapadia (40)	Cloth dealer (expedition leader)
Arun Samant (37)	Civil engineer
Victor Saunders (35)	Architect
Dhiren Toolsidas (20)	Engineering student
Stephen Venables (31)	Joiner
Dave Wilkinson (39)	Senior lecturer in Computer Studies

Expedition Scientist

Henry Osmaston (63)	Senior lecturer in Geography

Liaison Officer

2nd Lt Mahendra Singh

Porter-cooks

Harsinh
Harsinh
Pratapsinh

EXPEDITION DIARY

26 May	Dave and Stephen fly London-Bombay
27–31 May	Final preparations in Bombay
31 May–June 2	Overland party travels from Bombay to Srinagar
3–4 June	Overland party in Srinagar
4 June	Jim and Victor fly London-Delhi
5–6 June	Overland party travels from Srinagar to Leh
6 June	Air party flies to Leh, and full team (minus Henry) meets in Leh

7–11 June	Delays in Leh
12–13 June	Drive to Siachen Glacier snout
14–17 June	Load-ferrying to Dust Camp in Terong valley
19 June	Full team established at Snout Camp
21–23 June	Jim and Victor do recce to Advance Base
23 June	Full team and all luggage established at Base Camp (Mud Camp)
25 June	Full team settles at Advance Base (c. 5,000 metres)
26–27 June	Bad weather at Advance Base. Bhotias ferry loads from Mud Camp
28 June-2 July	Indifferent weather. Expedition splits up into small teams for reconnaissance of IBEX COL (c. 6,200 metres), RIMO I, west branch of N. Terong Glacier and Sondhi valley to SONDHI COL (c. 6,370 metres)
2 July	Full moon. Start of fine weather. Full team (minus Henry) meets at Advance Base for last time
4–10 July	Victor and Stephen attempt RIMO I (7,385 metres)
4 July	Henry arrives unexpectedly at Advance Base
6 July	Dave and Jim descend from RIMO I
8 July	Arun and Muslim climb SAFINA (5,975 metres)
7–13 July	Boga and Meena on South Rimo Glacier
11–16 July	Dave and Jim climb RIMO III (7,233 metres)
12 July	Arun and Dhiren climb SUNDBRAR (6,300 metres)
	Boga and Meena climb LHARIMO (6,070 metres)
13 July	Arun and Dhiren climb SONDHI (6,480 metres)
13–14 July	Victor and Stephen fix ropes on river cliff

15 July	Arun and Boga leave for Leh
	Muslim and Harsinh Senior climb
	DOAB (6,045 metres)
16 July	End of fine weather
	Jim, Henry and Victor leave for Leh
20 July	Weather improves again. Dave, Dhiren,
	Harish, Harsinh Junior, Muslim and
	Pratap leave for S. Terong. Stephen
	leaves for Shelkar Chorten
22 July	Stephen climbs CHORTEN PEAK
	(6,050 metres)
23 July	Dhiren and Harishreach
	TERONGCOL(c. 5,720 metres)
	Harsinh Junior and Muslim reach W
	ARSHI COL (c. 5,400 metres)
24 July	Stephen climbs NGABONG TERONG
	(6,180 metres)
	South Terong party returns to Mud
	Camp
25 July	Stephen returns to Mud Camp
26 July	Whole party starts river cliff crossing
27 July	Construction of Mahendra's Bridge
	Return to army base
29–30 July	Return to Leh
1 August	Flight to Delhi
2 August	Dave flies Delhi-London
August 4	Meena flies Delhi-London
	Rest of team return to Bombay

Appendix 4   Exploration and Mountaineering in the East Karakoram, 1821–1985

This table is intended to supplement the historical information in chapters 9 and 10. I am indebted to Harish Kapadia for his assistance, particularly for the painstaking work he has done in researching the records of recent expeditions to the area. As in all historical lists there will inevitably be unintentional omissions, but this does cover all the main events of which we are aware. In describing 'East Karakoram', I have defined the western limit of the area with a line running approximately north-east to southwest through Sia Kangri and the head of the Siachen Glacier. Several of the expeditions listed were primarily concerned with the Baltoro region further west, but are included in this list because they touched close to the eastern and northern limits of the Siachen (e.g. Conway's and Dyrenfurth's expeditions). Entries in italics refer to significant political events that have affected the area.

Most of the expeditions mentioned are referred to in the *Geographical Journal* (GJ), *Himalayan Journal* (HJ), Himalayan Club Newsletter (HCNL), *American Alpine Journal* (AAJ) or *Iwa-to-Yuki* (ITY) and the volume numbers of the relevant journals are mentioned. (Some of the expeditions have obviously been reported in more than one of these journals and have also been covered in the *Alpine Journal*. Further research into other foreign journals would unearth more details and photographs, but as a starting point the *Himalayan Journal* is the most useful single reference source for expeditions since 1929.)

The early explorations are headed under the names of individual explorers. This reduction of expeditions to individual leaders' names is done in the interests of simplicity and space-saving, and is not intended in any way to detract from the vital part played by their companions and by the Balti and Ladakhi porters who made their expeditions possible.

SV

1821	WILLIAM MOORCROFT crosses from Leh to Panamik in Nubra valley.
1837	GODFREY VIGNE visits Nubra valley from Leh. Too late in year to cross Saser La to Karakoram Pass.
1838	After wintering in Skardu, VIGNE makes second approach to Nubra. Sikh occupiers in Leh, suspicious of British intruders,

refuse him permission to return to Leh, hence his attempt to reach Nubra from Baltistan by the Saltoro Pass (Bilafond La). Attempt thwarted by storm and snow-covered crevasses.

1846   *Sikh Wars concluded by TREATY OF AMRITSAR. British govern-ment creates semi-autonomous state of 'Jammu, Kashmir and Ladak'. Effective sphere of British influence pushed north to Ladakh.*

1847   *LADAKH BORDER COMMISSION - Alexander Cunningham, Henry Strachey and Dr Thomas Thomson. During their recent occu-pation of Ladakh, the Sikhs had also invaded Tibet, where their army was routed. Now the British made their first attempt to delineate the eastern border of Ladakh.*

1848   THOMSON reaches Karakoram Pass.
STRACHEY reaches head of Nubra valley and travels two miles up Siachen Glacier. GJ 23

1861   GODWIN AUSTEN survey of Baltoro Glacier.

1862   E.C. RYALL produces Survey of India map with inaccurate rep-resentation of Siachen Glacier.

1889   FRANCIS YOUNGHUSBAND crosses Karakoram Pass to Yarkand and Shaksgam valleys. Nearly reaches Indira Col from north (Urdok Glacier).

1892   MARTIN CONWAY's Karakoram expedition follows Hispar and Biafo Glaciers to Baltoro. First ascent of Silver Throne and attempt on Baltoro Kangri.

1892   Survey of India map again gives inaccurate representation of Siachen Glacier.

1897   ARTHUR NEVE, a medical missionary, visits Nubra valley, Mamastong Glacier and climbs small peak near Saser La.

1908   NEVE thwarted by Nubra floods from reaching Siachen Glacier. GJ 38

1909   THOMAS LONGSTAFF crosses Saltoro Pass and discovers true extent of Siachen Glacier. Also visits snout of Rimo Glacier and returns to travel up Siachen from Nubra valley. GJ 35
DUKE OF ABRUZZI's Karakoram expedition. First full-scale attempt on K2. The first in a long line of ambitious Italian Karakoram expeditions which provided much of the data for the British Survey of India maps.

1911–12   BULLOCK WORKMAN East Karakoram. The last of the great Karakoram explorations by the William. In 1912 they cross the Saltoro Pass (now named Bilafond La) and descend the Lolofond Glacier (name taken from Balti porters who called Longstaff 'Lolaff') to the Siachen. Extensive survey of upper Siachen aided by British surveyor, Grant Peterkin, and ascents of minor peaks.

Younghusband's pass named Indira Col and a nearby pass Turkestan La. Unsuccessful attempts to reach head of Teram Shehr Glacier and to cross from the Siachen to the Baltoro. Party eventually exited by the Sia La and Kondus Glacier. The BWs discovered evidence of earlier local visitors to the Siachen. For analysis of their possible origin and likelihood of an ancient trade route over Siachen see the discussion between BWs and Longstaff at the RGS, quoted in GJ 43 (pp. 138–139 and 149–150.) GJ 43

1914   FILIPPO DE FILIPPI (previously a member of the Abruzzi 1909 expedition) makes first survey of the second largest glacier in the East Karakoram, the Rimo Glacier. Survey of Rimo peaks from north-east. Intended survey of Shaksgam valley halted by First World War.

1922   Dr P.H.C. VISSER explores southern approaches to Saser Kangri.

1926   KENNETH MASON surveys Shaksgam valley, via Karakoram Pass. Hindered by advanced Kyagar Glacier. GJ69

1929   DUKE OF SPOLETO's Karakoram expedition approaches Shaksgam valley from Mustagh Pass. Explores Urdok, Singhi, Staghar and Kyagar Glaciers, linking up with Younghusband's work of 1889 and Mason's 1926 survey. HJ 3

1929–1930   VISSER's second East Karakoram expedition. Explores La Yoghma Glacier on south side of Nubra valley. Visits Terong basin. Partial survey of North Terong and Shelkar Chorten Glaciers. Followed by exploration of glaciers round upper Shyok valley and crossing of Karakoram Pass, to winter in Yarkand. GJ 84

1930   Prof. GIOTTO DAINELLI explores Teram Shehr Glacier. Swift efficient approach up Nubra (before flooding) to Siachen and its junction with Teram Shehr. Continues up heavily crevassed Teram Shehr (which had defeated Bullock Workmans in 1912) to cross the 'Col Italia' to the Rimo Glacier. Returns via Saser La and Khardung La to Leh. HJ 4

1934   G.O. DYRENFURTH's international Karakoram expedition. First ascent of west, central, east and main summits of Queen Mary from Baltoro side. ('Queen Mary Peak' was the name given by the Bullock Workmans to the mountain now known as Sia Kangri.) HJ7

1935   VISSER's third East Karakoram expedition. Completes work of Younghusband (1889), Mason (1926) and Spoleto (1929) on glaciers descending north from East Karakoram watershed into Shaksgam valley. HJ7

| | British army expedition led by JAMES WALLER attempts Saltoro Kangri, approaching from south. Team includes a young officer, John Hunt (later of Everest fame), who spearheads a bold near-successful attempt on this massive peak, in the face of appalling weather. HJ 8 |

1937   ERIC SHIPTON's *Blank on the Map* expedition explores area north of K2, linking up with Younghusband/Mason/Visser explorations in Shaksgam valley.

1939   Lt PETER YOUNG visits Gyong La.

1946   J. ROBERTS reconnoitres southern approaches to Saser Kangri and climbs Lookout Peak. HJ 14

1947   *INDIAN INDEPENDENCE AND PARTITION. Proposed independent state of Jammu and Kashmir elects to join India, prompting Pakistan to invade from west, with the ready support of Muslim tribesmen*
R.C. SCHOMBERG fails to attain Siachen snout due to July/ August flooding of Nubra. Explores valley above Rongdu, southeast of Saser Kangri. HJ 15

1948   *Kashmir ceasefire line left the state divided, with Pakistan securing a narrow strip down the south-west border and the whole north-west corner, i.e. a large part of the upper Indus valley and the greater part of the Karakoram. The ceasefire line was left undefined at the point where it reached the Karakoram.*

For foreign mountaineers access to the Karakoram was now strictly controlled, particularly at the eastern end of the range. Pakistan allowed a few expeditions into the range, including a very few which were allowed on to the upper Siachen from Baltistan; but India kept the eastern approaches, via Leh and the Nubra valley, strictly closed to foreigners.

In the entries below an asterisk indicates an expedition approaching the East Karakoram from Pakistan.

1956   M.S. Kohli leads first Indian expedition to East Karakoram. Reconnoitres southern approaches to Saser Kangri and climbs Sakang Peak. HJ 25
*Austrian expedition climbs Sia Kangri West. HJ 20
CHINA OCCUPIES AKSAI CHIN – the large north-eastern corner of Ladakh. India now threatened by Chinese troops along her northern frontier from Ladakh in the west to Assam in the east.

1957   *British Imperial College expedition, led by Eric Shipton, crosses Bilafond La and explores Siachen, Teram Shehr and K12 glaciers, climbing small peaks, including Tawiz. HJ 21

1960	*British expedition explores south-west approaches to K12. HJ 23
1961	*Austrian expedition makes 1st ascent of Ghent via Kondus Glacier and Sia La. (Ghent was the name given by the Bullock Workmans to commemorate the Treaty of the Ghent, (which terminated hostilities between Britain and America in 1814.) HJ 23
1962	*INDO-CHINESE WAR. The main point of contention was the border in the eastern Himalaya, but there was also fighting in the Aksai Chin. India subsequently began a massive military build-up in Ladakh.*
	*Japanese-Pakistani expedition makes first ascent of Saltoro Kangri I. HJ 25
1965	*INDO-PAKISTANI WAR. Kashmir ceasefire line remains undefined where it reaches Karakoram.*
1962–1974	*Karakoram closed to all foreigners, save a few expeditions to the West Karakoram. Pakistan preoccupied with a period of turbulent politics, two wars with India and strengthening ties with China, symbolised by the construction of the Karakoram Highway and the ceding to China of the Shaksgam valley, north of the range.*
1970	Indian expedition reconnoitres Saser Kangri from south-west and climbs four outlying 6,000-metre peaks. HJ 30
1971	*INDO-PAKISTANI WAR. India gains strategic hill posts on main supply road to Ladakh. Kashmir ceasefire line remains undefined where it reaches Karakoram.*
1973	ITBF expedition makes first ascent of Saser Kangri I from the east (North Shukpa Kunchang Glacier) Formidable problems with summer flooding of rivers.
1974	*Austrian expedition climbs Sia Kangri. HCNL32, AAJ 49
	*Japanese expedition attempts Sherpi Kangri II. HCNL 31
	*Japanese expedition makes probable first ascent of K12, but two summiteers disappear on descent. HCNL 31
1975	*British expedition attempts Sherpi Kangri.
	*Japanese expedition repeats ascent of K12. No trace found of previous year's missing climbers, but ascent of K12 now undisputed. HCNL 31
	*Japanese expedition makes first ascents of Teram Kangri I and Teram Kangri II. HCNL 31, ITY 48
	*Japanese expedition attempts Saltoro Kangri I. HCNL 31
1976	*Japanese expedition makes first ascent of Sherpi Kangri I. HJ 35
1977	*Japanese expedition makes first ascent of central summit of Gharkun, near Gyong La. ITY 64
	*Japanese expedition makes first ascent of Apsaras I. HCNL 32

*Japanese expedition crosses Bilafond La and Turkestan La to make first ascent of Sing hi Kangri from north. HCNL 32

*Austrian expedition attempts Saltoro Kangri II. HCNL 32

*Austrian expedition makes first ascent of Ghent north-east from Kondus Glacier.

*Japanese expedition climbs Ghent northeast. HCNL 33

*Japanese expedition crosses Gyong La and Siachen to entrance of Terong valley. Attempt to continue up Terong valley to glacier and Rimo peaks stopped by problems with flooded river. NB excellent panorama photos of East Karakoram in this issue of ITY. ITY 64

*Japanese expedition attempts Chumik (S. of K12). ITY 67

Indian army expedition led by Col N. Kumar climbs Teram Kangri II. The first Indian expedition to venture on to the upper Siachen from Nubra. HJ 37

1979   *Japanese expedition made first ascent of Teram Kangri III. HCNL 33

*Japanese expedition climbs Sia Kangri and makes first crossing from Baltoro to Siachen Glacier, with 116 porters. This was the crossing which defeated the Bullock Workmans in 1912.) HCNL 33

Indian expedition makes second ascent of Saser Kangri I.

1980   *American team, led by Galen Rowell, make first complete ski traverse of Karakoram, linking Siachen, Baltoro, Biafo and Hispar Glaciers. The four men carry their own provisions from Kaphalu, only stopping once, at Askole, to re-provision during their six-week journey. An outstanding achievement, verging on the masochistic, summed up by one member: 'The trip was hardly enjoyable - it was an accomplishment'! The crux of the route is the Siachen-Baltoro crossing, via S. face of Sia Kangri and Conway's Saddle, where the Japanese employed 116 porters the previous summer. Only one thing mars the elegance of their achievement-politics prevents them from starting at the very eastern Indian-controlled end of the Siachen so they have to cut into the upper glacier from the Pakistani-controlled Bilafond La. AAJ 23/55

*Two-man Japanese team plans reconnaissance of Rimo peaks via Bilafond La and Siachen, but one man dies in crevasse accident near Bilafond La. ITY 81

*German expedition climbs Ghent. HCNL 34

Indian army expedition makes second ascent of Apsaras I. A massive exercise in logistics, approaching the Siachen from the Nubra valley: '68 members assisted by 20 porters ferried over 25 tonnes of equipment and rations across 12 camps'

| 1981 | *Dutch expedition attempts Saltoro Kangri II. HCNL 36 |

1981   *Dutch expedition attempts Saltoro Kangri II. HCNL 36
Col N. Kumar's second Indian army expedition to upper Siachen Glacier. Ascents of lndira Col, Turkestan La, and Sia Kangri. First of Saltoro Kangri II. HJ 39

1983   *American, French, German, Japanese and Korean parties allowed to trek from Pakistan over Bilafond La to Siachen and Sia La.

1984   *OUTBREAK OF HOSTILITIES BETWEEN INDIA AND PAKISTAN ON SIACHEN GLACIER. Indian army takes control of entire glacier.*

Indian army expedition makes second ascent of K12 approaching from Siachen Glacier. Something of a propaganda exercise, this is claimed as the 'first ascent of K12 were invalid, having originated in Pakistan.

Indian army makes first ascent of Rimo IV, from South Rimo Glacier.

Inda-Japanese expedition makes first ascent of Mamastong Kangri I. The first joint Foreign-Indian expedition allowed into the East Karakoram. HJ 41

1985   *Indian army retains control of entire Siachen. Indian Mountaineering Foundation publicises new regulations allowing up to three Foreign-Indian expeditions per year to visit Siachen area.*

Indo-British expedition visits Terong basin exploring several passes and climbing several peaks, including the first ascent of Rima III. Indo-Japanese expedition makes the first ascent of Saser Kangri II by NW Ridge, approaching from Nubra valley and Sakang Lungpa Glacier. Four Indian members reach a west summit, described as exactly the same height (7,518 metres) as the distant east summit. HJ 42.

Acknowledgements

The many sponsors and helpers of these two expeditions are acknowledged in Appendix 6, but I should like here to thank all those who have helped specifically with the preparation of this book:

Jim Fotheringham for writing the vital chapter on the first ascent of Rimo III and Henry Osmaston for allowing me to use his fascinating and entertaining scientific report.

Alec Spark for the drawings and maps; Henry Osmaston and Arun Samant for all the initial work on the East Karakoram maps.

Laetitia Powell, Jane Riley, Audrey Salkeld and various members of my family for checking and criticising the first draft.

The publishers, John Murray, for permission to quote a passage from Francis Younghusband's *Heart of a Continent*.

Pat Johnson, the Alpine Club librarian, for her help with the bibliography.

Simon Brown, Rob Collister, Lindsay Griffin and Paul Nunn for advice on the Kishtwar appendix.

Philip and Caroline Venables for their hospitality while I was writing Part One. James and Rachel Ogilvie for nurturing me through Part Two and for letting me loose on their brand new Amstrad word processor, which proved invaluable for typing and correcting the manuscript.

Mark Tully for his advice on the historical sections and Harish Kapadia, Bombay's most prolific letter writer, for his boundless enthusiasm, encouragement and meticulous checking of details.

Anna Powell, at Hodder & Stoughton, for much hard work and Margaret Body, my editor, for all her expert help and encouragement.

SV

About the Author

Stephen Venables is a mountaineer, writer, broadcaster and public speaker, and was the first Briton to climb Everest without supplementary oxygen. Everest was a thrilling highlight in a career that has taken Stephen right through the Himalaya, from Afghanistan to Tibet, making first ascents of many previously unknown mountains. His adventures have also taken him to the Rockies, the Andes, the Antarctic island South Georgia, East Africa, South Africa and of course the European Alps, where he has climbed and skied for over forty years. The stories of these travels have enthralled Stephen's lecture audiences all over the world. He has appeared in television documentaries for the BBC, ITV and National Geographic, presented for Radio 4 and appeared in the IMAX movie *Shackleton's Antarctic Adventure*. Stephen has also authored several best-selling books on climbing in the high mountains.

Printed in the USA
CPSIA information can be obtained
at www.ICGtesting.com
JSHW012016140824
68134JS00025B/2453